The Negro's Image in the South

CLAUDE H. NOLEN

The Negro's Image in the South

The Anatomy of White Supremacy

UNIVERSITY OF KENTUCKY PRESS, Lexington, 1967

For Jeanne

Acknowledgments

I AM HAPPY to express my gratitude to Professor Barnes F. Lathrop of the University of Texas for his invaluable and indispensable assistance in the writing of this book. Mrs. Ralph Krug of Austin was helpful from first draft to last.

C.H.N.

Contents

PART FOUR   Labor

Introduction

LONG BEFORE the American Revolution, Southern whites had come to believe that the Scriptures justified slavery and that their African slaves, though inferior beings, were more comfortable and happy than European peasants. A few of them even thought that they had chanced upon hard-working creatures which looked and acted like men but were not human. From the Revolution to about 1820, when aroused to activity by occasional attacks upon the "peculiar institution," proslavery thinkers often indignantly replied that the introduction of slavery was the work of avaricious New England Puritans, but that in time the South, if left alone, would work out the problem.

Around 1820, Southern leaders, stirred to aggressiveness by the fight to prevent the westward extension of slavery and by the increasingly heavy assaults of abolitionists on human bondage wherever it existed, began openly to justify slavery as a positive good. Publications appeared in the South praising slavery as an instrument of high civilization, with the Greeks and Romans as examples, and John C. Calhoun ceaselessly argued in national councils that the institution was an element of social welfare and good government that ought to be handed on to posterity.

During the thirty years of sectional strife culminating in the Civil War, proslavery thought reached its full development. In newspapers, periodicals, sermons, lectures, and books, Southern propagandists described the excellence of slavery and presented a portrait of the South as a society in which all that was best in this world could be found.[1]

Slavery needed no apology, apologists maintained, for when

the Bible spoke, there was an end to controversy. In the Old
Testament, numerous passages testified to God's approval of
slavery, and the very persons He singled out for His special
regard, notably Abraham, were owners of slaves. Since Christ
came to fulfill the law, not to destroy it, everything in the old
law that He did not change remained lawful. Furthermore,
precepts of the Apostles taught slaves to obey their masters.
In fact, said proslavery men, St. Paul's warning to servants to
obey their masters must have been called forth by the activities
of godless abolitionists.

According to those who searched the Scriptures for arguments
to use against Yankee abolitionists, slavery was an institution
of divine mercy. But for that institution, millions of Ham's
descendants in the South would have faced eternal damnation,
remaining strangers to the Gospel and knowing nothing of
God. So the Creator had blessed these savages by prompting
Southern Christians to become their masters. Northerners,
preferring to serve Mammon rather than God, had made huge
profits in the slave trade and then had shirked the responsibility of training and elevating the Negroes. Instead, they

[1] The following outline of proslavery thought is based on the essays by
Samuel A. Cartwright, "The Education, Labor, and Wealth of the South";
J. H. Hammond, "Slavery in the Light of Political Science"; Chancellor
Harper, "Slavery in the Light of Social Ethics"; Charles Hodge, "The
Bible Argument on Slavery"; Thornton Stringfellow, "The Bible Argument:
or, Slavery in the Light of Divine Revelation"—all in E. N. Elliot, ed.,
Cotton Is King and Pro-slavery Arguments (Augusta, Ga., 1860); Albert
T. Bledsoe, *An Essay on Liberty and Slavery* (Philadelphia, 1856); John
C. Calhoun, *A Disquisition on Government and Selections from the Dis-
course*, ed. by C. Gordon Post (New York, 1953); Langdon Cheves,
*Speech of the Honorable Langdon Cheves, delivered before the Delegates
of the Nashville Convention, on Friday, November 13, 1850* (Columbia,
S.C., 1850); Howell Cobb, *A Scriptural Examination of the Institution
of Slavery in the United States with Its Objects and Purposes* (Georgia,
1856); George Fitzhugh, *Sociology for the South, or the Failure of Free
Society* (Richmond, Va., 1854), and *Cannibals All! or, Slaves without
Masters* (Richmond, Va., 1857); James H. Hammond, *Selections from the
Letters and Speeches of James H. Hammond* (New York, 1866); and
William S. Jenkins, *Pro-slavery Thought in the Old South* (Chapel Hill,
1935).

heartlessly had turned their slaves loose to poverty, crime, and death, and, compounding the fault, were now encouraging abolitionists in the diabolical design to unleash even greater evil in the South. "It is impossible," wrote Howell Cobb,

to conceive the amount of mischief abolitionism has done, and is seeking to do. Its broad slime-trace is to be seen in every direction. It pervades the sanctuary of law, and strikes the balance from the hand of justice; it tramples upon the Constitution; it repudiates the Bible; it has rendered asunder the church of the living God; it sports with everything holy and sacred; it commits murders; it has progressed far in destroying the comity between the States; it now menaces the integrity of the Union itself! This, however, we trust, is as far as it will be allowed, by the patriotism of the people, to progress. A spirit so emphatically "devilish" demands that every patriot in the land should make haste to put it down.[2]

No wonder the defender of slavery believed that the assembly of a mob to chastise an abolitionist was as laudable as a rally of shepherds to drive the wolf from the fold!

Southern whites had great difficulty in reconciling the natural rights doctrine of the American Revolution with the existence of slavery. Most of them simply stated that the Caucasian enjoyed privileges by virtue of his membership in a superior race, while the inferior Negro came into the world with few, if any rights. Some whites, such as Albert T. Bledsoe, attempted to reconcile liberty and slavery by showing that the common good, especially the good of Negroes, demanded slavery. James Hammond, speaking for others, asserted that the institution of slavery was a social compact whereby the master exacted from the slave obedience and industry in return for peace, plenty, and security.

A large number of proslavery men rejected altogether the doctrine of natural rights. Of these thinkers who saw inequality everywhere in nature and society, John C. Calhoun was the greatest and George Fitzhugh the most astonishing. Fascinated

[2] *Scriptural Examination*, 17.

by the beauty and justice of slavery, Fitzhugh urged the North
to enslave its workers as a social reform. Southern masters, he
said, maintained the sick and the aged from the labor of the
strong and healthy, but Northern masters, like cannibals,
devoured the substance of their employees before abandoning
them to die. Instead of embracing slavery, Fitzhugh complained, the North was going mad. One wing of the Northern
libertarians, he wrote:

is in daily expectation of discovering a new Social Science, that
will remedy all the ills that human flesh is heir to. They belong
to the schools of Owen, Louis Blanc, Fourier, Comte, and the
German and French Socialists and Communists. The other wing
and probably the most numerous wing of the party, is composed
of the Millenial Christians—men who expect Christ, either in the
flesh or in the spirit, soon to reign on earth; the lion to lie down
with the lamb; every man to sit down under his own vine and fig
tree; all to have an interest in lands; marrying and giving in
marriage to cease; war to be abolished, and peace and good will
to reign among men. They are as intent on abolishing all Church
government and authority as the infidels. They would, equally
with them, trample on all law and government, because "liberty is,"
say they, "an inalienable right," and law, religion, and government
continue to protect slavery.[3]

Southerners who applauded Fitzhugh for his spirited attacks
on abolitionists were scandalized by his advocacy of slavery for
laborers of all races. White men were made for freedom they
believed, and black for slavery. That Negroes were an inferior
people who benefited by enslavement could be shown by the
most cursory examination of their history in Africa and in
America. In Africa they were forced to endure a life of ignorance, war, murder, polygamy, and paganism. Slaves there were
eaten, women were mere beasts of burden, and the worst forms
of heathenism prevailed. In the United States the African
enjoyed many blessings. Already a slave in Africa, no injustice
was done him when he was brought to the South a naked,

[3] *Cannibals All!* 146.

ignorant pagan but one remove from the brute. As a result of the laborious endeavors of the state, the church, and the master, his condition was ameliorated and he became a Christian, albeit a feeble one. But "it must be remembered," wrote Howell Cobb, "that we have to control a race of human beings who are under the influence of the most depraved and vicious propensities that ever marked the character of the debased: individuals of which race seem to be incapable of redemption, either by kindness or severity."[4] Still, the slave was elevated in the South. His disposition was softened, his intellect was sharpened, and his sensibilities were aroused by Christianity.

When emancipated (as in the British West Indies), Negroes would not work except occasionally, and so the planters were ruined. The morals of the Negroes disappeared with their industry, as was foretold by Calhoun, and they sighed for rest and sleep and satisfaction of a few animal wants. Lacking regular employment, they lived like brutes, looking only to the present.

If Southern Negroes were freed, they too would become vicious vagabonds, whom the states would have to maintain in poorhouses and jails until they perished under their vices or were expelled to Africa. Severing of the ties between white and black would cause the prejudice of race to become intense. Blacks now content with restrictions of privileges would resent their exclusion from society and from government and would clamor for "inalienable rights." Some dastardly whites would instigate them to claim racial equality and, by diabolical art, inflame their bad passions. But the effort to force the blacks into social and political equality with whites would forever fail, for the social order of the Southern states was founded on the virtue and intelligence of the white people—and there it would stand.

Biological science, like the Scriptures and history, provided the advocates of slavery with evidence from which they con-

[4] *Scriptural Examination*, 121.

cluded that the white and black races were nearly opposites.
In the veins of the white man, it was said, there coursed rich
red blood that flushed the face and brightened the countenance.
Light skin, thin lips, high nose, soft hair, and brilliant eyes
bespoke high intelligence, strength of will, and great energy
of mind and muscle. In the Negro, molasses blood of a dark
hue sluggishly circulated, scarcely penetrating the capillaries.
Black skin, thick lips, flat nose, and kinky hair revealed low
intelligence, weakness of will, and slothfulness of mind and
body. The typical Negro's nervous system was somewhat like
that of the monkey; his sense of smell was so acute that he
could detect snakes at a distance; when healthy, he gave off a
potent odor. The Negro's constitution was so well adapted to
heat that he instinctively covered his head with a blanket at
night and lay with his head, instead of his feet, to the fire.

Psychological differences between the races, signalized by
physiological differences, were obvious to every white observer.
The white man, it seemed, was a thinking being. The Negro,
on the other hand, was a creature of feeling almost devoid of
reflective faculties, and so unable to care for himself. The
relation of master and slave, therefore, naturally sprang up
between the two.

Though dull and weak of will, the African was eminently
qualified for labor in the field, where he was infinitely better
off than when dozing in his native jungles. The sentiments of
honor and pride were so utterly lacking in him that in the
plantation house, he coveted the opportunity to wait on table
or to brush a coat. Handicapped with a will so weak and
disposition so gentle, Negroes readily fell under the domination
of other races of men. Even an old man or a cripple, if of the
white race, could lead about a gang of a hundred or more
Negroes. The same ordinance which kept the spheres in their
orbits subjected the Negro to the white man.

African slaves were notoriously idle and improvident. If
free, they would never labor on a plantation. They loved

novelty and sensual excitement of all kinds—when awake. If
released from obligations, few would work while there was any
food to steal; many would roam about wild in the Southern
woods. Thus the white and black races could not exist together
on terms approaching equality. They differed in all traits which
characterized the varieties of the human species, and color
drew an indelible line of separation between them. Slavery was
not the mother, but the daughter, of degradation. It was the
offspring of that debasement which, for so many thousand
years, had been growing upon the black race.

The Negroes' degradation in morals led to petty thefts, to
falsehood, and to licentious relations between the sexes. Yet,
because of their nature, their failings deserved no harsher term
than that of weakness. And their failings were compensated
for by the virtue of loyalty.

Other marks of the Negroes' inferiority included: indifference
to personal liberty; want of domestic affections; submissiveness
to authority; weakness, timidity, cowardice; and improvidence.
It was obvious that Negroes were natural slaves and that it was
merciful to enslave them. From savagery they were subdued to
usefulness. The influence of Negro slavery upon whites was
also said to be good: their probity was made strict, their pride
of character increased, and their sense of honor strengthened.
The master, being responsible for the well-being of his depen-
dents, was encouraged to practice vigor and justice in governing
them. Thus the South produced great leaders.

In an effort to preserve slavery from advancing abolitionism,
Southern whites created the Confederacy, and when abolitionism pulled down the Confederacy with General Grant's mighty
armies, they did not thereupon surrender the attitudes which
had sustained their peculiar institution for two hundred years
and more. On the contrary, they clung to the belief that
Negroes, as members of an inferior race, could live in company
with white men only as subordinates. To justify measures to
reassert control over Negroes, slavery or no slavery, whites held

that the destiny of their race was either to conquer or to exterminate weaker races, never to allow them equality.

After the Civil War, blacks, on the other hand, attempted to throw off the vestiges of bondage and to take their place in Southern life as the whites' equals. But whites marshaled their forces and imposed on the struggling blacks a substitute for slavery. Uniting under the banner of white supremacy and employing violence and fraud, they turned Negroes out of government and away from the polls. To maintain political supremacy, they developed the Solid South and defended it against third party movements which threatened to bring Negroes back into politics. By statutory legislation and constitutional amendment they dispossessed Negroes of the suffrage, depriving them of the political means to change the social order.

Similarly, whites opposed the efforts of freedmen to attain equality through education. Some of them objected to any education for Negroes; almost all stood against racial integration in the schools. To avoid integration they promised "separate but equal" educational facilities, but in fact they segregated Negroes in inferior schools. As a substitute for higher education they offered "industrial education," hoping to prevent the rise of effective leaders among the oppressed and to make sure that the education blacks received did not encourage them to revolt.

As regards the economic order, Southern whites divided the labor force of their region into two classes, giving preference in the choice of work and in wages and conditions of labor to themselves. They used the machinery of the state to coerce black workers, and they threatened to supplant restive Negroes with immigrants or to deport them to Africa. The key to this policy, and to that of the entire structure of white supremacy, was, of course, the South's desire for cheap black labor.

My intention in this study has been to present a descriptive narrative of the mind of the South in relation to the Negro

during the period after the Civil War. While focusing attention on the popular ideology of white supremacy which ratio-
nalized the development of quasi-slavery in the New South,
I do not wish to say that Southern whites alone among Americans were racist nor that, where Negroes were concerned, they
knew nothing at all of justice and charity.

PART ONE

The Argument

CHAPTER ONE

Physical and Psychological Inheritance

IN A DEMOCRATIC climate of opinion, slavery could be justified only by positing differences in the innate characteristics of the white and black races so great that the black race must appear to be incapable of freedom and thus destined to serve the white race forever.[1] When the slaves were freed, men of the New South kept alive the proslavery thinking of their fathers, tinkering with it only to adjust it to altered conditions. Science, the Scriptures, the experience of mankind, they still alleged, showed that black men were born to be servants. In this way they reconciled democratic equality with servitude.

In their effort to prove the Negro an inferior creature, white supremacists developed analogies supposedly derived from biology. So they found the Negro to have a head thick as a goat's for absorbing blows, a skin that exuded copious perspiration with a distinctive stench, monkeylike arms, flat feet, a sensitive heel, a brutish physiognomy—all of which marked him as a creature useful for hard labor, but good for little else. Such a perversion of science, of course, allowed a devotee of racist biology to discover that while investigating the peculiar animal traits of the Negro, he had revealed an ape; a community conditioned to abhor the lust of a brute might without qualms burn an alleged rapist at the stake.

The first step in this foray into biology was to find the Negro mentally dull, and then to hunt for physiological characteristics which explained this trait. About the age of puberty, it was discovered, there occurred a rapid thickening of the skull, and the animal portion of the brain then became supreme, ruling over the adult Negro organism. This stunted cranial growth accounted for the black man's cultural immobility for thousands of years; as he was at creation's dawn, so he remained, without initiative, without inventiveness, without the ability to move forward.[2] The Negro had, so it seemed, always known about his thick head; for untold centuries he had used it as a weapon of attack, "as is the custom of rams."[3]

The Negro's face, like his cranium, revealed a great deal to the racist biologist. It expressed the simplicity of animal existence. Round features, tropical eyes, flashing smile—all marked the black man as tractable, emotional, and intellectually torpid. Perhaps, wrote a Southern lady in 1878, an infusion of Caucasian blood would dissipate the simian type, improving the shape of the retreating forehead, changing the contour of the jaw, and giving weight and power to the inactive brain.[4] Some specialists concentrated attention on the nose, the hair, or the eyes and ears in the hope that they would find evidence of the inferiority of the black race. A South Carolina physician, C. W. Kollock, reported that in studying the purest type of African in the United States, the coal-black variety of the Sea Islands, he had never found a true case of myopia. He did find one nearsighted black, but concluded that a complete

[1] For an exposition of this theme, see Gunnar Myrdal, *An American Dilemma* (New York, 1944).

[2] Hilary A. Herbert, "The Problems That Present Themselves," in Southern Society for the Promotion of the Study of Race Conditions and Problems in the South, *Race Problems of the South: Proceedings of the First Annual Conference* (Richmond, Va., 1900), 31; Thomas M. Norwood, *Address on the Negro* (Savannah, Ga., 1908), 8. See also William Stanton, *The Leopard's Spots: Scientific Attitudes toward Race in America, 1815-1859* (Chicago, 1960).

[3] Charles Carroll, *The Negro a Beast or in the Image of God?* (St. Louis, 1900), 46.

[4] Jenny Woodville, "Rambling Talks about the Negro," *Lippincott's Magazine*, XXII (1878), 621-26.

history of that particular family would turn up a white man somewhere, as it was well known that primitives were endowed with excellent vision.[5]

The black man's skin, the most obvious mark of inferiority, was believed to possess certain peculiar qualities other than distinctiveness in color. It secreted oil which kept it in a state of shine, thus deflecting intense solar rays. The pigment carried heat into the system, there driving water to the surface, which in evaporation dissipated body heat. The Negro made an excellent worker because he was eminently a sweating animal; but this remarkable sweating capacity, however useful in the field, caused him to be a pariah in white society, objectionable in the jury box, the legislature, or the drawing room. During Radical Reconstruction the "sweetness of loyalty perfumed the air" of legislature and political meeting, and white men held their noses.[6]

Skin characteristics helped explain why Negroes languished in the North and why at some future date they would be found only in the Lower South. Following this argument, which had been advanced by Louis Agassiz and echoed by others, Henry Gannett of the United States Geological Survey, a consultant to the United States Census Bureau, claimed in 1898 that since Negroes flourished only in regions of high

[5] Cited in George R. Stetson, "The Eye, the Ear, and the Commonweal of Whites and Blacks," *Liberia*, Bulletin No. 10 (February, 1897), 39.

[6] New Orleans *Crescent*, November 15, 1865; [Robert Buchanan], *Caliban: A Sequel to Ariel* (New York, 1868), 31; Robert Tomes, "About Heat," *Harper's Magazine*, XXXVIII (1869), 502; Carrollton *West Alabamian*, January 26, 1870; Fort Smith, Ark., *Herald*, September 17, 1870; [Bennett Puryear], *The Public School in Its Relation to the Negro* (Richmond, Va., 1877), 5; Carroll, *The Negro a Beast*, 62-63. Dark pigment, as an element in a more efficient mechanism for the dispersion of heat, may have survival value for tropical people; see Ruth Benedict, *Race: Science and Politics* (New York, 1959), 41; John Fraser Roberts, "A Geneticist's View of Human Variability," in Philip Mason, ed., *Man, Race and Darwin: Papers Read at a Joint Conference of the Royal Anthropological Institute of Great Britain and the Institute of Race Relations* (New York, 1960), 55; Harry Shapiro, *Race Mixture* (Paris, 1963), 30.

temperature, they were slowly congregating in the Gulf states. An analysis of census data convinced him that either Negroes must migrate southward or fail to maintain their numbers. Because he thought the ecological conditions of the Gulf states highly favorable to Negro population growth, Gannett surmised that this was their natural country.[7] Such an argument was not welcome to the whites of the Gulf region, who said that they already had quite enough black workers and too many black voters. Nevertheless, some white supremacists, aware that nearby Caribbean islands belonged to people of African origin,[8] endorsed the idea that Negroes would gravitate to the lower latitudes of the United States by divine enactment. Having reached their proper habitat, they would, however, discover white men already on the spot ready to direct them in the performance of that kind of labor best calculated to promote the interests of mankind.[9]

The inclination of white Southerners was to believe that the mark of race was stamped upon every organ and upon the whole organism. Physiological differences, they thought, were so great that treatment which restored the feverish white man to health made the Negro worse than before. A physician of Anniston, Alabama, to cite an instance, claimed that Negroes required double the dose of medicine used by whites.[10] If Negroes required strong medication, or were afflicted, as many thought, with peculiar diseases, it was because inferiority was stamped plainly on their physical being.

In assembling evidence to prove Negroes inferior, white Southerners faced the temptation to consign them to a lower order of creation. Some extremists drove Negroes to the very

[7] "The Negro's Present Condition," Southern States Farm Magazine, V (1898), 492-95. See also James Bryce, The American Commonwealth, 2 vols. (rev. ed., New York, 1910), 512-13.

[8] Frank Tannenbaum, Slave and Citizen: The Negro in the Americas (New York, 1947), 6-7.

[9] [Puryear], The Public School, 5.

[10] Carroll, The Negro a Beast, 61.

edge of the abyss separating man from monkey, and a few aberrants saw the Negroes as apes.

A New Orleans editor in 1866 described a "fine, likely lot of big strapping negroes—each with a face as black as ink, eyes and teeth as white as snow, hair as woolly as a poodle's, and a mouth as large as the Mammoth cave."[11] Such description came easily to this admirer of J. C. Nott's *Types of Mankind* (1854), which, he believed, established beyond reasonable doubt the separate origin of Negroes and demonstrated that domesticated blacks reverted to wildness when left to themselves. He thought to corroborate Nott by an account of a band of freedmen who, abandoning the highest degree of imitative civilization of which they were capable, had put on breechcloths and begun to worship toads and snakes along a bayou near the gulf.[12] A like-minded journalist in 1875 described Africa as a land where apelike men horribly caricatured humanity and where hideous customs and frightful suffering and death prevailed.[13]

Some newspapermen did not hastily abandon the notion of the separate creation of the races, evidently reflecting the opinion of a body of readers who preferred not to acknowledge any kinship with or responsibility for their black neighbors lest they seem deserving of the privileges accorded kinfolk. One of these in 1875 claimed that Mosaic history was the history of the Caucasian race only. How the other races came into existence was unknown, and need not be known, for if their muscles or their brains could be made to promote the comfort of Adam's descendants, they might be preserved; otherwise, they must eventually be exterminated.[14]

[11] New Orleans *Crescent*, March 19, 1866.

[12] *Ibid.*, July 16, 1866. For Nott's work, see Josiah Clark Nott and George R. Gliddon, *Types of Mankind* (Philadelphia, 1854); Stanton, *The Leopard's Spots*.

[13] *Southern Magazine*, XVI (1875), 320.

[14] *Sunny South*, November 6, 1875. See the reply by a reader upholding the unity of races, November 13, 1875, and restatements of the editor's position, December 9, 1875, October 12, 1889.

Joining the assault on the Negro's human worth, Charles Gayarré, an important political leader and historian of Louisiana, in 1877 denounced Radical Reconstruction, "when bipeds hardly superior to Caracalla's horse" were given judicial, legislative, and executive power. The Radical regime in Louisiana was "a kitchen uprising of impish dwarfs, of creeping things used to the chain of servitude, crouching under the flagellations of centuries," and dependent on federal support, for in themselves "there was flesh and blood, such as it was, but no intellectual and moral entity whatever."[15] A generation later, the notorious racist James K. Vardaman, governor of Mississippi and United States senator, spoke of the black race as a footstool barely human.[16]

Though a few Southerners were to be found arguing that the races were created separately, and fewer still supposed Negroes to be less than human, the inimitable John W. De Forest, novelist and official of the Freedmen's Bureau in South Carolina, testified to the commotion caused by the nonhuman theory: "There was a prodigious movement in the Southern mind in consequence of Dr. Cartwright's discovery that God created three kinds of beings, to wit, man, 'living creatures,' and beasts; and that the negroes, being evidently 'living creatures,' are lower than humans, though not so low as animals. This remarkable 'reading,' having been popularized by a writer signing as 'Ariel,' was used with great effect by Governor Perry [of South Carolina] against universal suffrage, much to the confusion of certain Radical pundits, who did not know what the Governor was talking about."[17]

"Ariel" published an array of "Biblical facts" in an attempt to show that the Negro was created as a beast, the slave of

15 "The Southern Question," *North American Review*, CXXV (1877), 482-84.
16 Archibald S. Coody, *The Race Question from the White Chief* (Vicksburg, Miss., 1944), 46-48.
17 *A Union Officer in the Reconstruction*, ed. by James H. Croushore and David Morris Potter (New Haven, Conn., 1948), 192.

Adam; that this beast was denied immortality; that it was the tempter in the Garden of Eden; that God destroys all nations which mix with the beast or allow it equality; and that mulattoes crucified Christ.[18]

"Prospero," unlike "Ariel," was willing to concede humanity of a low order to Negroes in the manner of "preadamic" creation. Negroes, as descendants of the preadamic men were closer to the chimpanzee than to the Anglo-Saxon. The Caucasian, head of all races, was tempted in the Garden of Eden by one of the "preadamites," called a serpent. Later Cain went out among these creatures, who welcomed the felon and gave him a wife. As punishment for the heinous crime of mixing the blood of the preadamite with the blood of Adam, the Creator sent the flood over the area occupied by these vile creatures; the unmixed preadamites, however, like the pure Caucasians, were spared. After the flood, Caucasians drove the Negroes into Africa. In the South the Caucasians again committed the sin of Cain, not by owning preadamites, but by amalgamating with them. For contaminating their blood with that of the lowest of humans, they were being punished by subjection to the accomplices of their crime.[19]

"Ariel" and "Prospero" in warping the Scriptures and science produced the monstrous type of offspring which they imagined the mulatto to be. Even so, their ideas had a flickering sort of viability. Charles Carroll, following "Ariel," endeavored to prove in 1900 that Negroes were lower animals; and Albert Stowe Lee-Craft in 1923 classified Southerners as superior Caucasians, inferior Negroes, and mulattoes or "mule niggers." Negroes, Lee-Craft wrote, could attain immortality if they obeyed the white man, but "mule niggers," being neither

[18] [Buckner H. Payne], *Ariel's Reply to the Rev. John A. Seiss, D.D., of Philadelphia; Also, His Reply to the Scientific Geologist and Other Learned Men in Their Attacks on the Credibility of the Mosaic Account of the Creation and of the Flood* (Nashville, 1876), 5-94.

[19] [Buchanan], *Caliban.*

white nor black and conceived in violation of divine law, were denied everlasting life.[20]

Carroll held that atheism erroneously taught "that all bipeds, with articulate speech, the erect posture, and well developed hand and foot, and the ability to make and handle tools, are men." The best scientific information on the anatomy of Negroes, he said, actually proved them to be apes. Carroll believed that everyone with a drop of Negro blood was nothing but an ape. All the red, yellow, and brown peoples were apes; they were offspring of the Caucasian human and the Negro beast.[21]

In the minds of the great body of Southern whites it sufficed to define Negroes not as lower animals but as inferior men swayed by passions ineradicable from the flesh that came to them from their ancestors. These defective psychological characteristics, too self-evident to require proof, all pointed to the natural dependence of Negroes upon whites; but to deny the Negro's humanity would, said Hilary Herbert, "bring damnation to the Southern people."[22]

To most whites, Negroes were improvident creatures of the present. Their daily round consisted of sleeping and waking, with a struggle between morning and evening to get enough to put into their mouths. Now and then they attended a religious meeting and perhaps experienced conversion. They dressed in rags six days and wore expensive clothes on the seventh; comfortably labored in broiling heat on a workday, yet indulged in the luxury of an umbrella on a holiday; cheerfully walked miles on weeknights to visit friends, then spent their earnings for a carriage drive on Sunday.[23]

[20] *The Devil's Inkwell: A Story of Humanity, Embracing Biblical Evidence Establishing Irrefutable and Utter Supremacy of the White Man on the Earth since the Beginning of Historical Time* (Houston, 1923), *passim*, esp. 32-46.

[21] *The Negro a Beast*, 46-193.

[22] In Southern Society, *Race Problems of the South*, 32. See also *Sunny South*, December 9, 1876; *Christian Advocate* (Nashville), May 2, 1891.

[23] Edward King, "The Great South: Southern Mountain Rambles: In

The Negro was peaceable and kindly—the fortunate possessor of a sweet and generous nature, the happiest mortal in existence. He delighted in church meetings, parades, craps, and midnight dances. No laborer in the world was so lighthearted and merry. His joy burst forth in music, for which he had a talent equal to that of the Italian. So he had been as a slave, and so he was, in lesser measure, after the restoration of white supremacy. But if he were disturbed by fanatics, then one could look in vain for the old song and dance or the hearty laughter. And the burden of responsibility which had come with freedom had had, it was sometimes argued, a melancholy effect: "while Cuffey has not laid down the shovel and the hoe, as he once thought he was going to do, he has almost entirely hung up the fiddle and the bow."[24]

Whites generally believed that when their defective tendencies were held in check, Negroes made good laborers. This point of view explains why the Negro, though damned, was praised as well. For agricultural labor, one Southerner wrote, Negroes were incomparably better than European immigrants, "better even than the olive pig-tails of the flowery Kingdom." Properly trained, inoculated with just conceptions of themselves and others, and so protected against the malignancy of modern philanthropy, they were still the best farmhands in the world.[25] In all kinds of toil they loved to excel. They were unequaled in splitting rails or lifting heavy weights; at home

---

Tennessee, Georgia, and South Carolina," *Scribner's Monthly*, VIII (1874), 16; Gayarré, *North American Review*, CXXV (1877), 490; J. B. Killebrew, "How to Deal with the Negro," *Southern States Farm Magazine*, V (1898), 485-86.

[24] Helen M. Ludlow, "Hampton Normal and Agricultural Institute," *Harper's Magazine*, XLVIII (1873), 684; [David Hunter Strother], "Our Negro Schools," *Harper's Magazine*, XLIX (1874), 433; Henry Watterson, "The Solid South," *North American Review*, CXXVIII (1879), 54; F. A. Shoup, "Has the Southern Pulpit Failed?" *North American Review*, CXXX (1880), 595. See also *Sunny South*, December 4, 1880; Jackson, Miss., *Clarion*, July 14, 1890; Killebrew, *Southern States Farm Magazine*, V (1898), 485.

[25] [Puryear], *The Public School*, 20.

in the fields, cutting sugarcane, picking cotton, hoeing tobacco, or harvesting rice; and efficient in quarries and tobacco warehouses, as stevedores and steamboathands, and indeed in all kinds of employment where great muscular strength was required or great heat was to be endured.[26]

Having the kindliest disposition of all workers, the Negro alone among laborers was docile in temper. He did not take offense nor seek revenge; among all the races there was none so loyal. Trained by the high intelligence of the Anglo-Saxon, the Southern Negro proved by his fidelity, his incomparable courtesy of manner, and his accommodating disposition that he occupied his true place in society.[27]

The emphasis on the Negro's happiness in the Southern pattern of thought is illustrated in the story about a clergyman from South Carolina whose everlasting topic was the felicity of Negroes under slavery. While traveling in England, he badgered his company beyond endurance in order to instruct them on the contentment of slaves in South Carolina. Losing patience, an Englishman asked, "My dear sir, if things are as you say, why not go back to South Carolina and become a slave?" The Carolinian flew into a rage and challenged the Englishman to a duel, but was not given satisfaction.[28] Like the defender of slavery, the Southerner at the close of the nineteenth century still believed that only the closely regulated Negro could be happy. In that year Clifton R. Breckinridge of Arkansas, a former member of Congress, asserted that the Negro at last regained happiness when the whites forged anew restraints from which he had been released by visionaries

26 New Orleans *Crescent*, October 18, 1865, January 6, 1868; Edward King, "The Great South: The South Carolina Problem: The Epoch of Transition," *Scribner's Monthly*, VIII (1874), 142; *Sunny South*, May 7, 1888; New Orleans *Picayune*, August 28, 1891; Killebrew, *Southern States Farm Magazine*, V (1898), 484.

27 Edward King, "The Great South: A Ramble in Virginia: From Bristol to the Sea," *Scribner's Monthly*, VII (1874), 674; Killebrew, *Southern States Farm Magazine*, V (1898), 484-85; J. R. Stratton, "Address," in Southern Society, *Race Problems of the South*, 150.

28 De Forest, *A Union Officer*, 176-77.

and opportunists. "The negro knows his place," Breckinridge said, "and he is happiest when assigned to it."[29]

As a defense against accusation from various quarters, whites desperately persuaded themselves that the exploited Negroes were happy. If in a Christian society a subordinate people were turbulent, dissatisfied, striving for improvement, this would show that it was not their nature to be ruled by another people. Necessarily dependent Negroes, slaves or semislaves, were said to be as lighthearted as children, while the radical, political Negro was denounced as a devil incarnate.[30]

Under external control the Negro might be good or he might be bad, for he was imitative and, like a chameleon, reflected the character of his white master. His greatest pride was identification with a white family of reputation, but his imitativeness and dependence could be exacerbating if his white master were a carpetbagger or, perhaps, a traitor to the South. In that case, evil influence could spread and contaminate the whole black mass. Thus the South was quickly incensed at white troublemakers and at the few wicked men of the Negro class.[31]

Along with other servile qualities, the Negro was said to inherit a disposition to obey. If United States troops were withdrawn, the Negroes would, according to ex-Confederates in 1867, submit themselves to the guidance of those who had always constituted the community. Only while coerced by federal authority had they ranged themselves against the white people. They had been forced to aid in the consummation of schemes of the very nature of which they were profoundly ignorant.[32] Later, after the restoration of white supremacy,

[29] "Lynching as a Penalty," in Southern Society, *Race Problems of the South*, 174-77.

[30] Watterson, *North American Review*, CXXVIII (1879), 54.

[31] New Orleans *Crescent*, August 3, 1866; Jackson, Miss., *Clarion*, July 14, 1870; Carrollton *West Alabamian*, January 31, 1872; *Sunny South*, July 24, 1886; editorial, "The Negro in the South," *Southern Bivouac*, IX (1887), 710-12.

[32] New Orleans *Crescent*, December 4, 1867.

Southerners pointed out that blacks had obeyed in turn the slaveholder, the temporarily stronger Union officials, and the "redeemers."[33] In short, Negroes were subject to power, and always to the greatest power. In this manner white Southerners explained that strange phenomenon—Negroes who became independent, even aggressive, during the period of Reconstruction. All they had actually done, said Southerners, was obey the power dominant at the moment.

Though obedient by nature, the Negro was an incorrigible thief. It was said that in every county of North Carolina in 1868 freedmen lived on the fruits of theft.[34] A Georgian observed in 1877 that Negroes, shouting on the way home from church, carried away pigs, turkey, chickens, melons, and roasting ears.[35] A citizen of Opelousas, Louisiana, reported in 1879 that in the Negro areas of St. Landry Parish the hogs and chickens were stolen from the barnyard and the corn from the fields. Still, the Louisiana planter and his family were too proud to do their own work and kept on hiring Negroes while getting poorer every day.[36] A Congregational minister of Tennessee declared in 1890 that the Negro's "most conspicuous saints have oftentimes been known to shout and exercise themselves with all the fervor of ecstatic joy until 2 o'clock in the morning, and then make a happy breakfast on some neighbor's shoat or chicken."[37]

Defenders of Southern blacks, such as the Reverend Henry J. Fox, president of the University of South Carolina during the Radical regime, objected to the notion that Negroes were congenital thieves, arguing that they had developed thieving habits under the patriarchal system of bondage. Indeed, Fox noted, they had become ingenious casuists: "If chicken eat

---

[33] Editorial, *Southern Bivouac*, IX (1887), 710-12.

[34] Wilmington, N.C., *Journal*, December 11, 1868.

[35] *Sunny South*, September 29, 1877.

[36] Louisville *Home and Farm*, June 15, 1879.

[37] N. M. Long, "Comparative Value of Man's Intellectual Powers" (delivered January 15, 1890), in *Sermons and Addresses* (Memphis, 1906), 243.

corn, only turn massa corn into massa chicken; he no tief. If hog root through potato rows, he no tief; only turn massa potato into massa hog. If nigger eat corn, and chicken, and hog, he no tief; all massa's yet." Under freedom, the black was giving up slave habits, Fox said, even though the South would not admit it.[38]

Petty thieving was only one of a legion of moral failings thought to characterize the colored man's psychology. A few Negroes were generally well behaved, at least when not under the domination of passion; usually they had been trained as slaves, or by parents who had been slaves. The vast body of the race, wrote Thomas Nelson Page in 1904, lay like a "sluggish mass of uncooled lava over a large section of the country, burying some sections and affecting the whole." Except for a minute fraction, the black race had not advanced at all in morality. Unfortunately, the fountain was tainted at the source. Negroes lacked any idea of morality because they lacked the instinct upon which such an idea could be founded.[39]

Perhaps it was unjust to censure the Negro for moral failings. If he left one mate and took another without marriage or divorce, was he not merely subject to his overpowering instincts? Did not sexual immorality characterize all black people, educated or ignorant, rich or poor? Was it not all but impossible to find a chaste Negro over fifteen? As everyone knew, the black preacher was as much an adulterer as anyone in his congregation.[40]

If Negroes were lazy and improvident, had no honor, experienced no shame, were thieves without conscience, it was because they surrendered, as they must, to the coarseness and vulgarity inseparable from the low grade of humanity bestowed upon them by African ancestors. "They're the meanest, triflingest creature a-goin'," one planter observed. "Thar ain't no good

[38] "The Negro," *Methodist Quarterly Review*, LVII (1875), 94.
[39] *The Negro: The Southerner's Problem* (New York, 1904), 62-64, 81. See also Watterson, *North American Review*, CXXVIII (1879), 47-58.
[40] Page, *The Negro*, 83-84.

side to 'em. You can't find a white streak in 'em, if you turn
'em wrong side outwards and back again. . . . All the men are
thieves, and all the women are prostitutes. It's their natur' to
be that way, and they never'll be no other way."[41]

When his bad nature erupted, it was like a volcano; the
Negro would do anything—commit arson, murder, or outrage
a child. He could dine heartily and sleep deeply with blood
on his hands. "A bad negro is the most horrible human
creature upon the earth," Charles H. Smith wrote in 1893,
"the most brutal and merciless"; even ministers or teachers
"are never made cowards by conscience, nor do they suffer the
stings of remorse."[42] Taking into consideration such slavery to
passion, it was in the interest of society that the Negro's
freedom be curbed.

With abundant reason the Negro scholar W. E. B. Du Bois
complained in 1897 that while sociologists gleefully counted
his bastards and his prostitutes, the soul of the black man was
darkened by vast despair. The Negro, Du Bois said, accepted
the degree of prejudice which was founded on just analysis,
but he was sickened by the "ridicule and systematic humiliation,
the distortion of fact and wanton license of fancy, the cynical
ignoring of the better and boisterous welcoming of the worse,
the all-pervading desire to inculcate disdain for everything
black."[43]

There was little Negroes could do to alter this false image
in the mind of the white man. By heroic efforts they might
as individuals overcome the temptations and handicaps inherent
in an almost hopeless environment.[44] Nevertheless, the white
South was determined to believe that they were inferior beings.

41 Cited in De Forest, A Union Officer, 101.
42 "Have American Negroes Too Much Freedom?" Forum, XVI (1893),
181. See also Noah K. Davis, "The Negro in the South," Forum, I
(1886), 130.
43 "Strivings of the Negro Race," Atlantic Monthly, LXXX (1897),
197.
44 For an interesting and sympathetic view of Negroes living in a hostile
social environment in Cincinnati, on the edge of the South, see Lafcadio
Hearn, Children of the Levee, ed. by O. W. Frost (Lexington, Ky., 1957).

CHAPTER TWO

Testimony of History

SOUTHERNERS looked to history as well as to biology for evidence to be used against the Negro. As they saw it, upon the character of each race history was grounded. The Creator had made Negroes to be servants of white men, and this original fact was of paramount importance in the whole history of Negro-white relations. Some up-to-date white supremacists, influenced by the theory of evolution, especially by the concept of social evolution, conceived of racial distinction as the product of natural forces. In whichever light the Southerner viewed the history of the races, he concluded that Negroes were inferior. Either they could never hope to attain equality, or they could at best do so only after eons of development.

The Southerner was never at home in appealing to Cartwright, Nott, and Darwin; science did not represent high enough authority. Grounded in the religious argument in support of slavery, and generally fundamentalist in belief, he was uncomfortable unless he could find divine support for his racist views. Behind the "voice of Nature" he looked for the will of God. In this spirit, Senator Garrett Davis of Kentucky stated that "the great God who created all races never intended the negro, the lowest," to have equal power with the highest, the white race.[1]

If the races were made unequal, then antagonism toward pretension on the part of the colored man was an "instinct of manhood, the elevation of the soul, the pride and dignity of race which God Almighty has implanted in the breast of every reasonable creature."[2] The white man had no shame to hide; he ought to proclaim his virtue from the housetop. Because the law of nature and the law of God had determined it, Negroes must work as bootblacks, cooks, farmhands—as menials of whatever sort until chaos should come again.[3]

Any attempt to change the Negro into what he could not be was like trying to change arteries, nerves, and bones. So thought Senator John T. Morgan of Alabama, who believed that race aversion rested upon ordinances that human power could neither amend nor repeal,[4] and Senator James B. Eustis of Louisiana, who said that he stood helpless to aid the black man because nature and God forbade him to. The Negro, Eustis believed, would have the right to appeal to the sense of justice of the American people to protect him against the arrogance and proscription which he had so long endured were it not that the unequal relations between the races had been fixed by divine law.[5] A leading Mississippian, Ethelbert Barksdale, observed that, unlike those rapscallions, carpetbaggers and scalawags, redeemers made no profane attempts to annul the distinctions which infinite wisdom had established between the Caucasian and the Negro.[6]

---

[1] Cited in "Monthly Record of Events," *Harper's Magazine*, XXXIV (1867), 398. Two years earlier, in January, 1864, Davis had endeavored to persuade the Senate to include in the proposed Thirteenth Amendment a provision which would have barred Negroes from office under the United States government. See James G. Blaine, *Twenty Years in Congress*, 2 vols. (Norwich, Conn., 1884), I, 505.

[2] Carrollton *West Alabamian*, March 9, 1870.

[3] [Puryear], *The Public School*, 9. See also "The Latin Races in America," *Southern Review*, IX (1871), 322-24; "The Best Government the World Ever Saw: or Christian Statesmanship," *Southern Review*, XIV (1874), 385-415, reprinted in Carrollton *West Alabamian*, August 26, 1874.

[4] "Shall Negro Majorities Rule?" *Forum*, VI (1888), 588.

[5] "Race Antagonism in the South," *Forum*, VI (1888), 147.

[6] "Reconstruction in Mississippi," in Hilary A. Herbert, ed., *Why the Solid South? or, Reconstruction and Its Results* (Baltimore, 1890), 343. See also W. Y. Atkinson, "The Atlanta Exposition," *North American Review*, CLXI (1895), 393.

Historical evidence subsequent to the creation of the races was assiduously offered to the public as proof that Negroes had been and were slavish. The historical and biological arguments complemented one another, but the historical argument was not only the more respectable but also the more plausible, for objective evidence of the backwardness of Negro societies certainly existed. Not even a New Englander could deny that Europe was more advanced than Africa, and few would analyze carefully the reasons why; it would suffice to assert that the Negro himself was at fault.

The white Southerner insisted that slavery, however bad it may have been for the white man, had offered nothing but good to the Negroes. Slavery had taught absolute savages to be skilled laborers in agriculture, in domestic arts, and, to some extent, in mechanical arts. Slavery had not been the cause of Negro inferiority, but the result; the only advances Negroes ever made had occurred in a state of slavery or quasi-slavery. When the influence and domination of a stronger race was lacking, they inevitably reverted to the original type. Since the dawn of history, the racist historian argued, Negroes had been elevated by their superiors in Egypt, in Rome, in the Spanish, Portuguese, Dutch, and English empires, and in the South. Presented with every opportunity to climb in the scale of civilization, they had never done so except under compulsion.[7] History demonstrated beyond the shadow of a doubt that Negroes were inferior.

In boasting that the American Negro was more advanced than the native African, the South admitted the possibility that the black race might develop increasing capacity for civilization. If it did, it must still remain thousands of years

[7] [Puryear], *The Public School*, 6; Thomas Nelson Page, "A Southerner on the Negro Question," *North American Review*, CLIV (1892), 401-403; Walter Hines Page, "The Last Hold of the Southern Bully," *Forum*, XVI (1893), 311; New Orleans *Picayune*, September 22, 1898; Paul B. Barringer, "The Negro and the Social Order," in Southern Society, *Race Problems of the South*, 183.

behind in the upward climb. In the ancient world the distinction between master and bondsman, even when both were of the same color, had resulted in mutual estrangement for 4,000 years. In the United States the social repugnance between the freeborn and freemade classes had been intensified by the fact that the bondsman was not only a slave but also a member of an inferior race. Four times 4,000 years might well be required before free blacks could hope to reach the level of their former masters. Nor was it possible to accelerate their movement. The white child inherited qualities implanted in the race during untold centuries of struggle toward the light of Caucasian civilization, and it was necessary for the Negro race to duplicate the experiences of the superior race before the Negro infant could come into the world on equal terms. White men felt, of course, that when Negroes had attained the heights whites then possessed, Caucasians would have ascended even more empyrean peaks.[8]

History was a record of extremely slow progress in civilization of originally barbarous people, with nothing abrupt, but rather a process of evolutionary development. In the United States there was juxtaposition of the most primitive and the most advanced, the most rudimentary and the most complex types of culture. Savages had been violently carried across the sea and put to work by masters who were several thousand years ahead of them in character and intellect. Though improvement had taken place, the great body of Negroes remained much what their ancestors had been in the tropical forests of the Congo. Suddenly, they were not only freed but also treated as fit to enjoy privileges which were thrust upon them when their highest form of pleasure had been "to caper to the strains of a banjo."[9]

[8] *Southern Review,* VI (1869), 100; Carrollton *West Alabamian,* June 1, 1870; William H. Ruffner, "Co-education of the White and Colored Races," *Scribner's Monthly,* VIII (1874), 86-87.

[9] Bryce, *The American Commonwealth,* II, 515-17. Other foreign observers of the American scene similarly were vulnerable to propaganda on

It was quite easy to assess the Negro's aptitude for civilized affairs, the Southerner imagined, inasmuch as he had had, since the beginning of time, a country all his own to develop. The same animals which were in Africa at the dawn of creation were still there. The same people were there, unable now as then to master the natural environment and develop the arts of civilization; "the same black, glossy, low-browed, wooly-headed, mighty-lipped, long-heeled natives who now possess its fertile plains, resemble their forefathers who sat down by the Nile and the Niger thousands of years ago, in their morals, social customs, laws, and business habits, as precisely as they resemble them in penetrating fragrance and personal comeliness."[10]

The king of Dahomey was said to be a tyrant loved for his tyranny, with three to four thousand wives and a reversionary interest in all the other females in his kingdom. His subjects were cowardly, cruel, and bloodthirsty, and given to lying and drunkenness. African villages were sinkholes of barbarism. The latest fashions were amusing: "How the People of All Classes Dress and Don't Dress There." The history of Africa was a static round of barbaric men succeeding barbaric men, because there was not a spark of innovation in their nature.[11]

The Negro's apologists could offer no excuse that time was lacking. Africa was ancient when England had been a waste. If it were claimed that the African environment was not conducive to the growth of culture, what did the Negro do to find a more suitable home? He would have been content to live and die in ignorance that the world extended beyond the woods in which he loafed. "It was only upon an invitation that he could not refuse, at the point of the blunderbuss, and under

the Negro. See, for example, Felix Klein, *In the Land of the Strenuous Life* (Chicago, 1905), 296-97.

[10] "The Best Government," *Southern Review*, XIV (1874), 385-415.

[11] Charleston, S.C., *News and Courier*, May 11, 1876; Charlottesville, Va., *Chronicle*, July 26, October 4, 1878; Jackson, Miss., *Clarion*, June 21, 1888.

the constraint of chains and handcuffs, that he turned up in
the character of an emigrant in foreign ports." Not he, but the
"brave old Pilgrim Fathers, and their pleasant posterity," who
had a "natural aptitude and appetite for man stealing," were
responsible for his presence in the South.[12]

Liberia, a creature of charity and a darling of philanthropy,
hardly differed from the Congo. It was nothing if not a failure.
Civilization had been created for the black man there, the
country founded for him by the Caucasian; Christendom had
given its prayers. Yet there were no factories in Liberia, no
boats, no beasts of burden, not even carts; there was no money
there. Altogether it presented a hopeless picture.[13]

Indeed, the Negroes had neglected Africa long enough; it
was time for the Caucasian to seize that dark continent and
to employ it in the uses of civilization. The partition of Africa
could hardly be ascribed solely to a lust for territory. The
tropical countries could not be left to the colored race. Progress came only from the energy, discipline, and efficiency of
men whose power was not the result of circumstances.[14] Unlike
the whites who had brought Negroes to America, perhaps a
few stout Caucasians should go to Africa to rule the blacks in
their jungle haunts, especially since valuable resources there
could be developed by native labor.

The doctrine of Manifest Destiny which produced the
imperialism of the closing decades of the nineteenth century
was, of course, advantageous to Southern white men in their
efforts to rule Negroes. Their belief that the incapacity of

12 "The Best Government," *Southern Review*, XIV (1874), 385-415.

13 Hilary Herbert, "Reconstruction in Alabama," in Herbert, ed., *Why
the Solid South?* 37; Jackson, Miss., *Clarion*, January 5, 1876; Page, *North
American Review*, CLIV (1892), 405.

14 J. L. M. Curry, *Difficulties, Complications, and Limitations Connected with the Education of the Negro* (Baltimore, 1895), 14. Doubtless
the rapid development of Africa would have been impossible without the
great technical knowledge of Europeans, some of whom wished to be
repaid with a permanent position of privilege. See Lucy Mair, "Tribalism
and Nationalism in Africa," in Mason, ed., *Man, Race, and Darwin*,
112-13.

primitives was demonstrated by history then received the endorsement of millions of Caucasians at home and abroad, North as well as South. Did not William McKinley, President of the United States and leader of the party for emancipation, call for the annexation of the Philippines in order to Christianize and civilize the American's little brown brother there?

In the history of neighboring Haiti and other Caribbean islands the racist historian discovered abundant material seeming to support his belief that civilization declined wherever Negro slaves gained freedom and dominance. As slaves, the Negroes of Haiti had contributed by their labor to the welfare of mankind. Upon gaining freedom, they began sliding into barbarism. Here was the old story of Negro government. Degeneration prevailed in Haiti, in Santo Domingo, and in all other countries where blacks enjoyed greater political power than whites, or where a few knavish whites used the blacks to ride into office. Negroes reverted to paganism and cannibalism and lived in unbroken desolation. In Haiti, perhaps 100,000 nominal Christians remained among 500,000 pagans.[15]

On this point, as on others involving Negroes, the Southern mind was unbelievably static. Immediately after the Civil War, the New Orleans *Crescent*, in condemning zealots who invaded the South to make the Negro "a voter, a magistrate, a judge, in short a white man," referred to Jamaican history as showing that it was as impossible to turn the African into a European as it was to make the leopard change its spots.[16] Thirty years or so later, Thomas Nelson Page observed that for a hundred years the Negro had been masquerading in governing Haiti, and a more fantastic mummery had never degraded a land. Under black rule, Santo Domingo had sunk into a state of primeval barbarism. Revolution succeeded revolution; massacre succeeded massacre. A country once wealthy was in ruin. Chris-

[15] New Orleans *Crescent*, December 9, 1865; Charleston, S.C., *News and Courier*, July 21, 1868; Carrollton *West Alabamian*, September 18, 1872, May 7, 1873; Jackson, Miss., *Clarion*, May 22, 1873.
[16] December 21, 1865.

tianity was giving way to voodooism. Such a riot of folly had never been witnessed save in those countries in which the Negroes themselves furnished the illustration.[17]

In discussing the history of the decline of free Negroes in the South, as in the Caribbean, the white man often used as illustration the freedmen's religious and labor history. In religion the Negro after the Civil War enjoyed greater freedom than in his other affairs and, said the white supremacist, the creation of Negro churches produced a lamentable spiritual decline, offering further proof that the ex-slave was unworthy of independence. Instructed by their masters, the slaves had been sober Christians, but upon becoming self-directed, they surrendered to their excitable natures, took the road to wild extravagance, and, in some cases, reverted to heathenism. Ethics was divorced from theology, and thieves and adulterers went uncensured in congregation and pulpit.[18]

One commentator spoke of a mass of sable humanity weltering in confusion and anarchy, every particle possessing "a soul imbued with superstition, woven into its grain as it were, never to be eradicated."[19] A congressman who wrote a piece on the advancing heathenism among Negroes in Liberty County, Georgia, claimed that it was refused publication in Northern papers on the grounds that Northern people would not believe it and that it was based on the prejudice of white men in the South.[20] Other accounts were not refused. In the pages of the *Century Magazine*, Bishop T. U. Dudley reached a Northern audience with the assertion that the Negroes' "religion is a superstition, their sacraments are fetiches, their

[17] *North American Review*, CLIV (1892), 405-406. See also G. O. Seilhamer, "Negro Life in Jamaica," *Harper's Magazine*, XLIV (1872), 553-61.

[18] Chevereux Gris, "The Negro in His Religious Aspect," *Southern Magazine*, XVII (1875), 501-502; Davis, *Forum*, I (1886), 130; Robert F. Campbell, *Some Aspects of the Race Problem in the South* (2d ed., Asheville, N.C., 1899), 23.

[19] Gris, *Southern Magazine*, XVII (1875), 501; see also *Sunny South*, September 28, 1889, March 15, 1890.

[20] Norwood, *Address on the Negro*, 12.

worship is a wild frenzy, and their morality a shame." The remedy was a resumption of white control regardless of the objections of some black ranters.[21]

The freedmen's labor history also pointed to their need for supervision. Complaints, loud and frequent, were heard that the freedman would not work, that he occupied, without cultivating, the soil, and that rich land was relapsing into jungle. This was especially true, it was said, in localities where Negroes had gained control of the land and made no use of it, living merely by fishing and hunting. The people of Charleston, South Carolina, referred to nearby Beaufort as the "capital of the Kingdom of Dahomey." This reversion to primitive civilization had been hastened by tutelage that had led the Negro to believe that if he would just sit still and open his mouth, Uncle Sam would see that he was fed.[22]

Not only were freedmen lazy, but they also manifested an uncontrollable tendency to roam about the country. Considering no agreement binding, they were restless, suspicious, and untrustworthy. At a crisis of the season the hands were as likely as not to disappear, "leaving their employer to do the best he could; and the best he could would be to hire other negro laborers, who, in their turn, would disappear when their labor was necessary."[23] They all went to town on Saturday almost as a religious duty, often to squander their earnings on whisky. A month before Christmas they would abandon the

[21] "How Shall We Help the Negro?" *Century Magazine*, VIII (1885), 279-80; see also D. Clay Lilly, "The Negro in Relation to Religion," in Southern Society, *Race Problems of the South*, 119-21.

[22] N. S. Shaler, "An Ex-Southerner in South Carolina," *Atlantic Monthly*, XXVI (1870), 60-61; Edwin De Leon, "Ruin and Reconstruction of the Southern States, a Record of Two Tours in 1868 and 1873," *Southern Magazine*, XIV (1874), 24-35; Edwin De Leon, "The New South," *Harper's Magazine*, XLVII (1874), 271; King, "South Carolina," *Scribner's Monthly*, VIII (1874), 129-60; Edward King, "The Great South: Down the Mississippi: The Labor Question: Arkansas," *Scribner's Monthly*, VIII (1874), 652; Joseph Le Conte, *The Race Problem in the South* (New York, 1892), *passim*.

[23] Joel Chandler Harris, in Charles A. Gardiner and others, "The Future of the Negro," *North American Review*, CXXXIX (1884), 87.

fields "to prepare for their annual frolic, and leave their employers with the bag to hold, and fill, too."[24]

Proslavery theorists had predicted that removed from the salutary control of slavery, American Negroes would not long survive. Some white supremacists of the New South believed that except for the development of quasi-slavery, history would have confirmed this prediction. The most sacred of rights, said the distinguished Southern geologist Joseph Le Conte, was "the right of the weak and the ignorant to the control and guidance of the strong and wise"; thus even in 1892, control of the Negro race by the white race was still absolutely necessary.[25] Since emancipation, Professor Paul Barringer of the University of Virginia noted in 1900, the Negro had been subjected to the "remorseless laws of nature, and being unfit to meet their demands here, he from that day, began to fall." Evidence to this effect was the well-known decline in the Negro's capacity for labor, and his accompanying impoverishment and increased death rate. "Unobtrusive but steady and persistent force was necessary to the continuance in welldoing of this race of pagans."[26] This same year the Reverend D. Clay Lilly urged his fellow Southerners to remember the lesson of history that their Negroes were mere children who labored well for others under humane discipline but were unequal to the grave responsibilities imposed upon them by freedom.[27]

In 1901 George T. Winston reviewed what racist historians claimed had happened to the Negro race in the South.[28] This North Carolina college president explained that following the abolition of slavery, a great change involving personal interest, moral influence, and social and economic relations had taken

[24] Carrollton West Alabamian, April 22, 1870.
[25] The Race Problem in the South, 360-61.
[26] In Southern Society, Race Problems of the South, 178-94.
[27] In Southern Society, Race Problems of the South, 118-19.
[28] "The Relation of the Whites to the Negroes," in America's Race Problems: Addresses at the Annual Meeting of the American Academy of Political and Social Science, Philadelphia, April Twelfth and Thirteenth, MCMI (Philadelphia, 1901), 105-18.

place. There was practically no social contact between the races except that which involved the Negroes and degraded whites. During slavery the two races had mingled, not as social equals, but in constant social relations. On every plantation the white and black children played together. It was a privilege for the white child to visit the slave cabins and listen to a real "Uncle Remus" delight him with the stories later immortalized by Joel Chandler Harris. Social intercourse had involved adults, too. White women came to the cabin to inspect the children, to direct work, and to show their interest in the slaves. It was this influence of the white race which had gradually transformed the savage into a semicivilized individual.

Upon emancipation the Negro had reverted to the idleness made possible by a mild climate, the abundance of game in forest and stream, and the bountiful supply of wild fruits and berries. As a consequence, he idled away his time and yet lived in tolerable comfort. The national government had strengthened this inherited inclination to laziness by distributing food and clothing to freedmen. In this way a vast and effective labor force was corrupted and became a miserable object of charity. During the dark night of Radical Reconstruction carpetbaggers and educational and religious visionaries overran the South, preaching social and political equality, destroying the friendship between the races, and giving the Negro "a consciousness of being unharnessed, unhitched, unbridled and unrestrained." Wild excesses followed.

When this destructive revolution was crushed, the Negroes were left with a burden of ignorance, incompetence, and criminality and with gloomy prospects for the future. Their only hope was to continue under the instruction and control of the whites, and remain there until the race problem should be finally solved. The alternative was for the Negro to remain a "dull and stupid draught animal," finally to vanish from history.

Winston's discussion of the dependence of the freedman upon the white Southerner was a distillation of the thoughts of the South on the Negro question. It was in substance an adaptation of the proslavery argument of the Old South to the conditions of quasi-slavery of the New South. Not an original thought was advanced by Winston,[29] and the history he presented was deceptive. Indeed, the South did not welcome original thought on the Negro problem and did not shrink from deception. It intended to keep the Negro in thralldom, and its leading spokesmen acknowledged as much, often in a fashion seductive enough to win a hearing among Yankees anxious to be deceived.

[29] Winston's ideas can be found in greater or less degree in nearly any item of white supremacy propaganda. The *Southern Review*, for example, spoke of Negroes as children who could prosper only under the "pupilage, control, guidance" of the whites; otherwise they were exposed to "want, idleness, and crime." "Congress versus the Constitution," IV (1868), 86. In the Atlanta *Constitution*, March 4, 1877, it was stated that the emancipated slave, after a fling, had been "sauntering toward the mansion," but he met a "tramp with a carpetbag on his shoulder," who turned him away from the old master; now finding sickness and death along the Radical road, he was coming back to his Southern master's home.

CHAPTER THREE

Amalgamation

AMALGAMATION of the races was a nagging worry in the South. Much theorizing on race relations stemmed from this basic fear. Given the belief that because of its God-given superiority, the master race ruled the servant race in justice, anything which tended to destroy the distinction between the sheep and the goats was unholy, unclean. Here was the root of the horrifying associations called into the consciousness by the prospect of racial amalgamation. Could white men despise—and use—their mulatto children, nephews and nieces, cousins, or spouses?

It is not surprising that the moment unacceptable suggestions were offered to solve the Negro problem the Southerner quickly raised the specter of social equality, resulting in amalgamation. "The next thing you know," he would say, "the niggers will be eating and sleeping with us." He knew that if white and colored people went to school together, worked in the same factories, sat in the same legislature—all on terms of equality— then it would no longer be possible to forestall amalgamation on the grounds that Negroes were not worthy to marry whites. This was the reason that whites of Alabama were shocked at the work of the "mongrel" constitutional convention of 1867 which authorized mixed schools and refused to prohibit racial intermarriage, that whites of Arkansas complained that their radical constitution of 1868 would lead to amalgamation, and that Georgians sighed with relief when their supreme court in 1869 declared interracial marriages forever null and void.[1]

By their Civil Rights or "Social Equality" bill of 1874, congressional Radicals proposed to poison the morals of the South and to leave the body alive that it might transmit corrupted blood.[2] Such proposals, it was said, encouraged rape. Thus a rumor rode on the winds in the fall of 1875, like ante bellum panic over imagined slave plots, that Negro militiamen in Washington County, Georgia, had planned an insurrection during which they would kill all the white men and ugly women and take the pretty white women for themselves. This "Georgia Insurrection," allegedly planned for a twelve-county area, chilled the blood of whites in Georgia and in neighboring states.[3]

A main attraction of the white man's party organized during Radical Reconstruction was its promise to protect the white man's family from the corruption fostered by amalgamationists. When white supremacy was reestablished, the Southern states enacted legislation to prohibit interracial marriages. The Hanover County Court in Virginia in 1879 sentenced a Negro, Edward Kenny, and his white spouse to five years in prison for the crime of intermarriage, which had been changed from a misdemeanor to a felony the year before. The United States Circuit Court of Richmond, presided over by the Republican Judge R. W. Hughes, who was "not lost to respect for his race and the laws ordained by his Maker,"[4] upheld the conviction, stating that the law applied equally to white and black, without distinction on the basis of "race, color, or previous condition." Although Negroes protested, whites maintained that the wisdom of the law was sustained by the history of the world and

---

[1] In Herbert, ed., *Why the Solid South?* 46; Fort Smith, Ark., *Herald*, February 22, 1868; Atlanta *Intelligencer*, clipped in Jackson, Miss., *Clarion*, July 8, 1869.

[2] Montgomery *Advertiser*, clipped in Carrollton *West Alabamian*, June 10, 1874.

[3] Carrollton *West Alabamian*, September 1, 1875; Jackson, Miss., *Clarion*, September 15, 1875.

[4] Jackson, Miss., *Clarion*, May 21, 1879.

the lessons of science.[5] A Georgia judge, thinking that punishment should fit the crime, advocated the death sentence for the Negro, and life imprisonment for the white, in cases of miscegenation.[6]

White Southerners convinced themselves that miscegenation was un-Christian. During Radical Reconstruction they recoiled in shame and horror before the hybrids who misrepresented them, declaring that providence had prescribed the position which black men were to occupy.[7] A quarter century later, when reviewing the evils of Reconstruction, they similarly clothed the South in righteousness while denouncing the "wicked defiance of the law of Almighty God to divide human beings into distinct races, and the institution of the beastly system of mongrelism usually called social equality." Only the vigilance, force, and courage of the white race in the South had prevented a repetition there of the histories of Haiti and Santo Domingo.[8]

To prevent amalgamation the Creator had, it was thought, implanted in each race an instinct of aversion toward all other races which tended to maintain the races in pristine purity. Only the worst members of each race were unresponsive to this instinct, said the chancellor of the University of Georgia, who expressed the utmost confidence that the best people, on the other hand, shuddered at the prospect of racial mixing. It had been plausibly suggested that intermingling would begin along the line of the highest development of the black and the

[5] Charlottesville, Va., *Chronicle*, May 2, 1879. The *Sunny South*, March 6, 1886, in a discussion of this case, brushed aside constitutional questions and took the high ground that race pollution was a crime which legislation should define as such.

[6] Norwood, *Address on the Negro*, 25-28. The editor of the Charlottesville, Va., *Chronicle*, May 2, 1879, however, while denouncing the crime, asked for executive clemency for the "degraded pair" if they would move far away, because gross unions of this sort outside matrimony were defined as misdemeanors.

[7] Fort Smith, Ark., *Herald*, May 2, 1868.

[8] Barksdale, in Herbert, ed., *Why the Solid South?* 330-49.

lowest of the white, but the sporadic cases of miscegenation had occurred among the lowest types of both races.[9]

The North Carolina leader Zebulon Vance believed that race aversion among the best people was even stronger in 1884 than it had been in 1865. Intermarriage then was regarded with so much disgust that when you found a white man or woman ready to marry a Negro, you could be sure the Negro would get the worst of the bargain.[10] Less inclined to insult the best people among the Negroes, Joel Chandler Harris claimed that aversion to intermarriage was as strong in one race as in the other, a fact demonstrated by the harsh criticism intelligent Negroes had leveled at Frederick Douglass for marrying a white woman.[11] Harris's view, though it was less flattering than the notion that the black race yearned to lose itself in the beautiful and masterful white race, was supported by A. G. Haygood, a leading Southern Methodist clergyman, who also commended Negroes for not desiring to mingle their blood with that of the whites.[12]

A Virginian, less sure of the power of instinct, asserted that the animus of the entire machinery of the federal government during Reconstruction had been to wear away race antagonism by promiscuous contact and so to degrade into mulattoes "the noblest type of the noblest race that ever floated on the tide of time." If the South were saved, it would be only because of antagonisms implanted in men by the Creator to protect purity of blood. But law might weaken instinct, so that both from the increasing strength of the law and the growing weakness of virtue, the race might be hopelessly ruined. To prevent such a development, Virginians must, by their public policy, reduce the temptation to commit the sin of amalgamation

[9] Walter B. Hill, "Uncle Tom without a Cabin," *Century Magazine*, V (1883-1884), 862.

[10] *North American Review*, CXXXIX (1884), 86.

[11] *Ibid.*, 87.

[12] "Introduction," in J. M. Hood, *Negro in the Christian Pulpit: or the Two Characters and Two Destinies as Delineated in Twenty-one Practical Sermons* (Raleigh, N.C., 1884), 5-6.

"against decency and morals, against race and blood, against God and nature."[13]

An officer of the Freedmen's Bureau, John W. De Forest, noting that only a few widowed, "low down wimmen" took Negro lovers, confirmed the observation of Governor Vance that miscegenation had declined under freedom. His explanation had nothing to do with instinct, however, but was based upon the conditions of increased segregation and heightened propaganda. Where prejudice had been cultivated by every possible appeal, only the worst degradation could lead a white woman "to listen to overtures of love from a 'nigger.' "[14] A generation later, Lord Bryce reported that the mixture of blood had diminished, a mixture which, he thought, may have been leavening the black mass with superior talent.[15] The thoroughgoing segregation of the New South, necessitated by the semifreedom of the blacks, was chiefly responsible for this slowdown in amalgamation, a process which had been going on as long as Negroes had lived among whites and which had produced, in addition to the large number of mulattoes, groups of "almost whites," called Guineas, Brass Ankles, Red Bones, Ramps, Issues, Red Legs, Melungeons, and Buckheads.[16]

Some Negroes and Yankees suggested that amalgamation would bring nothing worse than the blending of Caucasian and Negroid physical traits. This prediction was in itself shocking enough to the white Southerner, who was fond of contrasting Negro ugliness with Caucasian beauty. The novelist Thomas Dixon, for example, thought that "the big nostrils, flat nose, massive jaw, protruding lip and kinky hair will register their animal marks over the rarest beauty of any other race."[17] But the white supremacist believed that far more than esthetics was involved. Amalgamation would darken the future

13 [Puryear], *The Public School*, 14-15.
14 *A Union Officer*, 138.
15 *American Commonwealth*, II, 517.
16 Brewton Berry, *Almost White* (New York, 1963).
17 *The Leopard's Spots: A Romance of the White Man's Burden, 1865-1900* (New York, 1902), 382.

of the South, determined as it would be by a population low
in intelligence, lacking in capacity for self-government, and
weak in all other virtues of the Caucasian. The debased society
would falter and then go into decline until it reached the
midpoint between civilization and savagery, if indeed it could
stop short of brutish chaos.

Plentiful illustrations were offered to prove this point. Albert
T. Bledsoe, for example, read the ills of Mexico, and of the
whole of Latin America, in terms of mongrelism. Spanish blood
had been polluted by the Indian; therefore Mexico was condemned to bloodshed and strife.[18] Other writers diligently
searched out indisputable evidence of the bad consequences of
amalgamation. Charles A. Gardiner found that

the Griquas of South Africa, hybrids of Dutch colonists and Hot-
tentots; the Kruglis of Western Africa, of Turkish-Moorish descent;
the Zambos of western South America, mongrels of mixed European, negro, and indigenous American races; the Portuguese-Malay
half-castes of the East Indies; the English-Maori half-breeds of
New Zealand; the Dutch-Malay half-breeds of Java; the Mongolian
and Slavic mixture of Russian Asia; the Portuguese and negro
population of Brazil; and the Mestizos of Mexico; are all examples
of modern race fusion, but without an exception they disclose
results adverse to miscegenation. In no instance does the mixed
people show the mental vigor of the Caucasian parent stock, and
in most instances the mental and moral condition of the half-caste
is lower even than that of the inferior stock.[19]

The mulatto, as defined by the white, was the most effective
argument against racial intermarriage. Although Southerners,

[18] Editorial, "The Latin Races in America," *Southern Review*, IX
(1871), 322-24. Spaniards themselves entertained this fear of racial
debasement, though with less tenacity than Southerners. See Donald
Pierson, *Negroes in Brazil: A Study of Race Contact at Bahia* (Chicago,
1942), who deemphasizes race prejudice in Brazil but acknowledges its
existence; Stanley J. Stein, *Vassouras: A Brazilian Coffee County, 1850-1900*
(Cambridge, Mass., 1957); Lewis Hanke, *Aristotle and the American
Indians: A Study in Race Prejudice in the Modern World* (Chicago,
1959).

[19] *North American Review*, CXXXIX (1884), 80.

in order to stress the inferiority of the black race, were quick to point out that intelligent Negroes were mulattoes, they also consigned the mulatto to relative inferiority in order to encourage the white race to maintain its superiority. The real difficulty about mulattoes was that they were deemed more intelligent than blacks, more dissatisfied with menial labor, and more difficult to manage, in addition to the unpleasant fact that they were kinfolk who had been abandoned to degradation.

The mulatto, according to the Southern view, was peculiarly inflammable. From the white he inherited a refinement unfitting him for all indelicate work; from the black, a moral laxity, unquestionably a Negro trait. There might be hope for pure blacks, but there could be none for mulattoes, who were hybrids at once short-lived and sterile, which, if the stock were not replenished, would soon vanish. It was a common belief, supported by the authority of the great Louis Agassiz, that the hybrid was weaker, more susceptible to disease, and shorter lived than either of its progenitors.[20] As segregation tightened and amalgamation declined, the South hopefully anticipated the extinction of the mulatto breed.

Some idolators of race believed that Caucasian blood was so potent that the slightest degree lifted the mulatto above the pure Negro; others thought that a quarter white was inferior in intelligence to the fullblooded Negro; but most agreed that the mulatto, because of his kinship to the master race, aspired to equality with whites and, in consequence, stirred up the Negro, who otherwise was prevented by instinct from hoping for the unattainable. But it would be a mistake to admit mulattoes, let alone blacks, to white society; the structure of civilization erected by Anglo-Saxons could be maintained by no lesser people. Thus white Southerners thought of themselves as being burdened by contact with an

[20] Shaler, *Atlantic Monthly*, XXVI (1870), 57; Jackson, Miss., *Clarion*, November 3, 1870; R. Randolph Stevenson, *The Southern Side: or, Andersonville Prison* (Baltimore, 1876), 292.

alien race to whom they could not allow equality without
disintegrating their civilization and corrupting their master
race.[21]

It is not surprising that the South took elaborate precautions
against what it believed to be imminent destruction. Segregation of the races was designed in part to prevent amalgamation. So was the astonishingly complex etiquette that governed
the behavior of individuals of the two races when necessity
brought them into contact. Most carefully regulated was the
contact between Negro males and white females. Segregation
on the railways began with the setting aside of a "ladies' car"
to which white men were admitted, although Negro women as
well as men were excluded. Railways which permitted "filthy
negroes," "foul vermin," to enter Pullman cars occupied by
whites, especially by white ladies, encountered public hostility.[22]

In analyzing the "rape complex," W. J. Cash has pointed
out that the Southern woman was identified with the very
notion of the South and that an assault on the South would
be an assault on her.[23] There is no doubt that Southerners
thought the rape of a white woman by a Negro the most
horrible of crimes, justifying the most brutal punishment
imaginable. In dramatic fashion such rape challenged the
mastery and integrity of the white race. If control broke down
in this instance, all controls would collapse. Rape represented
the failure of the white man to defend his race against savage
insubordination. Refinement and virtue were challenged by
brutishness and vice. All society trembled, as it always does
when confronted by vicious crime, especially by rape and

[21] Shaler, *Atlantic Monthly*, XXVI (1870), 57; H. H. Goodloe, "The
Negro Problem," *Southern Magazine*, XIV (1874), 373-76; Gayarré,
North American Review, CXXV (1877), 490; Gardiner and others, *North
American Review*, CXXXIX (1884), 80; William P. Trent, "Dominant
Forces in Southern Life," *Atlantic Monthly*, LXXIX (1897), 48.

[22] Jackson, Miss., *Clarion*, September 8, 1870; Carrollton *West Alabamian*, April 7, 1875; Henry W. Grady, "In Plain Black and White; A
Reply to Mr. Cable," *Century Magazine*, VII (1885), 909-17.

[23] *The Mind of the South* (New York, 1941), 126.

murder. In this case, however, the possible collapse of the social order was more sharply revealed because this particular crime represented in the Southern mind not only the depravity of the Negro race but a fundamental challenge to white supremacy.[24]

A Southern college president expressed the collective fear and described the convulsive reaction of the white community in defense of its women and its honor:

The Southern woman with her helpless little children in solitary farm house no longer sleeps secure in the absence of her husband with doors unlocked but safely guarded by black men whose lives would be freely given in her defense. But now, when a knock is heard at the door, she shudders with nameless horror. The black brute is lurking in the dark, a monstrous beast, crazed with lust. His ferocity is almost demoniacal. A mad bull or a tiger could scarcely be more brutal. A whole community is now frenzied with horror, with blind and furious rage for vengeance. A stake is driven; the wretched brute, covered with oil, bruised and gashed, beaten and hacked and maimed, amid the jeers and shouts and curses, the tears and anger and joy, the prayers and the maledictions of thousands of civilized people, in the sight of the school-houses, court-houses and churches is burned to death.

.   .   .   .   .

I do not hesitate to say that more horrible crimes have been committed by the generation of Negroes that have grown up in the South since slavery than by the six preceding generations in slavery. And also that the worst cruelties of slavery all combined for two centuries were not equal to the savage barbarities inflicted in retaliation upon the Negroes by the whites during the last twenty years.[25]

The rape of Negro women, because it proved the continued mastery of the white, did not result in mob destruction of the criminal, although it was deplored because it foreshadowed obliteration of the color line. No doubt the fact that the

[24] Alexander C. King, "Lynching as a Penalty," in Southern Society, Race Problems of the South, 161-63; Jackson, Miss., Clarion, August 27, 1874.

[25] Winston, in America's Race Problems, 108-109.

white man could refuse to recognize his mulatto child and abandon it to the Negro community, while the white mother was bound to her child, helps explain this difference. In addition, the white man was given generalized authority over Negro women as well as men, while the Negro father of the mulatto child was of the subordinate group.[26]

The opponent of amalgamation was extraordinarily vigilant, lest the thing get started. The Protestant Episcopal diocesan convention, Columbia, South Carolina, in May, 1876, denied the request of the Negro parish of St. Mark's to admit its delegates, on the grounds that to give any encouragement to mulattoes would be to promote amalgamation of the races. A majority of lay delegates rejected the appeal of the bishop and a majority of the clergy to save the church from endorsing caste and heeded the report of a committee which noted that before the war, mulatto women had relations with white men, which they seemed to consider as very much like marriage. The results of such associations were numerous in the streets. It was this class which tempted to miscegenation. If miscegenation should be encouraged, then this class should be cherished and advanced. But since the Protestant Episcopal Church in the United States was based on the "unity of race," amalgamation was "opposed to the law of God and to civil policy." It was better to trust laymen who lived in the world than clergymen who ran after abstract principles. The argument that mulattoes would side with blacks was false; they had been classed as blacks since emancipation. Moreover, "would not immunities granted to mulattoes offer encouragement to the blacks to a mixture of races?" The committee reminded the delegates that the agitation of the Chinese question in California showed the importance of the question of race distinctions.[27]

26 John Dollard asserts that white men, by virtue of membership in the dominant race, had sexual access to Negro women. *Caste and Class in a Southern Town* (3d ed., New York, 1957), 134-39.

27 See "Report of the Majority Committee," in Charleston, S.C., *News*

Nine years later, in 1885, T. U. Dudley, Protestant Episcopal bishop of Kentucky, presented to the readers of *Century Magazine* substantially these same arguments. Remarking that the patriot stood appalled before the abysmal ignorance and moral incapacity of the black race, and that the halfcaste was both more debased in morals than the inferior Negro stock and less intelligent than the superior white stock, the bishop added: "Instinct and reason, history and philosophy, science and revelation, all alike cry out against the degradation of the race by the free commingling of the tribe which is highest with that which is lowest in the scale of development. The process of selection which nature indicates as the method of most rapid progress indignantly refuses to be thus set at naught. Our temporary ills of to-day may not be remedied by the permanent wrong of the whole family in heaven and earth."[28]

---

and Courier, May 13, 1876. For the developing controversy, see Charleston *News and Courier*, May 12-18, 1876.

[28] *Century Magazine*, VIII (1885), 273-75.

CHAPTER FOUR

Race Warfare

THE SOUTHERNER argued that diverse races when brought into contact either accommodate themselves to a superior-inferior relationship or engage in warfare for supremacy. As between Negro and white, biological and historical factors converged to give victory to the Caucasian race.

The function of this theory of race warfare was to excuse the use of violence in reducing the freedman to a status of subservience. If the white race was destined to war against the black race until the black race had been subdued, then the white man who forced the black man to acknowledge servitude was not morally responsible. The responsibility belonged to the race. Moreover, since nature and nature's God ordained the laws governing race, racial warfare had natural and divine sanction.

According to this theory, individuals were hardly more than manifestations of a race. They were recognized only to illustrate the characteristics of the race and then were promptly relegated to anonymity. On the other hand, the racist believed that every individual shared fully in the character of the race to which he belonged. Race theory in this way transmuted the white planter into the purest and strongest of masters, while it consigned the Negro cropper to the status of the humblest of servants. The Negro who was true to his race accepted subordination; the white man to remain true to his race must defend its honor unto death.

Shortly after the Civil War a white youth spoke up for a
true representative of the Negro race, Cato Allums: "He's just
as civil a nigger as need be. No gentleman ever had cause
to quarrel with him in no way, shape, nor manner. Wherever
Cato goes; if he meets a gentleman, he offs hat and says, 'Good
morning'; and if he sees a gentleman coming across the fields
he puts down the bars for him."[1] Cato had been conquered
like the free Negro in Joel Chandler Harris's "Free Joe and the
Rest of the World." Free Joe "realized the fact that though
he was free he was more helpless than any slave. Having no
owner every man was his master. He knew that he was the
object of suspicion, and therefore all his slender resources (ah!
how pitifully slender they were) were devoted to winning not
kindness and appreciation, but toleration; all his efforts were
in the direction of mitigating the circumstances that tended
to make his condition so much worse than that of the negroes
around him—negroes who had friends, because they had
masters."[2]

But what if Cato and Free Joe should demand the privileges
of freedom? By their very nature, it was thought, whites warred
against blacks until they overcame them. When the white
race moved into a region occupied by the black race, it assumed
possession as a right of nature. If the original settlers submitted, they were permitted to live in peace; if troublesome,
they were subdued; if permanently rebellious, they were exterminated.

Who in the South had not witnessed the docility of the
Negro, humble, trustful, and obedient? Even the Negro, coming from the crowd where he had been galvanized by inflam-
matory oratory, lost his courage when confronted by the white
man and, by his language and bearing, proclaimed his inferiority. Such a creature was no match for the unconquerable
race, which had been created to take possession of the globe and

[1] De Forest, A Union Officer, 4.
[2] Century Magazine, VII (1884), 120.

carry civilization to its every corner.[3] In 1879 Richard Taylor, formerly a lieutenant general in the Confederacy, remarked in his memoirs: "The breed to which these whites belong has for eight centuries been the master of the earth wherever it has planted its foot. A handful conquered and holds in subjection the crowded millions of India, another and smaller bridles the fierce Caffre tribes of South Africa. Place but a score of them on the middle course of the Congo, and they will rule unless exterminated; and all the armies and all the humanitarians can not change this, until the appointed time arrives for Ham to dominate Japhet."[4]

After the battle of Reconstruction had been won, Southerners congratulated Northerners on realizing that the white people of the South were engaged in a desperate race struggle and that "so-called outrages" were but the dutiful efforts of the superior race to conserve society. Since these incidents were only manifestations of a struggle for supremacy, white Southerners felt justified in denouncing black Southerners for having caused the spilling of so much blood by insanely attempting to dominate the white race.[5] The purpose of the violence which the South disguised as a natural virtue was the restoration of the old harmony which had been idealized as characterizing race relations under slavery. When Negroes were misled into thinking themselves equal to their betters, a clash followed and the Negroes suffered. As soon as they accepted respectful subordination, they were again treated with good-natured tolerance.[6]

[3] Gayarré, North American Review, CXXV (1877), 480-81. See also [Puryear], The Public School, 4-6.

[4] Destruction and Reconstruction: Personal Experiences of the Late War (New York, 1879), 250.

[5] Editorial, Southern Bivouac, IX (1887), 711; Eustis, Forum, VI (1888), 145; W. J. Northen, The Negro at the South: An Address before the Congregational Club, Boston, Massachusetts, May 22, 1899 (Atlanta, 1899), 15; Page, The Negro, viii, 20-49.

[6] Christian Advocate (Nashville), August 4, 1892; Killebrew, Southern States Farm Magazine, V (1898), 488; Page, The Negro, 51-55.

It sometimes happened, of course, that certain individuals or groups, frustrated by baffling conditions or psychological disorders, attacked defenseless Negroes as scapegoats, but the history of racial violence in the South proved that the usual occasion for violence was the real or imagined rebellion of Negroes against white supremacy. The disorder of racial violence was built into the exploitative social structure. Within the context of a general society dedicated to freedom, white supremacy was unattainable without violence and the threat of violence.

Every white man, it seemed, was a soldier in the Caucasian army. Thus the Ku Klux movement was portrayed as too clearly a popular movement to be attributed to any conspiracy. Moreover, the white man held a permanent commission to strike a sassy Negro or "nigger-lover." The private act of violence, like the act of a mob, asserted white supremacy and kept the Negro in his place; thus it constituted a patriotic and chivalrous deed. Some organization was necessary, however, to support the private soldier of the white race and to guarantee either that the Negro would not strike back or that he would wish he had not.[7]

The whole of white society gave birth occasionally to mobs which, in the South, had something of an organized, though evanescent, character; to semimilitary groups possessing more definite organization such as the Ku Klux Klan, the Pale Faces, and the Rifle Clubs; to the permanently organized political party; and to the most highly organized agency or society, the white man's government. Since white society or, according to another view, the Southern branch of the Caucasian race, was determined to conquer the Negro, the organizations which derived from the general community shared the same purpose.

[7] Cash, *The Mind of the South*, 128-29; William Garrett Brown, *The Lower South in American History* (New York, 1903), 195. At pp. 191-225 Brown offers a brilliantly written and extraordinarily naive apology for the Klan and kindred organizations.

In fact, the evanescent mob, the terroristic organizations, and the Democratic party of the South all worked together to conquer the freedman. The white man's government represented the victory attained.

The Caucasian army, like all armies, had recruiters. Such a one was Dr. James L. Thompson who, on order of the Pale Faces, delivered a speech at Lebanon, Tennessee, June 4, 1869, in which he told prospective recruits that the master race would fight to the bitter end against the wild fanaticism that would change the order of nature and place the inferior above the superior. "Pale Faces—pure white men of the Japhetic race, which alone nature's God has endowed with the capacity to attain the highest order of civilization" and "control the destinies of the world," Thompson invited to enlist in the secret brotherhoods.[8]

And the Caucasian army had heroes. General Martin W. Gary of Edgefield, South Carolina, for example, was so successful in the use of coercion to win elections that he was known in Edgefield as the "Hero of '76." In a speech during the campaign of 1878, and in the presence of Governor Wade Hampton, Gary stated that it was a mistake to consider the difference between the black and the white man a difference of politics instead of a difference in race. Whenever Caucasians united upon this issue, Negroes had to go to the wall. The Edgefield policy of terror was "based upon the history of the Islands of St. Domingo, Hayti and Mauritius, upon the instincts of human nature and correct political philosophy." This "straight-out" policy would prevail in 1878 as it had in 1876. The Democratic party would triumph because of the effectiveness of its military arm, the "Red Shirts." Although the greater "Hero of '76," Governor Wade Hampton, repudiated Gary's policy in a speech at Greenville, Hampton rode at the head of brigades of "Red Shirts," as he had two years earlier. General Gary continued unashamedly to acknowledge

[8] Carrollton *West Alabamian*, July 13, 1870.

the military-political policy which the white people of South Carolina and of the other Southern states had adopted, disclaimers to the contrary notwithstanding.[9]

That anti-Negro mobs represented the general community is shown by the fact that support from neighboring districts could be counted on in case of necessity. When the local blacks showed a disposition to resist in a body or when it seemed that they might win an engagement, white reinforcements moved into the threatened area to assure victory. This happened because the whites felt that they could in no case permit their mastery of the black race to be successfully challenged. Negroes must be convinced that they inevitably faced disaster whenever they rose in insurrection.

In September, 1868, thirty to forty men from Minden, Louisiana, went to Bossier Point to aid the local citizens quell an "insurrection."[10] The people of Grant Parish in 1873 fought a group of Negroes in the environs of Colfax in order "to preserve the peace." After the riot the old citizens remarked that the Negroes were never better behaved. "A nigger in that parish puts his hat under his arm now when he talks to a white man. They are just the most respectful things you ever saw. But before the fight, oh, Lord! there was no living with them." Reports that Negroes intended to murder white men and seize their wives had inflamed neighboring parishes and quickly brought reinforcements to help teach the Negroes a lesson. In this engagement the Army of North Louisiana of the Southern Department of the great Caucasian army broke through the Negroes' defenses at the courthouse, killing seventy to eighty of the black enemy while losing only two of its own.[11] During the "Tunica War" in north Mississippi in 1874, men from surrounding counties galloped in to strengthen the hard-

[9] Charleston, S.C., *News and Courier*, August 15, September 20, 1878.

[10] New Orleans *Picayune*, September 4, 1868.

[11] Letter from New Orleans to Cincinnati *Commercial*, printed in Carrollton *West Alabamian*, July 9, 1873; Jackson, Miss., *Clarion*, April 24, May 8, 1873.

pressed local whites, and a large force came from Memphis on a steamer that had evacuated white women and children from the scene of danger. Later that year in Vicksburg thirty-six Negroes and two whites were killed in a clash between local Negroes and whites who came from near and far.[12] In the Cain Hay Massacre in South Carolina in October, 1876, a body of whites was forced to retreat before the attack of disciplined Negroes, with the loss of several white men. When the news reached Charleston, indignation hardened every face and 150 men embarked on a steamer to counterattack.[13]

In October, 1882, a black insurrection was reported about to take place in Alabama. According to rumors, Negroes held secret meetings nightly and ominously planned an immense barbecue. Panic-stricken whites sent telegrams to Rome, Jacksonville, and other points along the railroad. Authorities at Anniston requested all white men to arm themselves and to stand in readiness. When the trouble was announced in the churches, the people rushed to their homes to prepare for the uprising. A mass meeting was held, guards were posted, and quiet prevailed.[14]

Battles between African and Caucasian races always ended in a rout, the Southerner boasted. In the Ellenton, South Carolina, riot of September, 1876, five to six hundred whites, hunting down a band of Negroes who had fired at a group of whites, killed six Negroes with no losses to their own force. It was supposed that this trouble resulted from the lynching of

[12] Jackson, Miss., *Clarion*, August 13, 27, 1874, December 10, 1874; Otis Singletary, *Negro Militia during Reconstruction* (Austin, Texas, 1957), 84-85.

[13] Charleston, S.C., *Journal of Commerce*, October 18, 1876. South Carolina was generally turbulent during the summer and fall of 1876 because of the military-political campaign to overthrow the Radical state government. See the Charleston *Journal of Commerce* and the Charleston *News and Courier* of these months for riots and rumors of riots. For a similar state of affairs in Louisiana, see the New Orleans *Picayune* during these same months. The *Picayune*, June 3, 1876, became alarmed that the state might be depopulated of its "most useful laborers."

[14] Atlanta *Constitution*, October 18, 1882.

an alleged rapist.[15] Across the South from Charleston, large crowds of armed men poured into Orange, Texas, in August, 1881, to help punish Negroes who had assaulted a white man. In the resulting fight six Negroes were killed, six to twelve wounded, and one hanged in front of Call's store, with the consequence that the Negroes were thereafter orderly.[16] In Carrollton, Mississippi, in 1886, one hundred mounted men crashed into the county courthouse and fired into a crowd of Negroes there assembled to support the prosecution of several whites in a case growing out of a shooting affray. Eleven Negroes were killed and nine others mortally wounded with no loss to the whites. A defender of the massacre explained that local Negroes had become so insolent that ladies were shoved from the sidewalks and gentlemen were forced to arm themselves when abroad at night. Deciding that it was time to act, the mounted men, "as protectors of the community," rid the land of a "dozen or more dangerous characters that were a disgrace and a drawback to any community."[17]

In the war of races lynch mobs played a significant part. Near Abbeville, South Carolina, in May, 1876, a mob of two to three hundred men armed with rifles, shotguns, and pistols put a "speedy end to the guilty wretches" alleged to have murdered a white couple. There was no secrecy. The prisoners were taken from the sheriff in broad daylight by a quiet, "orderly group." No one wore a mask, no one drank except from a well nearby, and no one shouted. The bodies, left exposed for fifty-two hours, were set upon by buzzards and finally buried by Negroes.[18]

This lynching incident points up the major purpose of anti-Negro mob action in the South. The white community of

[15] Charleston, S.C., *Journal of Commerce*, September 19, 1876.
[16] Houston *Post*, August 20, 1881.
[17] Jackson, Miss., *Clarion*, March 24, 31, 1886.
[18] Charleston, S.C., *News and Courier*, May 25, 1876. This case of leaving bodies to the buzzards was by no means unique; see, for example, Baton Rouge *Capitolian-Advocate*, September 23, 1882.

Abbeville judged that its interests were under attack by the entire Negro community, although only six men and two women (the women were driven from the county) were charged with the crime. If a mere eight individuals, distinguishable only as criminals, had been deemed responsible, the machinery of the law would have been set in motion. But the alleged criminals were regarded as representative of a subordinate race, who in murdering white people challenged the supremacy of the white community. A popular tribunal, therefore, passed sentence, and the white men of the community executed the criminals in such a way that the whole Negro community could not mistake the warning. The refusal to bury the dead was calculated to humiliate the Negroes and to force them to acknowledge responsibility for a crime made doubly horrible by its being perpetrated upon whites. The white community believed that it had discharged an onerous duty in vindication of the honor of the race.

Southerners usually defended lynching on the grounds that Radicals and Negroes were responsible and that silent and swift judgment had a salutary effect upon an impressionable population among whom laws and morals held feeble sway. Lynching, they said, was required by the most sacred considerations. Self-preservation was the first law of nature. Lynchers were often "among the most respectable portion of the community"—men whose good standing was a sufficient guarantee that they shed no blood except under the demand of necessity. Above all, lynching protected wives, mothers, sisters, and daughters from Negro brutes. Still, much of what was spoken of as Southern lawlessness was, according to the defense, in reality simply a determined effort to keep the lawmaking power in the hands of the virtuous.[19]

19 New Orleans *Crescent*, November 4, 1868; Wilmington, N.C., *Journal*, October 8, 1869; Jackson, Miss., *Clarion*, January 23, 1873; Charleston, S.C., *Journal of Commerce*, August 25, 1876; New Orleans *Picayune*, May 16, 30, 1876, July 18, 1887; Baton Rouge *Capitolian-Advocate*, September 19, November 31, 1882; George Braden, "Ku Klux

Many Southerners, horrified by lynching, condemned violence against Negroes. The courageous George Washington Cable was consistent in both opposing violence and objecting to white supremacy. Undoubtedly numerous "silent Southerners" were, as Cable asserted, equally consistent, though they did not dare speak out.[20] But most critics, like Walter Hines Page, the Reverend Atticus G. Haygood, W. P. Trent, and the Reverend Edgar Gardner Murphy, advocated white supremacy while denouncing violence.[21] These white supremacists might well have listened to the ex-slave Frederick Douglass: "When the negro is degraded and ignorant he conforms to a popular standard of what a negro should be. When he shakes off his rags and wretchedness and presumes to be a man, and a man among men, he contradicts this popular standard and becomes an offense to his surroundings."[22] Who was responsible for lynch law in the South? Not alone the mob, the public hangmen, who simply obeyed public sentiment. Responsibility also lay upon the men of wealth and respectability, the men of the press and the pulpit, who created and sustained public opinion. The North, too, shared the blame. It cooperated with the South in the establishment of white supremacy. It held Africans, Indians, and Mongolians in contempt.[23]

The arguments in support of lynching, and of the general theory of race warfare, indicate the determination of white Southerners to dominate black Southerners. In this respect

Klan, an Apology," *Southern Bivouac*, IV (1885), 103-109. Between 1889 and 1898 there were 1,351 lynchings in the South compared with 139 in the North and 110 in the West. National Association for the Advancement of Colored People, *Thirty Years of Lynching in the United States, 1889-1918* (New York, 1919), 8.

[20] "A Simpler Southern Question," *Forum*, VI (1888), 392-403.

[21] Page, *Forum*, XVI (1893), 303-14; Haygood, "The Black Shadow in the South," *Forum*, XVI (1893), 167-75; Trent, "Tendencies of Higher Life in the South," *Atlantic Monthly*, LXXIX (1897), 769; Murphy, *The White Man and the Negro at the South* (Philadelphia, 1900), 19-20.

[22] "Lynch Law in the South," *North American Review*, CLV (1892), 21.

[23] *Ibid.*, 20-25.

the white South was being consistent. The image of the Negro as an inferior to be held in subjection by the lordly Caucasian, constructed from scientific, scriptural, and historical materials, constituted the basic element in Negro-white relations from the Civil War until 1900 and beyond.

PART TWO

Politics

CHAPTER FIVE

Black Voters during Reconstruction

EMANCIPATION of slaves forced the nation to consider the question of Negro suffrage. Negroes and Indians had been the only large groups excluded from America's commitment to universal manhood suffrage; the Indians as savages and wards, the Negroes as slaves. A body of freemen without suffrage would be, like slavery itself, a contradiction of the American ideal. To remedy this defect, equalitarians, both white and black, initiated the Negro suffrage movement.

White Southerners responded with united opposition. Despite the loss of political influence which followed overwhelming defeat, they hoped to check the revolution which emancipation had brought upon them. They began at once to assert that freedmen were incompetent to exercise the right of suffrage. As free Negroes, said Virginians in the early summer of 1865, they were to be protected like unnaturalized foreigners, infants, and women, but vote they should not. Conservatives in Arkansas, too, denied that Negroes had any political rights whatever. The Florida Constitutional Convention of 1865 ordained that the laws of the state were to be made and executed by the white race alone. During 1865 South Carolinians agreed that Negroes should receive all those privileges essential to their new condition, not including suffrage, which they lacked the intelligence and virtue to understand. Voting was not a right but a privilege entrusted by the community to responsible individuals.[1]

In Tennessee, Negroes appealed to the state convention in

January, 1865, for the right to vote. Their petition was ignored, and they were soon, by the passage of a black code, treated as a peculiar class of inferior people. A Colored State Convention of August 6-11, 1866, then petitioned Congress for the liberties and privileges the state denied. A Memphian thought it better, however, for the black race to be swept away by a pestilence than to be enfranchised, believing the right to vote could as safely be given to monkeys as to Negroes.[2] General Benjamin G. Humphreys, recently pardoned by President Johnson upon his election as governor of Mississippi in November, 1865, thought that the several hundred thousand Negroes in Mississippi could not be admitted to political equality with the white race because the government of the state was and would ever be a government of white men.[3] Freedmen, the white people of Louisiana said, were protected by the black code, and the suffrage was not, as many Northerners thought, needed for their self-defense. If colored people voted and representation was based on population, the resulting black and white mosaic would end in anarchy and revolution. Furthermore, the right to vote was not a natural right, else women and children, excluded on the grounds of mental incompetence, would possess the right—they were far more intelligent than Negroes. If tests were necessary, the test of color, distinguishing as it did between the ignorant and the intelligent, was a more accurate test than any other that could be devised.[4]

During Presidential Reconstruction no move was made in any state of the Deep South to give Negroes the suffrage.

[1] John Preston McConnell, *Negroes and Their Treatment in Virginia from 1865 to 1867* (Pulaski, Va., 1910), 87; Paul Lewinson, *Race, Class, and Party: A History of Negro Suffrage and White Politics in the South* (New York, 1932), 37-42; Charleston, S.C., *Courier*, July 27, August 31, September 1, 1865.

[2] Memphis *Appeal*, February 26, 1867, cited in A. A. Taylor, *The Negro in Tennessee, 1865-1880* (Washington, 1941), 45.

[3] "Monthly Record of Events," *Harper's Magazine*, XXXII (1866), 125-27.

[4] New Orleans *Crescent*, December 5, 1865, March 22, 1866, November 20, 1867.

Mississippi rejected the Thirteenth Amendment; so also did Kentucky, fearing that it would be construed so as to give Congress power to enfranchise the freedmen. Alabama, Florida, and South Carolina attached riders to their ratification in an attempt to guard against such an interpretation. But the Southern states, unrepresented in Congress, were powerless to check the Negro suffrage movement. The first series of Reconstruction Acts, passed in February, March, and July, 1867, denied the legality of the Lincoln and Johnson governments, divided the South into military districts, and ordered new constitutional conventions, with Negro suffrage. In addition, Radicals forced the adoption of the Fifteenth Amendment, thus fastening upon the South universal suffrage in all its "hideous" consequences.[5]

Negroes had discovered their strength and were not to be put off with the simple privilege of voting, but were determined to have a proportionate division of offices, from members of Congress on down to the smallest state offices. As a consequence, ignorance and corruption seemed to strut with brazen effrontery where once intelligence and integrity modestly held sway. "It is infamy," wrote the Reverend Abram Ryan, the poet laureate of the Confederacy, "to give Negroes not only the vote, but the right to hold office. The 'Cuffies and Gumboes' will forsake their plantations . . . and seek . . . the offices which Congress has so generously opened to them." The ignorant horde of pauper barbarians would, Ryan predicted, demand money with which to build schools, colleges, hospitals, churches, and asylums.[6]

President Johnson endeared himself to Southern leaders, whom he had opposed as a Unionist, by endeavoring to halt the revolution against the white governments established under

[5] Wilmington, N.C., *Journal*, October 30, 1868; Lewinson, *Race, Class, and Party*, 36.

[6] *Banner of the South*, March 28, April 24, 1869. See also Fort Smith, Ark., *Herald*, August 24, 1867; Wilmington, N.C., *Journal*, December 29, 1868.

presidential auspices. In a message to Congress December 3, 1867, he denounced Negro suffrage and emphasized that it, together with punitive measures against Confederate leaders, opened the way to "Negro domination." The following year, in a message to the House of Representatives, June 20, 1868, Johnson raised constitutional objections against the Arkansas test oath, which read, "I accept the civil and political equality of all men, and agree not to attempt to deprive any person or persons, on account of race, color, or previous condition of servitude, of any political, civil, or religious right, privilege, or immunity enjoyed by any other class of men." He noted that a large proportion of the electors in all the states did "not believe in or accept the practical equality of Indians, Mongolians, or negroes, with the race to which they belong."[7] On this point Johnson's statement was too conservative; not one in a thousand Arkansas whites believed the Negro to be his equal.[8]

Though they could not prevent it, Negro suffrage was unacceptable to whites. An irrepressible conflict, it seemed, had been brought upon the South by the attempt to force Negro equality upon white people. Since Negroes must go to the wall in such a conflict, it was cruel of the politicians to lead them to destruction. This was so because the whites were the "only *people*" of the South, the blacks having never been accepted into the body politic. Said a Louisianian:

Of course the Radicals will say that they were made so by the potent influence of the late lamented Lincoln's proclamation and the reconstruction measures of a "trooly loil" Congress. But it takes something more than a proclamation, even though it be signed by the departed Lincoln, and than a statute, even though it be the act of a Radical Congress, to transform an ignorant, servile population into a "people." Legislative acts and military force may give the negroes something which is called a right to

7 A *Compilation of the Messages and Papers of the Presidents* (with additions), comp. by John D. Richardson, 20 vols. (New York, 1897-1929), VIII, 3762, 3848.

8 Fort Smith, Ark., *Herald,* January 18, 1868.

vote, and carpetbaggers and scalawags may lead them up to the polls and instruct them how to deposit their ballots; but no such expedients can ever make them anything else than an intrusive and anomalous element in a political community of white people, trained by tradition, by inheritance, and by custom to the exercise of political rights. Negroes may vote as much and as long as you please . . . ; they may put carpetbaggers and scalawags into pleasant and profitable places . . . ; but they will never constitute any portion of the people of Louisiana.[9]

Five years later, in 1873, a Northern observer saw no hope that Louisiana would admit that the Negro was competent to vote intelligently, or would ever be. Instead, white leaders in the state contented themselves with deriding their inferiors and, with anarchy at their doors, refused to make an effort toward an understanding between the races.[10]

A strong element in the South, very probably a heavy majority, unwaveringly opposed Negro suffrage in the decades after Appomattox. The most militant men of this group advocated violence to break up the Negro electorate, until such time as other means could be devised. Negro suffrage, an Alabamian stated, "is upon us in 1870, and, in the absence of civil commotions, it will be upon us in 1970."[11] Equally aggressive, a Georgian, the Reverend Abram Ryan, thundered: "This is a white man's Government, and upon this doctrine future political contests must be fought until the question is finally and irrevocably settled."[12] As the Southerner clung to the essentials of proslavery thought, and to the injustices it masked, he viewed the Fifteenth Amendment as that "great iniquity," that "boldly, daringly, and confessedly revolutionary" amendment, that "universal savage suffrage amendment."[13]

[9] New Orleans *Crescent*, November 1, 1868.

[10] Edward King, "The Great South: Old and New Louisiana: II," *Scribner's Monthly*, VII (1873), 148-49.

[11] Honeyville, Ala., *Examiner*, clipped in Carrollton *West Alabamian*, March 16, 1870.

[12] *Banner of the South*, September 25, 1869.

[13] *Ibid.*, April 24, May 8, 1869; Fort Smith, Ark., *Herald*, April 9, 1870; Carrollton *West Alabamian*, August 9, 1871.

Fearing that social equality was the logical consequence of political equality, a Virginian explained his allegiance to the white man's party: "I hain't no objection to the Republican party . . . it's the niggers . . . it's the *NIGGERS*."[14]

The South's continuing antagonism toward Negro suffrage as an unnatural thing found yet another expression in the *Southern Review* in 1874. The *Review* offered the constitution as proof that the people who made it had a heaven-sent capacity for self-government. Although the framers were drawn almost at random "from the ends of the earth, there was one thing—only one, but still *one*—in which they were all alike. They were all *white* people."[15] Sensible Negroes understood this. Aunt Silvey, for example, was reported to have told her people "to go long and tend to dere cotton patches and corn fields; dat's de kind o' votin' dey understan'."[16]

Unable to prevent the enfranchisement of freedmen, whites sought to dominate the unwanted voters. Even though white man's government was by definition opposed to the Negro's interests, Southerners hoped to obtain Negro support for it. Negroes for their part remembered the black codes, understood the motives of the white man's party, felt the stings of coercion, and had reason to fear that promises made them would be broken one by one as the Southern states were redeemed. They knew, moreover, that they had benefited more from the Radical governments, in which they participated, than they could from promised honest governments of the intelligent and virtuous classes.[17]

Negroes actually desired the privileges enjoyed by white people and hoped to secure them by political action. As delegates to Radical and Scalawag conventions from 1865 to 1867, they spoke on behalf of Negro-white equality. Colored voters convened in Lexington, Kentucky, in the spring of 1870

---

[14] Cited in Ludlow, *Harper's Magazine*, XLVIII (1873), 672.
[15] "The Best Government," *Southern Review*, XIV (1874), 385-415.
[16] *Sunny South*, March 20, 1875.
[17] See, for example, Jackson, Miss., *Clarion*, June 24, 1869.

and adopted a platform frankly avowing their desire for racial equality and asserting their political power to achieve this end. Declaring that in their district they held the balance of power, they demanded that white Radicals accept them as equals or get out of the Republican party, that Negro candidates be put forward, and that all weak-kneed white Radicals make way for white men who would acknowledge their equality with the Negro and then act it out.[18]

In Louisiana, in 1873, Negroes demanded as the price for support in overthrowing the Radical government what some whites thought of as a miserable program of Africanization. In this campaign a Committee of One Hundred promised to exercise moral influence to bring an end to discrimination in Louisiana and to support public school integration, equality in public accommodations and in employment opportunities, and full acceptance of Negroes in political affairs. In response to the abuse heaped upon the white unificationists from over the state and the South, General Beauregard replied: "We are bound to give this great experiment of republican self-government, on the basis of impartial suffrage, a fair trial; and as long as we assume a position antagonistic in principle to his rights, and thereby drive the colored man into opposition to us, if harm results, we must lay the blame upon ourselves."[19] A Negro voter, more impressed by the public clamor than by Beauregard's exhortation, informed the unificationists: "When you white gentlemen will agree to admit us to your society on equal terms, and not until then, we will agree to help you to elect men to office."[20]

[18] Carrollton West Alabamian, April 13, 1870. See also McConnell, Negroes and Their Treatment in Virginia, 28-29.

[19] Jackson, Miss., Clarion, July 2, 1873.

[20] Carrollton West Alabamian, August 6, 1873. To this end Negroes subordinated all other political aims. Elsie M. Lewis, "The Political Mind of the Negro, 1865-1900," Journal of Southern History, XXI (1955), 189-202. For the unification movement see Jackson, Miss., Clarion, July 26 through August 21, 1873; T. Harry Williams, "The Louisiana Unification Movement of 1873," Journal of Southern History, XI (1945), 349-69.

In view of the Negro's desire to gain the equality which Southern whites adamantly denied him, it is not surprising that attempts to use the Negro electorate as a prop for white supremacy on a Southwide basis failed and were abandoned in favor of disfranchisement. Before they were able to bring about disfranchisement, however, Southerners tried for many years to control colored voters, often expressing inability to understand their utter failure to induce even a corporal's guard to go Democratic. The usual explanation for failure was that "greedy cormorants" had turned the colored people against their former masters and white friends generally by cajoling and wheedling them into believing that theirs was a persecuted race.[21]

The Conservatives of Tennessee in 1867 opened a campaign to win colored votes by inviting Negroes to attend their convention in Nashville. A white leader then delivered a strong speech against Negro suffrage. A Negro, Joe Williams, followed with an obsequious speech which disgusted whites and infuriated his colored auditors. Many white delegates walked out when Negroes boldly offered suggestions, and the meeting ended in signal failure. An attempt to repair the damage by organizing a Colored Conservative Convention a few days later also failed. Conservatives, still hoping for Negro support, declared that Negroes were entitled to all the rights and privileges of citizens under both state and national law, whereupon the Conservatives nominated for governor Emerson Etheridge, who had expressed decidedly hostile views toward Negroes only a few days earlier. As evidence mounted that Negroes meant to vote for Radicals who offered constructive action rather than for Conservatives who made promises not to take away privileges already granted, the Conservatives decided either to dominate the Negro electorate or to suppress it. Conservative journals began to suggest the use of economic

---

[21] Wilmington, N.C., *Journal*, November 14, 1868; *Banner of the South*, December 4, 1869.

coercion, and white gangs initiated attacks against colored political gatherings, such as in Franklin, where they wounded twenty-three Negroes. After the Conservatives won control of the legislature in 1869, political power of the Negroes in Tennessee generally declined, leaving them to employ political meetings principally as a means to protest their loss of civil and political rights.[22]

The attempts of the whites to manage the Negro electorate in Tennessee conformed to a pattern observable throughout the South: whites made diffident gestures of political fraterniza- tion, offered promises made at the very least questionable by contrary expression and action, perceived their failure to gain substantial Negro support, and finally resorted to coercion. Upon regaining political control, whites continued to weaken the black electorate until they practically destroyed it.

In every Southern state during the first days of the Negro- white Reconstruction governments, local groups calling them- selves Conservatives had been formed to dispute political power with Negroes and carpetbaggers. Though at first disposed to seek Negro support, Conservatism soon began to draw the color line in its fight to pull down the carpetbagger-Negro govern- ments. Whites who had differed concerning important political questions were exhorted to bury their differences in a broad front against Radicals and Negroes.

The Conservatives became deeply involved in the national election of 1868 because they believed that if a Democratic President and Congress were chosen, the Radical program for the South would be set aside before it had fairly got underway. Early in 1868 politicians and editors were already engaged in exhorting the whites to gird for political battle. Nothing was more deplorable than Negro rule, they argued, and the only way to escape it was by united, determined action. People everywhere without regard to their past, whether they had

[22] Taylor, *The Negro in Tennessee*, 47-56, 65-71, 251.

been Whigs, Democrats, or Republicans, Confederate soldiers or Union, were said to be joining forces to defeat the project of the Negro-worshipers to Africanize the South.[23]

As the campaign progressed, rousing mass meetings were called, with enthusiastic speechmaking and the adoption of stirring resolutions. "By the help of God let us make the effort, and consecrate ourselves to the work," leaders urged. Be ready to register, they enjoined. Let every Democratic club be active; let good men come to the front. Organize with the discipline of an army. Encourage the timid; strengthen the weak; work strenuously, untiringly, unceasingly. It was the manifest duty of every citizen to win for Seymour and Blair.[24]

Grant's victory in this close election caused some to suggest compromise with the enemy, but the most effective voice heard in the South, even when the strategy was to woo Negro support for the Southern Democracy, continued to be that raised for white unity. During the state campaign in Mississippi in 1869, for example, the former Union Whigs and Secession Democrats were said to be fused into an impenetrable, invincible element with bands stronger than steel. In the face of common suffering and danger their union had become perfect, their harmony delightful.[25] "Let each man be a patriot and sacrifice on the altar of his country, for the good of the people," exhorted a Texan.[26]

White political warfare was the instrument to oust the robbers and barbarians from their stronghold. A political party was like a great army. In the interval between active campaigns straggling might be permitted, but when it became necessary

---

[23] New Orleans *Crescent*, January 31, 1868; Fort Smith, Ark., *Herald*, February 8, 29, 1868.

[24] Charleston, S.C., *Courier*, July 17, 1868; New Orleans *Picayune*, September 10, November 3, 1868; New Orleans *Crescent*, October 2, 1868; Wilmington, N.C., *Journal*, October 7, 14, 15, 28, 1868; Shreveport *Southwestern*, October 16, 1868.

[25] Jackson, Miss., *Clarion*, April 22, 1869.

[26] Austin *Democratic Statesman*, July 26, 1871.

to form for battle, all white men must move together as if they had but one soul. Duty demanded that each political warrior forget animosities or peculiarities of opinion for the sake of unity of action and party discipline. Like the great Prussian army of 1870 the army of the white man's party would enjoy crushing victory if every man enrolled in his political company, regiment, division, and corps.[27]

The Liberal Republican revolt presented an opportunity for the white man's party to manipulate a coalition to destroy Radical Reconstruction on the national level as it was in the process of doing on the state level. Profiting by splits among the Radicals, it had already undermined Radical rule in Tennessee, Virginia, North Carolina, and Georgia. Now division within the national Republican party offered the entire white South the opportunity to coalesce with Northern Democrats and Liberal Republicans to crush the Radicals once for all. Temporary fusion on the local level all over the South, even with Negroes, in conjunction with political factions in the North, could bring into power a friendly President and Congress which would deprive Radical organizations in the Southern states of the federal support requisite for them to withstand the single-minded opposition of the white man's party.

In the spring of 1871 Southerners began to take serious interest in the growing Liberal Republican criticism of the Grant administration. At this early date the white South was pleased by the disarray in the enemy camp but was still somewhat reluctant to join forces with Republicans of the Horace Greeley sort. Greeley recently had been denounced as author of more mischief in this country than any other man. He was classed as one of the murderous philanthropists who gloried in the slaughter of millions to obliterate natural distinctions in an inverted social order. He was viewed as a kindly old lunatic

[27] *Banner of the South*, February 19, March 5, 1870; Carrollton *West Alabamian*, August 17, 1870; Austin *Democratic Statesman*, summer and fall, 1871.

who preached guillotinism.[28] As soon as it became clear that
he would be the presidential candidate of the Liberal Republicans, the lunatic and murderous Greeley began to enjoy a
laudatory press. He was then presented as a doughty opponent
of thieving carpetbaggers, an admirer of Lee and Jackson and
Davis, and an influential advocate of amnesty for leaders of
the Confederacy. Far from being a centralizer, it was now
said, Greeley was a state rights man who, to halt the advance
of Radical ruin, had identified himself with Democrats as a
patriotic necessity to save the country.[29]

An architect of the coalition, B. H. Hill of Georgia, pointed
out that amnesty for Confederate leaders had been achieved
because of the Liberal Republicans, that federal control of local
elections had been prevented by a Liberal Republican-Democratic coalition, and that this coalition had denied Grant
authority to suspend the writ of habeas corpus in a campaign
to terrorize the South. Furthermore, Hill promised, the election of Greeley would carry in a Democratic House.[30]

A stumbling block to Southern participation in the Demo-
cratic-Liberal Republican coalition was the fact that the Northern elements therein objected to the nullification of the Fifteenth Amendment. The Liberal Republicans, convened at
Cincinnati, promised both impartial suffrage and local self-
government. John Quincy Adams II told the South in mid-
summer, 1871, that hostility to the Fifteenth Amendment,
which had created the strife necessary to sustain the Radicals,
was not worth gratifying at the risk of permanent Republican
rule. Defining the essence of democracy as the equality of all
men before the law, Adams asked, "But who dares face an
intelligent people with that testimony upon his lips, and

28 New Orleans *Crescent*, November 7, December 10, 1867, February
6, 1868, January 31, 1869; New Orleans *Picayune*, September 12, 1868;
Carrollton *West Alabamian*, June 7, 1870.
29 New Orleans *Picayune*, July 1, 1871, June 22, 1872; Jackson, Miss.,
Clarion, July 4, 1872; Charleston, S.C., *Courier*, July 11, 1872.
30 Carrollton *West Alabamian*, July 10, 1872.

denounce a measure which is too democratic for the Democrats only, because the enfranchised are black?"[31] White supremacists replied that Southern opposition to the Fifteenth Amendment was based upon principle and would continue despite Adams and the new Democracy. Many of them were willing, however, to postpone this issue, for "sooner or later the sweep of reaction will come."[32]

In the meantime, leaders of the movement to restore white supremacy by electing Greeley promised to protect the Negro's rights, including his exercise of the suffrage. Such a promise was made not so much to attract colored votes as to bring in conservative Republicans, especially those of the old native Union element. Cassius M. Clay, a former antislavery and pro-Union leader of Kentucky, was one who responded to appeals of this sort and came out for Greeley as the man to overcome the subjection of intelligence and property to ignorance and pauperism. Another who renounced Grantism and declared for Greeley was the Scalawag judge of Mississippi, William M. Hancock.[33]

While promoting coalition, Southern whites were determined to protect their own unity. The people were warned to spurn overtures from mongrelizers at home but to stand behind the Liberal Republican-Democratic national ticket. The irascible Robert Toombs, who had at first viewed the scheme to unite with the Liberal Republicans as destructive of Southern honor, at last concluded that the split in the national Republicans provided the opportunity for the white man's party to triumph in the South without compromising its integrity. There were exigencies, he thought, in which the South might support an enemy to break the enemy's lines. Fusion was in the interest of redemption and did not comprehend any local Radicals

[31] *Ibid.*, June 7, 1871.
[32] Mobile *Register*, clipped in Carrollton *West Alabamian*, June 7, 1871.
[33] Fort Smith, Ark., *Herald*, July 29, 1871; Carrollton *West Alabamian*, February 7, 1872; Jackson, Miss., *Clarion*, August 8, 1872; New Orleans *Picayune*, September 22, 1872.

who had anything to do with misrule. Toombs spoke for Southern whites in general, who had no intention of abandoning their goal of ruling the Negroes.[34]

Chary as they were of fusion at home, white Southerners hoped, nevertheless, to gain enough Negro votes to install their own executives in the statehouses and to make Greeley chief executive. Negroes were invited to help elect honest men who had the capital to make their labor productive and who stood fully committed to the Radical constitutions. The colored people were informed that black rule was never known to promote the welfare of any Negro population, that the contrary was true, but that the Negroes would be elevated up to the middle ground, though subordinate to whites, if they would help elect the right ticket.[35]

Appeals were made to Negroes on the basis that the South's allies were the Negroes' friends. The adherence of Charles Sumner to the Greeley Republicans was celebrated because, it was supposed, colored people would follow the lead of their great champion. In addition, letters to the editors of Democratic organs from local Negroes announcing support for the Democratic ticket and the formation of Greeley clubs were expected to swing black votes.[36] Despite hopes that the colored people would break loose from partisan trammels, one of them, Senator H. R. Revels of Mississippi, warned:

Greeley . . . was friendly to us and worked for us, but now, after having done so much, he has deserted us. He has called all Democrats thieves, yet today he is with them and is trying to get them into power. When he was our friend we loved and respected him, but now that he is with our *enemies* we cannot follow him. . . . We loved Mr. Sumner and honored him for his great services to

[34] Fort Smith, Ark., *Herald*, April 13, 1872; *Southern Review*, XI (1872), 474; Atlanta *Constitution*, June 28, 1872; New Orleans *Picayune*, August 27, 1872; Jackson, Miss., *Clarion*, July 4, 10, 1872.

[35] Charleston, S.C., *Courier*, July 9, September 30, 1872; New Orleans *Picayune*, August 15, 1872.

[36] See Jackson, Miss., *Clarion*, Charleston *Courier*, and New Orleans *Picayune* during July, August, and September, 1872.

us. . . . He hates General Grant with a fierce, vengeful hate, so bitterly that to gratify his personal feelings *he would sacrifice the entire colored race, and throw them back into the hands of their enemies.* When Charles Sumner changes from the Sumner of the past, he must understand most thoroughly that the colored people will not follow him.[37]

Lest appeals have little effect, threats were tried. Negroes were warned to vote Democratic or else. Radical electioneering endangered peace between the two races; an exclusive black man's party would force the whites to follow the Negro's example, with a consequent war of races. Negroes could save themselves from complete disaster only by dividing themselves politically, for they alone could allay the apprehension of a conflict of races. If they chose to support disgraceful government, the South would find ways to control nine-tenths of the vote, the Negroes would suffer the fate of the Indians, or the South would become politically Mexicanized and the Negroes, like the Mexican Indians, would be exploited by the few who voted them.[38]

Neither the names of Greeley and Sumner nor appeals and threats had the desired effect. Following Grant's victory a disgruntled coalitionist complained that on the night preceding the election Negroes assembled at a "Loyal League Den" in Rankin County, Mississippi, and "commenced a hideous uproar, with volleys of musketry, drum-beating and other warlike demonstrations, which were kept up until morning," the object of which was to intimidate colored persons from voting the right ticket.[39] According to a dismayed political strategist, Greeley was defeated by 700,000 colored votes.[40] Although Negro votes continued to be sought—or forced—for some years to come, the failure to win substantial Negro support in 1872

[37] Jackson, Miss., *Clarion,* August 22, 1872.
[38] New Orleans *Picayune,* August 1, 9, September 10, 14, 1872; Charleston, S.C., *Courier,* November 1, 1872.
[39] Jackson, Miss., *Clarion,* November 15, 1872.
[40] Charleston, S.C., *Courier,* November 7, 1872.

gave encouragement to the straight-out white Democrats who meant to destroy the Negro electorate.

Had Southern whites been sincere in their promises to accept Negroes as fellow citizens, the subsequent history of the South would have been radically altered. There can, however, be no doubt that the actual dominant interest of the South was to negate the Negro electorate upon the collapse of Radicalism, that Liberal Republicans were aware of this intention but hoped for the best, and that the mass of Negroes had no choice but to support the Grant Republicans in defense of their rights. In consequence, Grant won most of the Southern electoral votes, while Cleveland, taking advantage of later Republican disorganization, won them all.[41] By 1884, however, the Negro electorate in the South had been made ineffective by the white man's party. The election of 1872, therefore, is especially significant in that it indicates that the South's political beliefs and aims had not substantially changed since the enactment of the black codes. This election promised a dismal future.

Although consolidation of native whites was the key element in the strategy to overthrow Negro-based Radicalism, in some states whites not only had to overcome misgivings concerning their assault on justice, but also had to confront a numerical majority of the Negro electorate. If these whites could not attract Negro support, their alternative, given the objective of white man's rule, was to make war on Negro voters.

The dilemma facing whites of conciliation or conquest, and its final resolution, particularly in Louisiana, Mississippi, and South Carolina, is clearly revealed in the shift in policy in Mississippi. Until 1874 the Jackson *Clarion* favored conciliating Negro citizens. But in the summer of that year it began to go over to the white-liners. On August 13 it protested that

[41] If possible, the Liberal Republicans, or Independents, celebrated Cleveland's victory with more enthusiasm than the Democrats. See Allan Nevins, *Grover Cleveland: A Study in Courage* (New York, 1932), 188.

the white line was a dangerous policy, yet it praised the brutal white triumph in Vicksburg. At the same time the *Clarion* pointed out that a compromise ticket had beaten the straight-outs in Okolona. Reminded that when they failed to support Greeley in 1872, Negroes had forfeited privileges pledged by whites, the *Clarion* replied that a war on the principle of equality was a war on the constitutional amendments to which the faith of the nation had been pledged. By October, however, the *Clarion* was ready to support conciliation or conquest, depending on which seemed to be the surest way for each locality to crush Radicalism. In hasty retreat from its former position it began to claim that differences between the conciliators and conquerors did not amount to much, as both sought good government in which only whites would hold office. In December, asserting that Negroes had drawn the color line in spite of the patience of whites, the *Clarion* became a full-fledged white line organ and, at the end of the month, was advocating bloodshed during the coming political campaign.

For some time the *Clarion* excused itself for abandoning its former policy of racial conciliation by blaming Negroes for causing whites to band together. It was, stated the *Clarion*, one thing to urge the white people to draw the color line and throw down the gage, but quite a different thing to accept it in self-defense. Thus whites were urged to arrest alarming tendencies toward domination by Negroes, who, puffed up with a sense of superiority, refused to be conciliated. In July, 1875, having become a hard advocate of the white man's party, the *Clarion* celebrated the "glorious gatherings" of white supremacists over the state and spoke of their voice as "the voice of God." During the summer and fall of this year it blamed Negroes for the numerous race riots in reality precipitated by the white supremacy campaign, and encouraged whites to bolder attacks by assuring them that President Grant would not intervene in the state's affairs. On October 27 the *Clarion* offered its thanks to military-political clubs for cheers received during a great procession past its offices. These conquerors did indeed owe hurrahs to the leading organ of legitimation for the war against representative government they were then successfully conducting.[42]

Aware of the necessity to secure national acquiescence in the fall of Reconstruction in Mississippi, one of the most persuasive of white supremacists, Senator L. Q. C. Lamar, aided by Senator J. B. Gordon of Georgia, delivered a series of speeches in the North during the early part of 1875, calling on the people of that section to pay no heed to fomentors of trouble in the South. The white people of his region, Lamar said, accepted the abolition of slavery and Negro suffrage and now wished to live in liberty and union with their Northern brethren. Even while Lamar was conducting his diplomatic mission to assure nonintervention, his straight-out constituents were hard at work. Believing with General J. Z. George that the tendency of the times was toward fraternization between the North and the South, white leaders held taxpayers' conventions and organized Democratic clubs to get out the white vote and to prevent Negroes from voting. They developed an effective statewide military-political organization, a local unit of which was that of Tippah County under the leadership of Colonels W. C. Falkner and D. B. Wright and Captains Thomas Spright, T. B. Winston, and Francis A. Wolff.

During the campaign racial clashes occurred throughout the state, at Yazoo City, at Jackson, in Tallahatchie County, at Coahoma, and in other places, the worst one at Clinton during the first week in September. The Clinton riot, properly described in the white press as a battle, began as an interference with a political gathering of two thousand Negroes and twenty whites. Clinton whites, reinforced from Vicksburg and other nearby towns, smashed the Negro political group and roamed

[42] Jackson, Miss., *Clarion*, July, 1874, through December, 1875, particularly August 13, 27, October 1, December 10, 31, 1874, April 21, May 19, July 4, 21, 28, August 11, 18, September 8, 22, 29, October 13, 27, 1875.

the countryside in cavalry units killing and terrorizing Negroes, many of whom were compelled to sleep in the woods for safety. When the Radical Governor Adelbert Ames dispatched the militia to Clinton, he was accused of organizing murder, rapine, a war of races, in an otherwise peaceful state. As a consequence, new military clubs were formed and old ones strengthened. Superbly organized, energized by an excruciating mass emotion, on occasion striking with violence, General George's army "redeemed" Mississippi in November, 1875.[43]

Save in Florida, Louisiana, and South Carolina, Radical regimes had been overthrown by 1876. During the campaign of this year in the unredeemed states the white man's party continued to appeal for Negro support against Negro domination, all the while waging a campaign of terror. In February, 1876, white leaders assured Negroes that they had no reason to believe Radical charges that a redeemed government would take away their voting privileges by means of an educational qualification. They went on to deny the assertion of Republicans that the Democracy of the state was intolerant of the political equality of the colored people. Despite these assurances, the white man's party conducted a slashing attack on the colored people in their successful campaign of 1876 to break up Negro-white government in Louisiana.[44]

In South Carolina, redeemers planned their campaign on the Mississippi model. Former Governor Benjamin F. Perry of South Carolina, promising that all Negroes who joined the whites would be treated with respect, denied that the triumph of the Democratic party would mean barring the colored man

[43] *Ibid.*, January through November, 1875. See especially issues of March 25, May 5, August 11, 18, September 8, 15, 22, 29, October 13, 20, 27.

[44] New Orleans *Picayune*, February 22, 1876. For the campaign see the *Picayune*, summer and fall, 1876; Fanny Z. Lovell Bone, *Louisiana in the Disputed Election of 1876* (Baton Rouge, n.d.). For a justification of white violence consult Stuart Omer Landry, *The Battle of Liberty Place: The Overthrow of Carpet-bag Rule in New Orleans, September 14, 1874* (New Orleans, 1955).

from aspiring to anything above hewing wood and drawing water. Perry hinted, however, that an errant Negro electorate faced disfranchisement. Edward McCrady, on the other hand, stated that for weal or woe Negroes who had the suffrage would be protected in its exercise, and Wade Hampton said at Abbeville that he did not want the votes of whites who expected privileges denied to colored people.[45] While Hampton was making promises, Democrats, by means of the Red Shirts, applied "force without violence." At Abbeville three thousand mounted Red Shirts, forming a procession three miles long, rode with Hampton. Negroes who supported the Radicals were declared to be enemies of whites, and the Edgefield trio, Andrew P. Butler, Martin W. Gary, and Benjamin Tillman, believing that an ounce of fear was worth a pound of persuasion, agitated for violence and intimidation. Thus Tillman's men "executed" Simon Coker, the Negro state senator from Barnwell, for making an "incendiary speech." By such tactics Hampton's victory by a narrow margin of 1,134 votes was made possible; Edgefield's shotgun policy turned a potential Negro majority of several thousands into a Democratic majority of 3,134. At Landrum's Store Precinct, Tillman's mob kept Negroes from voting, while allowing white strangers to vote. The result was the return of 211 Democratic and 2 Republican votes, instead of the 180 Republican and 104 Democratic votes of two years earlier.[46] Thus was the South redeemed.

[45] Charleston, S.C., *Journal of Commerce*, August 24, 1876; Charleston, S.C., *News and Courier*, August 26, September 21, October 3, 1876. For Hampton's policy toward the Negroes see H. M. Jarrell, *Wade Hampton and the Negro: The Road Not Taken* (Columbia, S.C., 1949).

[46] Francis Butler Simkins, *Pitchfork Ben Tillman: South Carolinian* (Baton Rouge, 1944), 61-67; Charleston, S.C., *News and Courier*, September 25, October 19, 1876. For details of the campaign see the *News and Courier*, summer and fall, 1876.

CHAPTER SIX

Solid South

UNITY GAINED and victory achieved, it might seem that pressure to maintain a solid white bloc would have been relaxed. But restriction of political freedom was maintained because control of Negroes required unanimity among whites. If the North after 1876 promised at least temporary abandonment of federal intervention in Southern elections, it offered no guarantee that dissident whites and Negroes would not develop formidable alliances against the ruling groups within the states. Whenever a considerable portion of whites grew restive, such internal political revolts threatened white supremacy. The practical but illegal exclusion of Negroes from the suffrage created a powerful bloc of potential votes which insurgents were tempted to bring into play in support of a party seeking economic and social goals rejected by the leaders of the white man's party. This being so, much of the propaganda to maintain white unity was designed to weaken the appeal of insurgent parties, usually agrarian-labor coalitions, which, in calling out the Negro vote, threatened to sacrifice white supremacy.

The struggle to preserve unity began as soon as whites regained control in the Southern states. In 1870 North Carolinians were warned that redemption recently gained already was seriously threatened by wily enemies who lay in wait until divisions among Conservatives and Democrats should afford them opportunities to return to power in North Carolina and to entrench themselves more deeply in other Southern states.

All discussion of party differences was deprecated, including such matters as the relative value of the Democratic or the Whig wings of the white man's party, and white North Carolinians were urged to remember the villainy of their enemies and to support the Democratic party without reservation.[1]

The white people of other Southern states readily entertained the same uncomplicated argument. For example, the able Georgia leader, Benjamin H. Hill, in an address in October, 1872, called for unity among Democrats to protect the unblemished fruits of redemption from miserable Radicals, who were secretly plotting to take advantage of white dissension in order to regain the places from which they had recently been expelled. United, Hill promised, Georgians would enjoy such a crushing victory that from political leprosies they would be forever free.[2] Two years later, Arkansas Conservatives warned that minstrel Radicalism was only napping, ready to leap upon its prey whenever the people should be off guard. Bolting, or even discontent with a platform broad enough to comprehend all whites, was proclaimed to be associated with intolerable selfishness, ambition, or perversity. The uncluttered platform for Arkansas whites was: "A Whiteman's Government." Alabamians similarly stood on a platform of "Union, Harmony, Concession" within the one great family of white people. During the campaign of 1876, whites who refused to vote the straight Democratic ticket because certain nominees did not suit them were told to support the whole ticket or depart as undesirables.[3]

Following the election of 1876 the Southerner continued to wear with pride his straitjacket of unity because the Negro question was, he said, a question of the preservation of civiliza-

[1] Wilmington, N.C., *Journal*, August 20, 1870.

[2] Charleston, S.C., *Courier*, October 3, 1872.

[3] Fort Smith, Ark., *Herald*, July 18, September 11, 1874, April 22, 1876; Carrollton *West Alabamian*, March 19, June 14, July 29, 1876; Charleston, S.C., *Journal of Commerce*, August 30, 1876.

tion and the purity of a superior race. Unity in the cause of home rule was not only the South's glory, but the nation's best hope for the salvation of republican institutions. In consequence, both United States senators from Georgia and five of the eight representatives, who had formerly been Whigs, became loyal Democrats with faces turned against the Hayes scheme to attach the old Whigs to a white Republican party in the South. Similarly in Hinds County, Mississippi, white men formed unsullied ranks against the devilish combination of scurrilous whites and anarchic black-liners. In 1878 Louisianians were urged to do their political duty or face the humiliating return of Reconstruction vassalage. Young voters, it seemed, attached themselves to the side of honesty and truth despite the machinations of some old rascals and, during the election of 1878, loyal Southerners turned out en masse to support even those candidates whom they did not like in order to give no encouragement to Radical Republican adversaries in new disguise.[4]

Mississippians were told that while white unanimity meant justice to every class and race, self-willed and ambitious whites embraced the hideous body of the "Black Viper" to build a mongrel concern on the ruins of good government. Such propaganda was, by itself, insufficient to sustain white supremacy. In Yazoo County in 1879, for example, a mob of several hundred armed merchants, planters, and other respectable men in the county, seeing insurgency reviving in the Negro electorate, required on pain of death the Independent candidate, Captain H. M. Dixon, to sign a statement of withdrawal, which, safe from the threatening mob, he repudiated. A short

---

[4] Gayarré, *North American Review*, CXXV (1877), 479; Atlanta *Constitution*, March 13, 15, 1877; Jackson, Miss., *Clarion*, October 24, 31, 1877; Charlottesville, Va., *Chronicle*, October 11, 1878; Fort Smith, Ark., *Herald*, October 28, 1878; New Orleans *Picayune*, October 5, 23, 31, 1878. Vincent P. De Santis discusses this Republican strategy in "President Hayes's Southern Policy," *Journal of Southern History*, XXI (1955), 476-94.

time later, Dixon was shot and killed. Still, Independents were able to gain control in a few counties during the period 1879-1885, but this threat to the "safety, honor and welfare of the State" could not be tolerated for long.[5]

In a reply to the demand of insurgents and Negroes for "a free ballot, a fair count, and a full vote," white supremacists activated their military-political companies. In 1883 the "Capital City Light Guards" sent a detachment to help the men of Copiah County overthrow Independents there who had, it was said, reproduced the extravagance and misrule from which the state had suffered prior to the revolution of 1875. The "Red Spirited Brandy Wine Tigers" of Copiah County, like the "Meridian Rifles," the "Hill City Guards," and the "Winona Rifles," kept themselves in good condition to combat African rule. Thus, by 1885, Mississippi's errant counties had been reconquered by the white man's party.[6]

In Virginia, whites had won control of the legislature in 1870, after which they had initiated a program that nullified the black electorate. Hoping to prevent the dissolution of the white bloc and the formation of a small farmer-Republican-Negro coalition, a Conservative warned in 1877 that if a Negro was competent to vote, he was "fit to eat with us at our tables, to sleep in our beds, to be invited into our parlors, and to do all acts and things which a white man may do."[7] But two years later, small farmers and others of modest means, led by the former Confederate General William Mahone and known as Readjusters, revived the Negro vote and defeated the Conservatives on the issues of economic liberalism and civil rights. Readjusters then partially repudiated the state debt, abolished the poll tax as a requirement for voting, established a state college for Negroes, increased public school appropriations, and

[5] Jackson, Miss., *Clarion*, June 18, 30, August 6, 20, 27, 1879, December 17, 1884.

[6] *Ibid.*, September 29, 1881, November 7, 1883, August 13, September 17, October 1, 8, 15, 1884, July 1, November 4, 1885.

[7] [Puryear], *The Public School*, 14.

adopted other measures desired by practically all Negroes and a strong contingent of whites.[8]

This disaster of Independency in Virginia served as a warning to other Southern states. Mahone, it seemed, threw himself into the arms of Negroes and bad elements of the white population in order to maintain his strength. As a result, it was alleged, corrupt men assumed office, bitterness and strife affected social life, and all decent people came to despise Mahone:

In other words it is the triumph of Radicalism, and all who have suffered the humiliation and seen the abominable incidents of that regime in Louisiana will need no further description. We thus perceive how society in the reconstructed states is always hanging on the edge of an abyss in which there is always recurrent danger of being precipitated. Virginia had successfully emerged from the disorders incident to reconstruction and had entered on a hopeful pathway of progress and material advancement. But our recreant sons backed by the Administration, and using the votes of ignorant freedmen have precipitated her again in the ignominy of a new reconstruction.[9]

In consequence, Louisiana voters in 1882 as in 1876 were admonished to spurn all overtures to divide against the public interest or face the degradation of carpetbagger-Negro government with its miserable baggage of corruption, tyranny, and unnatural notions of social equality.[10]

The election of 1882 frightened leaders in other Southern states also. In South Carolina it was observed that the Green-

[8] Charles E. Wynes, *Race Relations in Virginia, 1870-1902* (Charlottesville, Va., 1961), 16-38. For the view that white Readjusters were traitors to the state and the Negroes ignorant victims of demagogues, see Richard L. Morton, *The Negro in Virginia Politics, 1865-1902* (Charlottesville, Va., 1919), 98-126.

[9] Baton Rouge *Capitolian-Advocate*, August 8, 1882. Arthur supported the economic radicals in Virginia in the hope of reviving the Republican party in the South. Vincent De Santis, "President Arthur and the Independent Movements in the South in 1882," *Journal of Southern History*, XIX (1953), 352-53.

[10] Baton Rouge *Capitolian-Advocate*, September 14, 15, 21, October 9, 10, 13, November 2, 1882.

back Labor Reform party was forced to offer terms to the
Radicals. Conservatives claimed that this coalition would,
unless the people spurned the evil embrace of Radicalism,
result in the overthrow of white government and subsequent
mongrelization of the state. According to Hampton, the danger
from wolves in sheep's clothing was as great as in 1876: "I tell
you that he who is not with us . . . is a traitor to the State."[11]
Editors joined in berating supporters of the "Greenback-Negro,"
the "African," or the "Greenback-Radical" party.[12] In Georgia,
Independency was, after a struggle, signally rebuked all through
the state by the election of Alexander H. Stephens, former Vice
President of the Confederacy, as governor.[13]

In 1883 the white man's party of Virginia launched an
aggressive campaign against Readjusters. Benefiting from racial
encounters, especially the Danville Riot of November 4, 1883,
straight-out whites regained control of the state government.
J. L. M. Curry, then a professor in Richmond College and a
leading Conservative, described the public reaction to news of
victory: "Old men wept. The young were hilarious. The women
thanked God."[14] Former Confederate General Jubal A. Early
declared that Negroes must learn from this defeat to behave
themselves and keep in their places.[15]

Although Independency might appear rebuked, in 1890 the
agrarian movement marked its greatest success in the South,
winning a major victory in Georgia, electing the state president
of the Farmers' Alliance governor in Tennessee, and committing
to the Alliance many United States representatives and several
senators. In this contest, statutory disfranchisement proved
insufficient to keep Negroes from voting. In some localities,
planters and agrarians vied in marching their own colored

[11] Charleston, S.C., *News and Courier*, October 13, 1882.
[12] *Ibid.*, October 14, 28, November 8, 1882.
[13] Atlanta *Constitution*, October 6, 1882.
[14] J. L. M. Curry to R. C. Winthrop, November 8, 1883, cited in
Wynes, *Race Relations in Virginia*, 36.
[15] Wynes, *Race Relations in Virginia*, 32.

supporters to the polls and in intimidating those of the opposing faction.[16]

In South Carolina in 1890 a Conservative faction led by Alexander Haskell sought to call out the disfranchised Negroes to defeat the Alliance Democrat Benjamin Tillman, but the insurgents in this case were strong enough to prevent Negroes from deciding the election. Although the Haskellites had intimidated Negroes, they campaigned on the promises of racial justice made by Hampton in 1876. To compound the irony, Tillman made threats against colored voters, but Hampton supported Tillman's election on the ground that every Democratic administration since 1876 had been honest. Many followers of Hampton in 1876 met the dilemma by switching from sharp criticism of Tillman to unqualified support of him. They claimed that the welfare of the nation and of South Carolina depended upon white supremacy, and in South Carolina, white supremacy could only be maintained by the people remaining solidly Democratic. The leaders of the Haskell movement were admittedly earnest, thoughtful, and patriotic men, but they had become Independents, and as such must be defeated. The real question at issue was whether to vote for the white people or the Negroes. Negroes, having been made to understand the folly and danger in "meddling" in the white people's quarrel, did not participate in the election heavily enough to affect the outcome, which was a victory for Tillman.[17]

Two years later, in 1892, politicians called to the attention of South Carolina whites the object of the federal elections bill, or "force bill," defeated a year earlier but still a threat. The force bill was designed, they said, to make the Southern states Republican, following which segregated schools would be abolished, heavy taxes levied to educate Negroes, legislation

[16] Lewinson, *Race, Class, and Party*, 76-78; Theodore Saloutos, *Farmer Movements in the South, 1865-1933* (Berkeley, Calif., 1960), 132.

[17] Charleston, S.C., *News and Courier*, October 18, 24, 27, 31, November 3, 5, 1890.

enacted making it a crime to discriminate against the employment of Negroes, laws against miscegenation repealed, and
other action destructive of the Southern social order taken. As
there was no peace nor safety for the South as long as a force
bill was possible, it was necessary for all true Southerners to
vote Democratic. Everything that had been gained since
Reconstruction would be lost if whites, forgetting the danger
to their supremacy, voted Third Party, Alliance, or Conservative.[18]

After the defeat of Populism in the national election of 1896,
it seemed to W. P. Trent that a Southerner could be an
Independent without being too rudely stared at. He imagined
that freedom of speech and action were becoming more assured
except in one particular, the advocacy of Negro equality.[19] The
difficulty was that Independents were usually forced to seek
Negro support if they hoped to unseat the ruling party, and
by seeking such support they invited ostracism as advocates of
Negro equality.

This happened in North Carolina in 1898, where the chief
issue to white supremacists was the white man or the Negro.
The state seemed to them overrun by an ignorant and vicious
element of Negro Republicans and base Populists, from governor to township council. As a result, it was said, white women
in black districts were afraid to walk the streets. Newbern and
other towns in the east became Africanized, and as many
Negroes as white men sat on the juries in Craven County.
Women were told that they could do something about this
state of affairs by spurning the advances of men who supported
the fusionists. After white men's unions were developed in
country districts and were joined by many former Populists
who feared Negro domination, white men reasserted their
supremacy.[20] This brief success in North Carolina of a third

18 *Ibid.*, October 26, November 6, 1892.
19 *Atlantic Monthly*, LXXIX (1897), 52.
20 Charleston, S.C., *News and Courier*, August 26, 1898.

party coalition of whites and Negroes was the last in the South of the period. When the Populists failed, or when they gained control of the white man's party, their leaders usually turned against the Negro.[21]

White supremacy had been so endangered by desertion from the Democratic party that Conservatives who despised the Tillmans and Bryans and favored the gold standard, high tariffs, and expansion, nevertheless voted for Bryan because they could not support Southern electors for McKinley who were likely to be Negroes and disreputable whites.[22] Later, at the beginning of the "New Age" following McKinley's victory over Bryan in 1900, some Southern businessmen felt that they might be able to join the Conservative Republicans. "There is," a Memphian wrote, "no longer a miscegenated, populite, democratic party standing in threatening attitude to frighten and disturb and check business enterprise."[23]

Neither Conservative industrialists nor Populist farmers and laborers were permitted to undermine white supremacy. However the Independents were looked at—as advocates of a white man's government who inadvertently courted defeat by splitting the white vote in the face of the united Negro electorate or as advocates of an outright bargain with Negroes—they were considered dangerous. Thus Southern leaders battled against Independency as a crime. Practically, what political freedom Southern whites enjoyed could be exercised only in the making of restricted Democratic policy and in the selection of candidates in the white primary.

Southerners frequently ascribed white solidarity to the prior solidarity of a black mass that promised to destroy civilization. The former carpetbagger Albion Tourgee found, however, the

[21] C. Vann Woodward, *The Burden of Southern History* (Baton Rouge, 1960), 156-57.

[22] Charleston, S.C., *News and Courier*, November 1, 3, 4, 11, 1896. See especially November 5, 6, 19, 1900.

[23] William Robert Moore, *An Open Letter to the Young Men and Boys of the Southern States* (Memphis, 1900), 2.

excuses of white Southerners to be identical with those formerly adduced in favor of slavery. They were urged, he said, "by the same class of our people, with the same unanimity, the same positiveness, and the same arrogant assumption of infallibility as of old."[24] Actually it was Negro solidarity that was defensive, Tourgee stated: "No race can separate into parties or factions while its rights and liberties are assailed by another on the ground of race alone. Their rights must be freely admitted before they will dare to surrender whatever power there may be in cohesion. To do otherwise would be an act of stupendous and incredible folly. One might as well expect a herd of sheep to separate in the presence of wolves."[25]

Nevertheless, white Southerners thought of themselves as having united in self-defense against the aggressions of barbarian cohorts of Negroes. They claimed that the South had taken the course of secession to maintain state rights; that the war had solved the problem of the relation of the states to the federal government without destroying the rights of states; but that the ballot had then been conferred upon a horde of ignorant and immoral Negroes, incapable of self-direction. This calamity, at last acknowledged as such in the North, made the Solid South a necessity and crystallized it into being. White voters had resisted the domination through the ballot of an ignorant and inferior people, by force at first and then by legislation when this became possible.[26]

[24] "Shall White Minorities Rule?" *Forum*, VII (1889), 144.
[25] *Ibid.*, 153.
[26] See, for example, Charles W. Dabney, *The Meaning of the Solid South; an Address at the Commencement of the University of Alabama, May 26, 1909* (n.p., 1909), 3-9.

CHAPTER SEVEN

Disfranchisement

WHITE SOUTHERNERS had rejected Negro suffrage during Presidential Reconstruction and had used illegal means, including violence, to thwart its effects in the struggle against carpetbagger government. Having created a solid front in successful political warfare during Reconstruction, and defended that unity against internal revolt, they were prepared to evolve a plan to force Negroes altogether out of politics.

On March 16, 1874, following the defeat of the Radical state government, Governor Richard Coke of Texas remarked in a message to the legislature that in the state there were 40,000 black voters, natural followers in their simplicity and ignorance of the trickster and the demagogue. The governor then suggested that changes be made in the state constitution to deal with this threat to white man's government.[1] Redeemers in other states also speculated whether it should become an object of the Democratic party to effect the disfranchisement of Negroes. Unwilling to consider the question debatable, some of them demanded immediate action. "It is urgent that decisive measures be adopted now," J. C. Delavigne wrote in 1875, "because the matter gets worse and worse by a delay that brings no compensating advantage."[2] After the successful campaign in South Carolina against Radicals and Negroes in 1876, during which the party of redemption had solicited Negro votes, disfranchisers declared that Negroes were utterly incapable of understanding the workings of republican institutions. Six years later, seeing no improvement in the capacity of the black race, they pronounced the experiment in Negro suffrage a failure.[3]

In calling for disfranchisement, many whites somehow deceived themselves into thinking that by advocating collective hypocrisy, they were reformers. They argued that the enormous potential Negro vote under existing laws afforded a field for the arts of the demagogue and the briber such as the world had never seen, and predicted that if something were not done, the whole of Southern politics would take on a rotten cast. Accordingly, for reform and honesty's sake, H. H. Chalmers in 1881 recommended tests to disfranchise Negroes.[4] In 1882, with disfranchisement in mind, a Louisianian looked forward to the restoration of "purity" to the ballot, and a Texan, following Cleveland's victory in 1884, demanded the repeal of meddlesome federal election legislation because Negro suffrage had replaced peace with rioting and the laws were unconstitutional, anyway. Other Southerners hopefully anticipated the day when it should be unnecessary to bribe or bulldoze Negro voters, "when the white man is to have all that he asks for, . . . because it belongs to him." In the late 1880s more and more whites publicly argued that unless universal suffrage were abandoned, free government would come to an end; since the ballot was a mighty engine of power, the federal government could, by insisting on Negro suffrage, cause the overthrow of Southern culture.[5]

[1] *Governors' Messages: Coke to Ross, 1874-1891*, ed. by Archive and History Department, Texas State Library (Austin, Texas, 1916), 43. Texas later relied upon statutory law rather than constitutional amendment to disfranchise Negroes.

[2] "The Troubles in the South," *Southern Magazine*, XVI (1875), 518.

[3] Charleston, S.C., *News and Courier*, November 10, 1876, November 13, 1882.

[4] "The Effects of Negro Suffrage," *North American Review*, CXXXII (1881), 244-48. See also Alexander Winchell, "The Experiment of Negro Suffrage," *North American Review*, CXXXVI (1883), 119-34.

[5] Baton Rouge *Capitolian-Advocate*, August 30, December 11, 1882; Houston *Chronicle*, December 30, 1884; New Orleans *Picayune*, October 14, 1887; *Sunny South*, January 28, 1888; Jackson, Miss., *Clarion*, June 28, 1888.

Senator John T. Morgan of Alabama, representing a bold Southern position, appealed to the nation in 1888, two years before the enactment of the "Mississippi Plan," to accept practical disfranchisement. Believing that democracy was suited to whites only, Senator Morgan advised the South to use whatever means necessary to disfranchise Negroes.[6] Like Morgan, "Senex" of Mississippi defended the widespread violation of state and national constitutions. "If for the protection of our lives, liberties and property," he wrote, "we are forced to stand guard constantly, and employ moral and physical repression, we can only regret the necessity that impels us."[7]

Prominent Southerners who denied that Negroes were being deprived of the suffrage were not lacking. No one, Senator L. Q. C. Lamar of Mississippi asserted in 1879, desired more than Southerners to see Negroes made a worthy element in political life. There was, to be sure, a natural tendency on the part of former masters to use absolute authority to develop the freedman according to their own idea of what was good for him. But Democrats meant to train freedmen in politics. In the meantime, Lamar explained, Negro voters supported their former masters as blindly as they had once followed the Radicals. Senator Wade Hampton of South Carolina agreed that Southern Democrats, instead of disfranchising Negroes, were giving them direction. As Negroes became more intelligent, they would gather behind native white leaders, a result which was as sure as any other natural law.[8] James G. Blaine, debating with Lamar and Hampton, denied the claim of his opponents that Negroes exercised the right of franchise undisturbed: "So long as the negro vote was effective in the South in defeating the Democracy, the leaders of that party denounced and opposed it. They withdrew their opposition just at the

---

[6] *Forum*, VI (1888), 591-95.

[7] Jackson, Miss., *Clarion*, January 24, 1889.

[8] James G. Blaine and others, "Ought the Negro to Be Disfranchised? Ought He to Have Been Enfranchised?" *North American Review*, CXXVIII (1879), 232-41.

moment when, by fraud, intimidation, violence, and murder, free suffrage on the part of the negro in the South is fatally impaired."[9]

Despite protestations that black voters were undisturbed, critics of the South viewed the radical decline in the number of votes cast by Negroes as evidence of the violation of the Fifteenth Amendment. Alfred H. Colquitt of Georgia answered them in 1887 by denying, as Lamar had done eight years before, that the South was antagonistic toward the Negro voter. The declining vote he attributed to a loss of interest in politics, delinquency in taxes which barred Negroes from voting, the Southern labor system, and the great distance to polling places characteristic of rural country.[10]

Unlike Southerners writing for Northern publication, those writing for home consumption were prepared to admit the truth of Blaine's allegation that the whites controlled the Negro vote by intimidation and violence. They rejected, however, the notion that the letter of the law should be respected and that public questions should be determined by majority vote. Because such a course was fraught with danger, "a free ballot and a fair count" was unacceptable to the South: "It would seem that intimidation or bribery—bad as either confessedly is —is unavoidable. If the Conservatives cannot rule numbers— and in few communities is it the case that they can—they must assert their saving power in some other way. States have been saved in the past by men who carried out their plans in the face of the few righteous who denounced their ways as demoralizing, and in spite of the many who were ever ready to complain of any invasion of the freedom of the franchise."[11] Patriotic white men, it was said, controlled South Carolina by depriving Negroes of the franchise. The decline in the gubernatorial vote in South Carolina from 170,000 in 1876 to only 33,154 in

---

[9] *Ibid.*, 282.
[10] "Is the Negro Vote Suppressed?" *Forum*, IV (1887), 268-78.
[11] *Sunny South*, July 28, 1888. See also Baton Rouge *Capitolian-Advocate*, August 12, 1882.

1886 was no accident; it was a result of white political mastery of South Carolina's Negroes.[12]   In 1890 a member of the Mississippi Constitutional Convention frankly acknowledged that violation of the Fifteenth Amendment was the usual thing in his state: "Sir, it is no secret that there has not been a full vote and a fair count in Mississippi since 1875—that we have been preserving the ascendancy of the white people by revolutionary methods. In plain words, we have been stuffing ballot boxes, committing perjury and here and there in the State carrying the elections by fraud and violence until the whole machinery for elections was about to rot down."[13]

George W. Cable was not persuaded either that the South had refrained from interfering with Negro suffrage or that the "experiment" was a failure and ought to be terminated. Cable asserted that whenever Negroes had been given a chance, they had proven their worth. Only where liberties had been bitterly fought and successfully nullified through Reconstruction, had they since been condemned and freely proclaimed to have been fairly tried and found wanting. The greater part of the wealth and intelligence of the South had opposed Negro suffrage, Cable said, and held out "desperately against it and for the preservation of unequal public privileges and class domination."[14]

To bring about the practical disfranchisement against which Cable struggled, trickery, in addition to violence, was employed. Polling sites were chosen at great distances from Negro communities; lists of colored voters "lost"; polling places changed

[12] Charleston, S.C., *News and Courier*, December 26, 1890. The *News and Courier* had stated on July 22, 1882, that "finesse and stratagem" were necessary to convert a minority into a majority to prevent the return of the horrors of Radicalism. In this way the Republican vote was reduced from 91,870 in 1876 to 13,740 in 1888, and the Negro was eliminated as a factor in South Carolina politics. See George B. Tindall, *South Carolina Negroes, 1877-1900* (Columbia, S.C., 1962), 73.

[13] Jackson, Miss., *Clarion*, September 11, 1890.

[14] *Forum*, VI (1888), 393-403. Cable quoted a governor of Alabama as saying that what he was interested in was not a "free ballot and fair count" but a "fair ballot and a free count." *Ibid.*, 403.

without notice, or proposed changes promised and not made; ballot boxes stuffed and the count manipulated; and bribery practiced. To these methods were added state control of local government to undercut Negro majorities, poll-tax require-ments, disfranchisement for being convicted of petty larceny or publicly whipped, confusing registration schemes, and com-plication of balloting.[15]

After less than a quarter century of Negro suffrage, containing less than a decade when the Negro vote amounted to much, during which Negroes seldom voted without interference or had their ballots fairly counted, and before those born five years after the war were old enough to vote, the South began to disfranchise Negroes under cover of constitutional amendment. By the spring of 1890 it was well known that in the Mississippi Constitutional Convention to meet later in the summer, the overshadowing question would be that of suffrage. Whites in other Southern states agreed that this issue was of paramount importance. The history of the last twenty-five years had empha-sized the fact that it was "extremely difficult to maintain republican government where ignorance predominates or at least holds the balance of power." The enfranchisement of Negroes had been a blunder worse than a crime that had introduced a constant strain to preserve decent government. Southerners expected the Mississippi convention to be a beacon to guide other states in a movement to save both whites and Negroes from Republican conspirators in Congress who sought to place Southern states under the domination of their Negro population. Thus Mississippians had undertaken to solve the problem of the age.[16]

The chairman of the Mississippi Constitutional Convention, in initiating the move to disfranchise Negroes, asked, "Who knows better than the gentlemen before me what is the occasion

[15] Lewinson, *Race, Class, and Party*, 65; Wynes, *Race Relations in Virginia*, 26.
[16] *Sunny South*, April 5, 26, 1890; New Orleans *Picayune*, August 12, 13, 1890.

and the object of this solemn assembly?" "You are confronted by a colossal fact which cannot be obscured by the clouds of maudlin sentiment of pseudo philanthropy," he continued. Noting the existence in Mississippi of two distinct and opposite types of mankind, he posed the problem of how it should be arranged so that they might live together harmoniously. Reminding Negroes of their good friends, the whites, the chairman explained how God had made each race desire to control the other but had given the white race the advantage, since white rule "always meant prosperity and happiness, prosperity and happiness to all races." White rule, therefore, "may be said to be a law of God."[17]

The delegates, receiving the signal for which they had been waiting, provided in article XII, section 244, of the constitution that every elector shall "be able to read any section of the Constitution of this State; or he shall be able to understand the same when read to him, or give a reasonable interpretation thereof."[18] Thus minor officials in local communities received authorization to maintain white rule by interpreting the Negro electorate out of existence.

Five years after Mississippi initiated the movement to exclude Negroes from politics through constitutional devices, South Carolina incorporated the Mississippi Plan into its constitution. Benjamin Tillman, the chief figure in the disfranchising convention, readily admitted that South Carolinians mastered the blacks by shotguns. Under his leadership most eligible Negroes were prevented from voting for delegates to the convention. Whites hoped that the new constitution would make fraud alone sufficient to disfranchise blacks, though Tillman himself perceived that force remained the ultimate arbiter in white supremacy politics in South Carolina.[19]

In 1902 Virginia joined the list of states disfranchising

[17] Mississippi Constitutional Convention, 1890, *Journal of the Convention* (Jackson, Miss., 1890), 9-10.
[18] *Ibid.*, 676.
[19] Simkins, *Pitchfork Ben Tillman*, 285-309.

Negroes "legally." The Virginia movement was hurried by the fact that in 1898, in *Williams* v. *Mississippi*, the United States Supreme Court had upheld the Mississippi prototype of the constitution Virginians had in mind. The author of the disfranchising clause of the Virginia constitution, Carter Glass, remarked: "Discrimination! Why, that is precisely what we propose; that, exactly, is what this convention was elected for —to discriminate to the very extremity of permissible action under the limitations of the Federal Constitution, with a view to the elimination of every Negro voter who can be gotten rid of."[20]

In addition to South Carolina and Virginia, five other Southern states followed Mississippi's lead between 1895 and 1910;[21] the others continued to rely on statutory methods to bar Negroes from the polls. The requirements of the eight states with disfranchising constitutions were similar. They perpetuated provisions of the statutory codes. A poll tax or other taxes must be paid. Registration was to take place far in advance of elections, and a tax receipt must be presented. The ability to read and write, or to interpret the state or federal constitution, was a standard qualification. In addition, residence requirements were extended throughout the South, and the list of crimes involving disfranchisement lengthened to include petty offenses to which Negroes seemed prone.[22]

Disfranchisement was the key to the subordination of Southern Negroes. Without political influence they watched helplessly as their masters used the machinery of the state against them in every area of society, providing the conditions and discipline to maintain quasi-slavery, including the toleration

[20] *Virginia Convention Debates, 1901-1902*, 3076-77, cited in Lewinson, *Race, Class, and Party*, 86.

[21] The whites of Natal, South Africa, also followed the Mississippi pattern. See Kenneth Kirkwood, "Darwin and Durham: Some Problems of Race and Politics in the Multi-Racial Societies of the Commonwealth and Colonial Empire," in Mason, ed., *Man, Race, and Darwin*, 101.

[22] Lewinson, *Race, Class, and Party*, 80-81.

of lynch mobs and other forms of occasional violence. With free use of the suffrage, Negroes would have helped govern the whole of society, as they had during Reconstruction, and could have effectively opposed those measures designed to hold them in an exploitable black caste. The so-called redemption of the South and its late-born twin, disfranchisement, were but expressions of prejudice used, though many whites did not know it, as a means to perpetuate white domination over black.

While disfranchisement was becoming an established system, spokesmen of the region assured themselves and everyone else that the South had taken a stand from which it would not move. And they were quite successful in persuading the American people to leave them and their Negroes alone. Hilary A. Herbert, for example, in 1890 edited an influential work on the Solid South the purpose of which was to show that federal intervention to protect the Negro was revolutionary in its tendencies and bad for business.[23] Other Southerners, such as the well-known classical scholar Basil Gildersleeve, defended the South on the ground that the grand principle of state rights was incarnate in the life of the Southern people.[24]

Southerners justified the subjugation of Negroes as inevitable. Everyone of deep thought, they said, had foreseen this result. Africans who had been transported to America as cheap labor by an imperious people were and always had been a subservient and inferior race. The Southern people had simply made intelligence overpower ignorance.[25] If intelligence and property were to rule in the Pacific islands, Dr. E. E. Hoss of the

[23] *Why the Solid South?* H. G. Turner, for example, writing on "Reconstruction in Georgia," pointed out the extraordinary increase in taxation under the Radicals and declared that redemption was a victory of those who had always been masters over those who had always been servants. *Ibid.*, 139.

[24] "The Creed of the Old South," *Atlantic Monthly*, LXIX (1892), 81-83.

[25] S. S. P. Patterson, "Municipal Primaries in the South," *Sewanee Review*, II (1894), 449-51.

Christian Advocate asked, "why not in American common-wealths?"[26]

Southern leaders often made sashays into the North to confirm and strengthen the racial prejudice in that quarter as a defense against possible intervention in Southern "domestic affairs." One of them, W. J. Northen, ex-governor of Georgia, in an address in 1899 before the Congregational Club in Boston, formerly the heart of enemy country, castigated the North for the sin of Negro suffrage. "If the avenues to division and hate and blood and carnage, outrages and lynchings and violence and mobs" had been opened up through Negro suffrage, whose sin was it? "Not the sin of the South, but the sin of the North."[27]

Apparently the way to end the shame of violence against Negro voters was to achieve the end sought—control—by legal disfranchisement. Since whites were unalterably opposed to Negroes' having a hand in government and would employ violence to prevent it, why not let them use the engines of the state to exclude the blacks from political life? In this way turbulent groups acting without official sanction and dangerous to peace and good order would be dissolved by the state's assuming their function.

The Southerner, looking back over the course of his region's history since emancipation, explained that Northerners were guilty of three gross errors in fostering Negro participation in politics: the assumptions that all men are equal, that the national government must sustain Negroes against their enemies, and that the interests of white and black were opposed. But the Southerner had always maintained that these were fundamental errors. The North, he believed, at length wisely surrendered Negroes to white guardianship.[28] The historian

26 *Christian Advocate* (Nashville), February 17, 1898. See also November 3, December 1, 1898.

27 *The Negro at the South*, 16. See also Basil W. Duke, *Reminiscences of General Basil W. Duke, C.S.A.* (New York, 1911), 242.

28 Page, *The Negro*, 31-47.

P. A. Bruce felt relieved that the North had bowed to Southern demands, because the methods formerly used to suppress the Negro vote had been demoralizing, even though the South had believed that the mass of Negroes were as incapable of voting intelligently "as the mules and oxen that draw the plows and wagons; and that from a patriotic point of view, it was as obligatory to suppress their vote as it would have been to suppress the votes of all the Southern mules and oxen, had a Republican Congress, in the spirit of Caligula . . . seen proper to confer the suffrage on these animals."[29] Charles W. Dabney found that wise leadership had replaced sometimes criminal methods of controlling the Negro vote "by Constitutional laws, based on the reserved power of the States to regulate the franchise," and that this settlement was universally recognized, North as well as South, as the final word on the subject.[30]

The exclusion of Negroes from the body of the electorate was supposed to be followed by many beneficial consequences. Peace and order, friendship, and a spirit of mutual helpfulness between the races; continued and improved education for Negroes; their increase in prosperity; honest and efficient government, untouched by partisanship and demagoguery—all these were momentarily awaited now that a great evil in Southern society had been ended.

Governor J. M. Stone of Mississippi was pleased to inform the nation of the imminent suppression of lawlessness in the South following the removal of the cause, Negro suffrage. Inharmonious relations between the races, he said, were due largely to political causes, which in Mississippi were rapidly diminishing under the operation of the constitution of 1890. Since Negro majorities had been eliminated, lawlessness was subsiding, and there was no reason to believe it would reappear. Governor Stone further predicted that caste prejudice, which

[29] *The Rise of the New South* (Philadelphia, 1905), 448.
[30] *The Meaning of the Solid South*, 3. See also Duke, *Reminiscences*, 415.

still obstructed just administration of criminal jurisprudence, would also gradually decline.[31]

Other optimists looked forward to the end of one-party dominance in the South. The solidarity of whites, having achieved the purpose of preventing Negro domination, would disintegrate under the pressure of divergent white interests hitherto submerged in the face of the great evil.[32] Even those concerned with a more favorable appreciation of Southern history professed to believe that with the disappearance of the race question from politics an advance would be made toward a dispassionate view of past events.[33]

Negroes were confidently expected to benefit from disfranchisement because, it was said, their welfare was contingent upon the supremacy of intelligence and property. Since whites possessed "ninety-nine one-hundredths of the culture and nineteen-twentieths" of the property, to them belonged the South's government. If the Negro was the Southerner's ward and Negro suffrage in the white man's hands, and if these things ought to be so, as the whole country believed, "then in God's name and in all candor," the Reverend Edgar G. Murphy asked, "why may we not say so?"[34]

A minority of Southerners recognized that opposition to Negro equality had unfortunate consequences for Southern whites themselves. Political thought, they realized, became so hedged in by commitment to white supremacy that free play of the intellect could not be tolerated. Walter Hines Page observed that the South's political energy was spent in preventing Negroes from voting, leaving no vigor for other tasks.

[31] "The Suppression of Lawlessness in the South," *North American Review*, CLVIII (1894), 502-503.

[32] B. J. Ramage, "The Dissolution of the Solid South," *Sewanee Review*, IV (1896), 502.

[33] United Confederate Veterans' Historical Committee, "Southern History," in "Proceedings of Charleston Reunion," *Confederate Veteran*, VII (1899), 248.

[34] *The White Man and the Negro*, 27-29. See also Charles B. Galloway, *The South and the Negro* (New York, 1904), 10.

Thus commonplace men were elevated to leadership.[35] William P. Trent, too, criticized the dead uniformity of Southern thought and the failure to recognize the transcendent importance of criticism to the accomplishment of reform. He complained especially of the despotic sway of party, which "put mountebanks into the gubernatorial chair, and stained the judicial ermine with homicidal blood."[36] A decade earlier, George W. Cable had shown the cramping effects of white supremacy in political thought. Southern propagandists, he wrote, contented themselves with the assumption that Negroes, supported by a large class in the North, wanted Negro supremacy. When challenged, these apologists remained silent until someone asked a subordinate question: "Is the negro contented and prosperous? Is he allowed to vote? Is his vote fairly counted? Has he all his civil rights? Are outbreaks due to political causes? Then their answers are abundant again."[37] Even the white supremacists Thomas Nelson Page and P. A. Bruce regretted that the Negro question absorbed the energies of the people, excluded consideration of every other question, and contributed to the decline in political knowledge in the South.[38]

Newspaper editors, powerful defenders of white supremacy and leading instruments in the impoverishment of Southern political thought, also occasionally became disturbed over the tyranny to which the citizen was subjected. The editor of the New Orleans *Picayune*, for example, declared: "The absolute necessity of maintaining the supremacy of the Democratic party in these States has made men submissive to the form of party management which has deprived the Democracy of the power of self-direction. Self perpetuating committees, rings and cliques have captured the party machinery and rendered

[35] *Forum*, XVI (1893), 304.
[36] *Atlantic Monthly*, LXXIX (1897), 51-52, 769.
[37] *Forum*, VI (1888), 399.
[38] Page, *North American Review*, CLIV (1892), 26; Bruce, *Rise of the New South*, 446.

popular nominations well nigh impossible. This is the new danger with which . . . the Southern people have to deal."[39] Others complained of the disposition to denounce anyone having the hardihood to condemn any party act. "The lash, wielded not by the best, but often by the worst men, is applied without mercy or stint to all who are forced by conscientious convictions to refuse obedience."[40] Still others worried that in depriving Negroes of the suffrage the South had invented rules which operated against white people who should have that right; but the danger from "even a negro minority in the hands of desperate white men is in effect as bad as a negro majority under the control of negro or carpet-bag leaders."[41]

How was the South able to get away with violating the Fifteenth Amendment and reversing the course of events launched by the Radicals in 1866? Actual or threatened intervention by the federal government in Southern politics did indeed delay formal disfranchisement of Negroes until Mississippi acted in 1890. Yet the truth was that the federal government had begun very soon after the Negro was enfranchised a long retreat in the face of Southern determination to restore white supremacy. By the end of the century, public opinion in the nation had been conditioned to accept what a young Northern scholar, subsequently a distinguished constitutional historian, called the false operation of laws that appeared to have been drawn up with indiscriminate fairness. Republicans relinquished the Negro problem as a party question because they had come to believe "that domination by the ignorant blacks of the Gulf States is something to be dreaded."[42]

[39] July 18, 1887.
[40] *Sunny South*, September 8, 1888.
[41] Charleston, S.C., *News and Courier*, November 9, 1900.
[42] Andrew C. McLaughlin, "Mississippi and the Negro Question," *Atlantic Monthly*, LXX (1892), 828. For an excellent account of platform pledges of the Republican party, and of its diffident attempts, relatively easily checked by the alliance of Northern and Southern Democrats, to enact a federal election law or "force bill" to protect the Southern Negro electorate, see Edward P. Clark, "The Solid South Dissolving,"

A year after the election compromise of 1876, the historian James Parton, while dismissing notions of racial inequality, said that the cruelest stroke ever dealt the Negro other than enslavement "was hurling him all unprepared into politics."[43] Eight years later, in 1886, a disappointed Radical noted that a pall of good feeling toward the South had spread over the country because of race malice in the North.[44] Lyman Abbott, formerly a passionate advocate of Negro suffrage said: "We have tried the experiment of giving the Negro suffrage first and education afterward, and bitterly has the country suffered from our blunder."[45] The Liberal Republican Moorfield Storey, later one of the founders of the National Association for the Advancement of Colored People, doubtless spoke for a large segment of the educated North in defending Negro suffrage while acquiescing in its denial: "We of the North perhaps wisely have left the negro to assert his rights, believing that 'who would be free himself must strike the first blow.'" The gradual gains Negroes were making encouraged Storey to refrain from urging federal interference in the belief that it would be impossible long to deny their right to vote, for they would in time be readmitted to suffrage under the educational qualifications of the Southern constitutions and would be sought as allies by white political rebels.[46]

Forum, XXII (1896), 263-74. See also Vincent P. De Santis, *Republicans Face the Southern Question: The New Departure Years, 1877-1897* (Baltimore, 1959).

[43] "Antipathy to the Negro," *North American Review*, CXXVII (1878), 491.

[44] Eugene Marechal Camp, "Our African Contingent," *Forum*, I (1886), 570. Negroes hoped to counteract growing Northern indifference by agitating through the medium of the Afro-American League, which they established in 1887. Emma Lou Thornbrough, "The National Afro-American League, 1887-1908," *Journal of Southern History*, XXVII (1961), 494-512.

[45] Cited in Moorfield Storey, *Negro Suffrage Is Not a Failure: An Address before the New England Suffrage Conference, March 30, 1903* (Boston, 1903), 4.

[46] *Negro Suffrage Is Not a Failure*, 17.

Thus ended the phase which began even as Reconstruction began and which, as C. Vann Woodward has pointed out, was marked by the withdrawal of federal troops, the giving up of the attempt to guarantee civil and political equality to the freedmen, and the acquiescence of the North in the South's demand that the Negro's status be left to the disposition of the Southern white people.[47] Nevertheless, as Storey's views indicated, the American people had perhaps postponed rather than abandoned the burdensome struggle to realize more perfectly the democratic ideal.

[47] *The Strange Career of Jim Crow* (2d rev. ed., New York, 1966), 6.

PART THREE

Education

CHAPTER EIGHT

Control of Education during Reconstruction

AFTER EMANCIPATION Negroes of all ages and degrees of intelligence displayed unrestrained eagerness for education and made remarkable efforts to learn, flocking to schools wherever established. They hungered for the intellectual stimulation withheld during slavery, or perhaps imagined that equality with whites could be speedily attained through book learning. They all knew that education was a major hallmark of the white man's civilization and its possession a requirement for political and social progress.

To satisfy the freedman's educational needs, Northern teachers pressed into the South behind advancing Union armies and founded schools in towns and on plantations. By 1869 nearly ten thousand of these teachers were engaged in dispelling slavish ignorance and uprooting obsequious habits from the minds and characters of former slaves.[1] They were supported by seventy-nine freedmen's aid societies or commissions and educational associations, such as the American Missionary Association, the Freedmen's Aid Society of the Methodist Episcopal Church (North), and the New England Freedmen's Aid Society, most of which had abolitionist roots. The reforming societies in turn received aid and encouragement from the Freedmen's Bureau. Besides establishing its own schools, the bureau offered protection to the teachers of missionary and benevolent associations, supplied them with transportation and quarters, and met the costs of erecting or renting their school buildings. The bureau's director, O. O. Howard, devoted more attention to the education of freedmen than to any other aspect of his work.[2]

Most of the Northern teachers were motivated by a religious or humanitarian desire to uplift the Negroes and to renovate the entire structure of Southern society. A Freedmen's Bureau inspector described them as "a band of missionaries who have come from the Christian homes of the land—following the example of their Divine Master—going about doing good."[3] A few of the "Yankee emissaries," guided by less worthy motives, looked for financial returns from tuition, or, perhaps, political opportunities.[4]

Whatever their motivation, Northern teachers openly challenged the caste system of the South. The New England Educational Commission for Freedmen in 1863 sent its missionaries South to teach Negroes to relinquish the habits of slavery and to learn the responsibilities of free men.[5] Edward

---

[1] Henry Lee Swint, *The Northern Teacher in the South* (Nashville, 1941), 3. The Western Freedmen's Aid Society sent teachers into Chattanooga behind the Union army, and a party of Northern teachers moved into Charleston as Beauregard retreated. See Gilbert E. Govan and James W. Livingood, "Chattanooga under Military Occupation, 1863-1865," *Journal of Southern History*, XVII (1951), 23-47, and Elizabeth G. Rice, "A Yankee Teacher in the South," *Century Magazine*, XL (1901), 151-54.

[2] Swint, *The Northern Teacher in the South*, 3-15. In out-of-the-way Texas, General Howard's agent, E. M. Gregory, organized Negro schools under the charge of teachers supplied by the American Missionary Society. Frederick Eby, *The Development of Education in Texas* (New York, 1925), 264. Between 1867 and 1869 the bureau helped the American Missionary Society to the extent of approximately $37,000 in the education of Alabama Negroes. Horace Mann Bond, *Negro Education in Alabama: A Study in Cotton and Steel* (Washington, D.C., 1939), 83.

[3] Cited in Swint, *The Northern Teacher in the South*, 43.

[4] *Ibid.*, 53-57. If an occasional teacher sought an income from the Freedmen's Bureau by opening a school, few of them could have been attracted by tuition from students at $0.25 to $1.25 per month. Vernon Lane Wharton, *The Negro in Mississippi, 1865-1890* (Chapel Hill, 1947), 45-46; Govan and Livingood, *Journal of Southern History*, XVII (1951), 45. In Alabama some of the teachers got themselves promoted to the Radical legislature. Bond, *Negro Education in Alabama*, 95.

[5] *First Annual Report of the Educational Commission for Freedmen with Extracts of Letters of Teachers and Superintendents* (Boston, 1863), 10.

L. Pierce, a Treasury Department agent among the freedmen of Port Royal, South Carolina, pointed out in his reports of the same year that the new schools aimed to undermine racial subordination: "The reading of the English language . . . is being taught to thousands, so that whatever military or political calamities may be in store, this precious knowledge can never be eradicated. Ideas and habits have been planted, under the growth of which these people are to be fitted for responsibilities of citizenship, and in equal degree unfitted for any restoration to what they have been."[6] In March, 1862, Pierce had exhorted a group of teachers and labor superintendents on board the steamer *Atlantic*, as they neared shore in the Sea Islands, that "never did a vessel bear a colony on a nobler mission, not even the Mayflower, when she conveyed the Pilgrims to Plymouth."[7]

Many of the Yankee teachers associated with Negroes and urged them to demand the rights of free men. Most of them were attached to the Republican party; a few organized the freedmen for the party of emancipation.[8] The aggressive Quaker, Cornelia Hancock, militantly strove against the "violent rebels" of South Carolina. She denounced President Johnson for protecting the "secesh" from punishments they richly deserved and excoriated officers of the Freedmen's Bureau for concessions to disloyal Southerners. She demanded that Negroes be given the franchise and protected in its exercise. Worst of all, she rowed across Charleston harbor in the company of Negro soldiers.[9] Although many of the Northern teachers were neither so bold nor so exasperating to native whites,[10] still they acted on the dictum that the North could "have no permanent peace with the South but by Americanizing it, by compelling

[6] *The Freedmen of Port Royal, South Carolina: Official Reports of Edward L. Pierce* (New York, 1863), 323.
[7] "Freedmen at Port Royal," *Atlantic Monthly*, XII (1863), 298.
[8] Swint, *The Northern Teacher in the South*, 84-85.
[9] *The South after Gettysburg: Letters of Cornelia Hancock, 1863-1868*, ed. by Henrietta Stratton Jaquette (New York, 1956), 195-210.
[10] See, for example, Galbraith B. Perry, *Twelve Years among the Colored People* (New York, 1884), 88-91, and Maria Waterbury, *Seven Years among the Freedmen* (Chicago, 1890), *passim*.

it, if need be, to accept the idea, and with it the safety of democracy."[11]

Southern whites reacted sharply against Yankee schools for Negroes because, as James Russell Lowell predicted in 1865, "if they must lose slavery, they will make a shift to be comfortable on the best substitute they can find in a system of caste."[12] The education of Negroes in an atmosphere of democracy during the fluid conditions after the war did indeed threaten to prevent the hardening of caste as a contradiction of emancipation. Schooling prepared Negroes to function in politics like any other enlightened citizenry and trained them to fill those positions in the economic order for which they were individually capable. Native whites, therefore, haughtily ignored or insulted Yankee teachers and cast every obstacle in their way.

Southerners refused to accept the Northern teachers as tenants and, by threatening to burn out any family which offered them shelter, forced them to live in public buildings and churches. Storekeepers refused to sell them food or charged exorbitant prices. Even in churches the teachers met rebuff, and on the street they were liable to gross insult. A group of college students in Lexington, Virginia, habitually greeted a missionary teacher as that "damned Yankee bitch of a nigger teacher." Mobs of various sorts, including the Ku Klux Klan, attacked the freedman's mentors, whipped many of them, and coated others with tar and cotton. During the presidential campaign of 1868, persecution quickened, and following the Radical victory of that year, Southerners launched a veritable reign of terror against the missionaries. Maria Waterbury was forced to seek refuge in a railway car, as in a fortress, in

[11] James Russell Lowell, *Political Essays* (Cambridge, Mass., 1871), 260. Lyman Abbott, executive secretary of the American Union Commission, declared that the slaveholding aristocracy must be destroyed and genuine democracy built up in its place. Ira V. Brown, "Lyman Abbott and Freedmen's Aid, 1865-1869," *Journal of Southern History*, XV (1949), 23.
[12] *Political Essays*, 259.

Jackson, Tennessee, and was driven from community to community. Despised and insulted, teachers in North Carolina had "as much to undergo, as if they were in Turkey." A teacher in Bastrop County, Texas, was taken from his home at night, tied to a tree, and whipped nearly to death, and his school was set on fire. Thirty-seven Negro schoolhouses were burned by Tennesseans in 1869; teachers were mobbed, beaten, and paraded about with ropes around their necks. In Mississippi and Alabama, Yankee teachers found it impossible to teach in plantation country and were forced into the cities. Cornelia Hancock responded to the persecution by charging that South Carolinians would be "glad if a consuming fire would come over the land and annihilate both the contrabands and their teachers."[13]

Once the decision that Negroes were to be educated had been made by the federal government in cooperation with private agencies and confirmed by the carpetbagger governments, opposition to Negro education was gradually transformed into opposition to the "wrong" kind of education.[14] As a result, Southern women did not face antagonism as teachers of colored children; they offered the kind of instruction designed to keep Negroes in their place. Many white people came to believe that the best defense against revolutionary education was to establish themselves in control of Negro education. They argued that it was to the South's interest to commit the

[13] Swint, *The Northern Teacher in the South*, 109. A Negro of Chambers County, Alabama, was allegedly killed for permitting a white teacher to room in his home. Bond, *Negro Education in Alabama*, 117; Waterbury, *Seven Years among the Freedmen*, 50-54, 116, 130-35; Albion Tourgee, *A Fool's Errand*, ed. by John Hope Franklin (Cambridge, Mass., 1961), 50; "Report of the State Superintendent of Public Education to the United States Bureau of Education, October 28, 1871," in Frederick Eby, ed., *Education in Texas: Source Materials* (Austin, Texas, 1918), 543-45; Taylor, *The Negro in Tennessee*, 90, 101-102, 180-81; Hancock, *The South after Gettysburg*, 234-35.

[14] General O. O. Howard of the Freedmen's Bureau declared that this qualified support of Negro education "may be called a new form of opposition." *Report of the Commissioner of the Bureau of Refugees, Freedmen and Abandoned Lands for the Year 1866* (Washington, 1866), 13.

Negro youth to the guidance of virtuous teachers; else educational posts would be occupied by subversives from Yankeedom who revered Beast Butler and scoffed at the name of Robert E. Lee and who organized a system of plunder and a hell of anarchy.[15]

The Southern white teacher might also be able to stem the tide of feminism, socialism, and other isms brought from the North. Publicists therefore urged native white women to enter the teaching ranks to roll back Radicalism by instructing their charges in the ideals of the South.[16] These native white teachers, whether or not they were conscious propagandists of caste, did not participate freely in the life of Negroes; instead, they trained students to adapt themselves to the racist social order. When black teachers were at last deemed safe within a system managed by whites, even they instructed students to think what white people expected Negroes to think. If they showed dissatisfaction with the status quo, the white community reacted swiftly and effectively, as in Mississippi in 1882 when some Negro teachers were branded as "Radical emissaries under the guise of school teachers" and thus forced to cease political activity.[17]

Although effective opinion was unalterably opposed to the education of Negroes by revolutionaries, North or South, some native whites accepted the Negroes as free and urged that they be assisted in developing a school system—in separation from whites, to be sure, but a system decidedly evolutionary and ultimately destructive of caste. In 1866 the Texas Teachers' Convention declared: "In every neighborhood, on every plantation, and at all suitable places, let the negro, with the aid of the Southern people, build up schools. The negroes will contribute from their own labor and small resources. But white

[15] Jackson, Miss., *Clarion*, June 21, 1870; Carrollton *West Alabamian*, May 31, 1871; Bond, *Negro Education in Alabama*, 117-18.

[16] New Orleans *Crescent*, June 15, 1866; Fort Smith, Ark., *Herald*, June 17, 1871.

[17] Jackson, Miss., *Clarion*, September 13, 27, November 1, 1882; Carter G. Woodson, *The Mis-education of the Negro* (Washington, 1933), 23-27.

people must also help. In every way let the negro see that the Southern whites are his best friends. We must rise above the prejudices and avarices growing out of our past relations to the negro and recent political events and be just and magnanimous."[18]

A feeble group of whites reasoned that the demands of justice required education for slaves now released from their bonds and advanced to a plane of equality with other citizens. A few thought that freedmen should have access to education because, uninstructed and free, they would constitute a grave danger to society; some argued that rudimentary training was necessary to equip freedmen to perform the common labor to which nature had consigned them. Scattered individuals were so favorably disposed toward the new education that they rendered aid to the missionary societies. But to offer assistance in the face of general opposition in the communities where they lived required a moral heroism not possessed by all who were sympathetic.[19]

The poor whites, no longer buttressed by slavery, objected to a policy which promised to obliterate distinction between them and the blacks. But white supremacy propagandists were seldom of the poor class, and members of the upper classes were prone to excuse themselves, despite their greater responsibility for discrimination, by placing the blame on their scrubby neighbors whose daily affairs brought them into contact with the even more submerged black folk. Though the poor whites did not elaborate a social philosophy, control the government of the South, or profit much from white supremacy, the more high-toned gentleman was ever ready to suggest that if it were not for the "red neck," "cracker," or "sand-hiller," the Negro would find the South a happy country.

[18] Cited in Eby, *The Development of Education in Texas,* 265.
[19] *Fifth Annual Report of the General Assembly's Committee on Freedmen of the Presbyterian Church in the United States of America, May, 1870* (Pittsburgh, 1870), 19; McConnell, *Negroes and Their Treatment in Virginia,* 91-92; Bond, *Negro Education in Alabama,* 111-14.

The majority of Southerners of all classes were in fact responsible for erecting barriers to the education of Negroes. Maria Waterbury, who came to Mississippi to elevate the freedmen, encountered adamant resistance from every rank in society, from the planter of large affairs and his elegant wife down to the unkempt and ignorant "poor white trash." "How strange it is!" said a Northern traveler on a Mississippi steamboat to Miss Waterbury, "These southern people use such splendid manners, and are so hospitable, but . . . if you attempt to teach a colored person, they'll have nothing to do with you, and wonder what you're down here interfering with 'our niggers' for."[20] A white woman of the "trashy" sort, on the other hand, responded: "Ye's got a right smart skule yere, a mighty sight o' niggers! Drefful pest, tu; orter be teeched. 'T ante no sin tu teech 'm to reed, but dey's niggers, an' ye must keep 'em under; *min'* an' keep 'em *under*. . . . You all cum down yer' an' teech dese black 'uns, but who'll teech *my chillen? Dey needs tu l'arn tu reed tu.*"[21]

The judgment that Northern teachers were either fanatics or knaves whose mission it was to sow tares of hate and evil in the minds of their Negro pupils became deeply embedded in the Southern mind. Years later, when the Yankee teacher was only an unpleasant memory, a prominent Southerner who administered Northern money for Southern-controlled Negro education complained of the disastrously kind philanthropy which had pampered vagabond mendicants and had multiplied private schools instead of supporting public education under

20 *Seven Years among the Freedmen,* 58-59.
21 *Ibid.,* 106-107. For the attitudes of Southerners of all classes on Negro education, see also Daniel J. Whitener, "Public Education in North Carolina during Reconstruction, 1865-1876," in Fletcher M. Green, ed., *Essays in Southern History* (Chapel Hill, 1949), 73; Edward King, "The Great South: Glimpses of Texas: II," *Scribner's Monthly,* VII (1874), 423-24; *ibid.,* "Pictures from Florida," IX (1874), 1-31; *ibid.,* "Notes on Kentucky and Tennessee," IX (1874), 148; McConnell, *Negroes and Their Treatment in Virginia,* 92; Taylor, *The Negro in Tennessee,* 177; Charles William Dabney, *Universal Education in the South,* 2 vols. (Chapel Hill, 1936), I, 113.

the supervision of the Southern states.[22] An Alabama judge, also looking back from the vantage point of victory, condemned the carpetbagger educators for teaching freedmen that their labor had enriched the master whose wealth in justice belonged to them alone and that they were due all rights which others enjoyed, even the right to take in marriage the white man's daughter.[23] Booker T. Washington and his students at Tuskegee witnessed a distressing instance of the unleashing of hatred for the Yankee teacher when a Confederate veteran threw aside his prepared address, after listening to the Negro Bishop John C. Dancy praise New England teachers who had come South after the war, and declared to the audience: "I want to give you niggers a few words of plain talk and advice. No such address as you have just listened to is going to do you any good; it's just going to spoil you. You had better not listen to such speeches. You might just as well understand that this is a white man's country, as far as the South is concerned, and we are going to make you keep your place. Understand that. I have nothing more to say."[24]

By 1870 most of the Northern teachers had left the South. They had bridged the gap until the Radical governments could set up free public school systems. Their schools had enrolled only a small portion of the Negroes during a brief period, but their achievement was commendable. They initiated the education of freedmen, provided a nucleus for the development of the colored public school system, and established a number of colleges which became the chief source for Negro professionals, especially teachers.[25]

[22] Curry, *Difficulties, Complications, and Limitations,* 12-13.

[23] Norwood, *Address on the Negro,* 5.

[24] Cited in Samuel R. Spencer, Jr., *Booker T. Washington and the Negro's Place in American Life* (Boston, 1955), 187-88.

[25] W. E. B. Du Bois, *Black Reconstruction: An Essay toward a History of the Part Which Black Folk Played in the Attempt to Reconstruct Democracy in America, 1860-1880* (New York, 1935), 648; Brown, *Journal of Southern History,* XV (1949), 36-37; Bond, *Negro Education in Alabama,* 84-86, 94-95.

The white-controlled governments of presidential Reconstruction displayed only the slightest inclination to educate freedmen. The Texas constitution of 1866 specified that the public school fund be used exclusively for the education of white students. It also provided that the legislature might levy taxes for public education and that such taxes paid by Negroes be used for educating Africans and their children. Although the constitution stated that it should be a duty of the legislature to encourage schools among Negroes, nothing of the sort was done by the government which followed. The Johnson legislature in Florida also required freedmen to pay for their own education. Schools for Negroes were to be supported by a tax of one dollar upon all male persons of color, supplemented by tuition to be collected from each pupil. The superintendent was to establish colored schools when the number of children in any county should warrant it, provided funds were sufficient to meet the expense.[26]

With the enfranchisement of Negroes and the overthrow of the Johnson governments, Radical conventions in all the Southern states provided for the establishment of free public school systems. Of this achievement, F. J. Moses, Jr., Radical governor of South Carolina, said: "No greater eulogy can be written upon the reconstructed administration of government in South Carolina than that when it came into power it was a statutory offense against the law of the land to impart even the rudiments of a common school education to a South Carolinian, because, forsooth, he was black, while the reconstructed government has made it a statutory offense to hinder or prevent any child in the State, of whatever color, from obtaining a common school education. Nay, we have even gone further, and demanded by our Constitution, that their attendance at school be compulsory."[27]

The carpetbagger superintendent of education in Texas simi-

26 Eby, *The Development of Education in Texas*, 265-66; Du Bois, *Black Reconstruction*, 654.
27 Cited in Du Bois, *Black Reconstruction*, 651.

larly expressed the flaming spirit of social revolution behind the Radical program to educate Negroes at public expense:

A civilization vitalized and energized by free school is our chief need, and the education of youth our primary duty. Let the community in its organized capacity provide the bread of knowledge for all its children, and leaven with intelligence the whole mass of society.

There is nothing we ought not to do, there is no effort we ought not to make; there is no sacrifice, whether of money or of prejudice, we ought not to yield, rather than allow a generation into whose hands the ballot and the government is gravitating, to remain unfitted for their duties and destiny.[28]

The financial resources of the Southern states, though in considerable measure destroyed by the Civil War and hard pressed to sustain the ordinary governmental expenses of Reconstruction, offered the impoverished freedmen the means to support a more comprehensive system of education than they could otherwise establish. The few millions supplied by the United States government through the agency of the Freedmen's Bureau, combined with the gifts of interested Northern associations and the contributions of the Negroes themselves, did no more than initiate and help along colored education.

The idea that they should finance Negro schools was vehemently rejected by propertyholders such as Judge John Hancock, who told a Democratic gathering in Texas: "Of all the wicked schemes ever devised by the wit of knaves to tyrannize over the people, to subjugate them soul, body, and State, and to rob them of their property for the enrichment of a worthless horde of strolling mendicants, this abominable school system seems to be the most complete."[29]

The establishment of free schools for Negroes constituted a serious long-range attack upon caste, but the most significant attempt to overthrow at once the social structure of the South

[28] Superintendent of Public Instruction E. M. Wheelock to Governor E. M. Pease, May 30, 1868, in Eby, ed., *Education in Texas*, 481.
[29] Austin *Democratic Statesman*, August 3, 1871.

was the effort to integrate Negro and white children in the schoolroom. School integration was first attempted by Northern teachers who expected to bring the races together on a voluntary basis and thus initiate a peaceful revolution.

Johnson's inauguration was celebrated in Charleston, South Carolina, by the semi-integration of the city's Yankee schools. A school in Jacksonville, Florida, was opened by Northern teachers to children of both races with temporary success. But this school, like those in Charleston, was sustained by military forces and conducted by outside teachers. The New England Freedmen's Aid Society promised to maintain no school from which pupils should be excluded because of race, and imagined that the principle had been established in 1866. But this attempt at racially mixed education was such a signal failure that the society was hard pressed to show a handful of whites attending school with Negroes in such scattered places as Alexandria, Virginia, Raleigh, North Carolina, Columbus, Georgia, and Port Orange, Florida. By January, 1868, the New England Freedmen's Aid Society implied defeat of its integration policy by noting that prejudice still kept the whites away from schools to which colored children were admitted. General O. O. Howard's decision that the Freedmen's Bureau would erect and repair only those schools open to both races failed to help the missionaries bring about integration.[30]

In every Southern state at the outset of Radical ascendancy the question of mixed schools was a matter of considerable debate and strong feeling. Alabama's Radical constitution provided for schools which all the children could attend free of charge. The legislature in 1870 decreed separate schools except where unanimous consent of parents and guardians permitted integration. The Arkansas convention stipulated that all children were to receive free instruction, and the legislature adopted

[30] Du Bois, *Black Reconstruction*, 643-54; *Freedman's Record*, II (1866), 17-18, III (1867), 26, 70, 190, IV (1868), 3-22; Freedmen's Bureau, *Circular No. 30* (Washington, 1867).

a "separate but equal" school law. The Georgia convention provided for free education for all children; again the legislature followed with "separate but equal" legislation. The Mississippi legislature in 1870 opened the schools of the state to all youth without distinction, but authorities interpreted the law to permit separate schools with "equal advantages." The constitution of Texas forbade discrimination but ignored the question of segregated or integrated schools, causing hysterical conjectures as to the intentions of the Radicals. In South Carolina, attempts to integrate the blind, deaf, and dumb school and the state university met dramatic failure. While the bust of John C. Calhoun looked down on the change with astonishment, students at the University of South Carolina erased their names from booklists to prevent them from being next to Negro signatures and, with the faculty, departed from the university upon the admission of Negroes.[31]

In Louisiana, segregated public schools were prohibited. Still only a few of them inaugurated integration. Social ostracism was applied and violence flared. The children of Lieutenant Governor P. B. S. Pinchback were escorted to a white school by a policeman, but run off when the policeman disappeared. A white boycott of schools which admitted Negroes was an effective means of combating integration. Nevertheless, integration was not completely defeated in New Orleans until the overthrow of "Negro government" following the election of 1876.[32]

[31] Stephen B. Weeks, *History of Public Education in Alabama* (Washington, 1915), 87; Stephen B. Weeks, *History of Public Education in Arkansas* (Washington, 1912), 54, 115-16; Dorothy Orr, *A History of Education in Georgia* (Chapel Hill, 1950), 182; Edgar W. Knight, *Public Education in the South* (New York, 1922), 324; Eby, *The Development of Education in Texas*, 266; F. B. Simkins and R. H. Woody, *South Carolina during Reconstruction* (Chapel Hill, 1932), 439-40; King, *Scribner's Monthly*, VIII (1874), 156-58.

[32] Du Bois, *Black Reconstruction*, 660; Edward King, "The Great South: Louisiana," *Scribner's Monthly*, VII (1873), 27; Louis R. Harlan, "Desegregation in New Orleans Public Schools during Reconstruction," *American Historical Review*, LXVII (1962), 663-75.

Negroes wanted integrated schools. They desired the advantage of association with white children, and they wanted this
proof of equality; segregation, as they well knew, was grounded
upon a belief in the inequality of races. In addition they
realized that the expense of maintaining two school systems
weakened the quality of education.

Negroes often gathered in conventions to declare their support of school integration. In July, 1873, at a meeting in Texas
they bluntly accused the whites of steadfast opposition to
their political, educational, and social progress, "with a blind
spirit of malignant opposition not calculated to inspire us with
either confidence or affection." This convention demanded
the passage of the civil rights bill and promised to agitate the
question until Negroes were guaranteed their rights. "We
would far prefer to have received these boons as a voluntary
offering from our white fellow-citizens," the convention declared.
Unfortunately, Southern white men were determined to leave
the colored people nothing to be grateful for, "as every right
we enjoy has been forced from their grasp, in the face of stern
opposition and openly expressed hatred." But the convention
did not despair. It once again appealed for mutual cooperation
"for the advancement of the interests of our state and the
welfare of its citizens."[33] Subsequent conventions in 1874,
1879, and 1883 urgently requested legislation to secure Negro
educational rights and place them beyond the control of the
white man's party or any other party.[34]

In response to demands of Negroes and their friends for
school integration, the white South advanced the popular
argument that integration could not be enforced or could be
enforced only by a consolidated, tyrannical government contra-
dicting the vision of the Founding Fathers. Both races would

[33] "Colored Men's Convention, July 3-4, 1873," in Eby, ed., *Education
in Texas*, 581-84.
[34] Carrollton *West Alabamian*, July 8, 1874; Jackson, Miss., *Clarion*,
May 21, 1879, October 3, 1883; Harlan, *American Historical Review*,
LXVII (1962), 672.

suffer from mixed education, especially the white race, which would at once be corrupted in morals and ultimately destroyed by mongrelization. In any case, Southerners would not submit. If Radicals wanted their precious philosophy of universal education to prevail, then they could save the public school system below the Mason-Dixon line only by conceding separate education of the races under the direction of local whites.

The white South, as we have seen, was inclined to claim divine approval of its caste system, keeping a good conscience and throwing up an unassailable barrier to the schemes of infidels in the process. In the Arkansas constitutional convention of 1868, John M. Bradley demanded to know "in the name of God, in the name of your fathers and mothers, and of your sons who sleep in the graves of heroes" whether "you now prepare to thrust into the same common school with your child and mine, the children of the Negro. Will you endorse that monstrous instrument which prepares to take advantage of the necessities of widows, and of poverty-stricken men, who cannot afford to send their children elsewhere, to compel them to thrust these children, for three months in the year, among the offspring of a race whom God, by writing an indelible mark upon their head and foot and brain, had pronounced the social inferiors of your sons and daughters?"[35] During the debate on the civil rights bill in 1874, Southerners in Congress argued that the states had the authority to keep the races apart in schools and elsewhere because God had "stamped the fiat of his condemnation" upon mixed marriages.[36] Lest integration result in amalgamation, not a few whites threatened, the South was prepared to exterminate the Negroes.[37]

A most compelling reason offered in defense of separate

[35] Arkansas Constitutional Convention (1868), *Proceedings* (Little Rock, 1868), 660-61.

[36] Alfred H. Kelly, "The Congressional Controversy over School Segregation, 1867-1875," *American Historical Review*, LXIV (1959), 553.

[37] T. M. Logan, "The Opposition in the South to the Free School System," *Journal of Social Sciences*, IX (1878), 95.

schools was that strife always accompanied attempts to mix the races. This was indeed true because the use of violence was the effective means for controlling Negroes. Social strife obviously was not caused by Negroes, but by whites who violently resisted school integration, or any other kind of integration. The white man, in consequence, could not find language severe enough for persons who excited the colored people to hope for racial equality. Wise men therefore did not prate about liberty and equality, knowing social turbulence to be the result, but attained their goals in a practical way—by means of segregated education.[38]

Bitterly opposed as they were to racial equality, white supremacists threatened to destroy the new system of public schools rather than see them integrated. The demand of the Alabama press to abolish public schools in the event of the passage of Sumner's civil rights bill was practically unanimous. The "little dirty, greasy, filthy, odoriferous descendants of Ham" would be educated, if at all, by their parents, not at white expense and in the same schools with Anglo-Saxon children. Whites would tear down with their own hands school buildings, sooner than submit. If the bill became law, one editor said, the question would be "How to get rid of the Negro race."[39] The school system in the former slave states, threatened the segregationist, would last as long as would be required to go through the forms of law needed to destroy it. Everybody knew it, black and white, and therefore the blacks did not desire mixed schools, nor did the real friends of universal education. Such a law would turn more than a million and a half children out of school. What man could bear that responsibility?[40]

[38] Ruffner, *Scribner's Monthly*, VIII (1874), 88-90; New Orleans *Crescent*, October 18, 1867; Carrollton *West Alabamian*, October 7, 1874.
[39] "Alabama Press on Civil Rights," in Carrollton *West Alabamian*, June 17, 1874.
[40] Ruffner, *Scribner's Monthly*, VIII (1874), 89. See also Jackson, Miss., *Clarion*, June 19, 1873, August 1, 1877.

Whether or not Negroes were willing to abandon the goal of integration in order to save the public school, their white Republican allies in the South were. The files of the New Orleans *Republican* between 1871 and 1874 demonstrate how Republican enthusiasm for mixed schools rapidly waned.[41] In Louisiana it appeared Republicans preferred segregated education to none, and peace to turbulence. In Mississippi the ex-Confederate Colonel R. W. Flournoy, a stanch advocate of school integration, denounced "pretended Republicans, who are not above seeking the votes of the colored people to give them office, but are mean enough to turn upon their benefactors and deny them the privileges of other citizens."[42]

Trustees of the Peabody Fund played an important role in cooperating with the South on this question. In a letter to the Louisiana state superintendent of schools on July 10, 1869, Barnas Sears, general agent of the fund, expressed a willingness to help the state, if the two races were placed in separate schools, but if the public schools were attended by colored children alone, the Peabody Fund must look after the white children. Later, in justification for helping white children only, Sears explained to the protesting superintendent of schools that his board had no objection to mixed education, but as the white people of Louisiana did, the Peabody Fund was compelled to offer assistance to the neglected whites only. Despite their ostensible neutrality, the trustees used their influence with Congress to defeat the mixed school clause of the civil rights bill of 1875 because, they supposed, public education in the South was at stake.[43]

From 1872 to 1875 a few congressional Radicals, notably

[41] See particularly the issues of July 8, 1871, September 16, 1873, December 16, 17, 1874.

[42] Jackson, Miss., *Clarion*, June 19, 1873.

[43] Barnas Sears to R. M. Lusher, July 10, 1869, in New Orleans *Picayune*, July 27, 1869; J. L. M. Curry, *A Brief Sketch of George Peabody and a History of the Peabody Education Fund through Thirty Years* (Cambridge, Mass., 1898), 61-65; Kelly, *American Historical Review*, LXIV (1959), 553-54.

Charles Sumner in the Senate and Benjamin F. Butler in the House, endeavored to secure the passage of a civil rights bill with a school integration clause. Despite repeated attempts to reinforce Southern integrationists with federal power, Sumner died before his bill could be enacted, and then it was barely more than a memorial to him, with the school clause deleted. As E. L. Godkin, who had objected to policemen's dragging white men's children to colored schools in Louisiana, said, "Indeed, it is a harmless bill."[44]

Integration failed on the private, the state, and the national levels. Doubtless threats to end public education swayed Northerners and Negroes too. The free school idea was then riding a strong groundswell of public sentiment; it appealed to millions as the sure guarantee of republican government. The injection into the voter lists of masses of ignorant Negroes, together with a flood of immigrants, powerfully stimulated faith in public education. Should the South refuse to develop its public schools, a crowd of poor whites might join the Negro contingent and the foreign-born in an onslaught on republican institutions. Since the public school idea had far more adherents than Negro equality could muster, the choice, if it was a choice, was made in favor of public education—with segregation.

Perhaps the "separate but equal" provision for educating Negroes was not altogether a defeat. Negro schools might otherwise have been quietly allowed to languish. Furthermore, the controversy over mixing of the races forced the South to promise equal facilities in order to forestall national intervention. Although the promise was broken, Negro children were not excluded from the schools to the degree that their fathers were barred from the polls.

Once whites regained supremacy in state politics, they set up two school systems radically different in effect upon white

[44] *Nation*, VII (1868), 203, XX (1875), 141; Kelly, *American Historical Review*, LXIV (1959), 537-63.

and Negro children. The purpose and effects of segregation in maintaining Negro subordination were so apparent that Southerners felt bound to defend the policy long after their victory over the Radicals. For example, Henry W. Grady stated in 1885 that the South, once it was assured that the school would "not be made the hot-bed of false and pernicious ideas, or the scene of unwise associations," cordially supported Negro education. The blacks were perfectly happy in their own schools; indeed they "insist that the separation shall be carried further, and the few white teachers . . . supplanted by negro teachers."[45] Edgar Gardner Murphy, executive secretary of the Southern Education Board, in an address to the National Education Association in 1903, said, "The doctrine of race integrity, the rejection of the policy of racial fusion is, perhaps the fundamental dogma of southern life." This dogma of the segregation of races was approved and sustained by the masses of people, white and black, "as the elementary working hypothesis of civilization in our southern states." Under conditions where Negroes were in the majority, "the abandonment of a dual system of public education and the enforcement of a scheme of coeducation for the races would involve, not the training of the children of the weaker race in the atmosphere and under the associations of the stronger, but the attempted training of the children of the stronger race in the atmosphere and under the associations of the weaker." Although the white race should elevate the Negro race through some contact, the "point of helpful contact must not be placed among the masses of the young, and the leverage of interracial co-operation must not seek its fulcrum upon the tender receptivities and the unguarded immaturities of childhood."[46]

[45] *Century Magazine*, VII (1885), 912.
[46] "The Schools of the People," in *Journal of the Proceedings of the National Education Association, 1903* (Chicago, 1903), 129-31.

CHAPTER NINE

Attitudes toward Negro Education in the New South

SOUTHERNERS did not gladly concede formal education to Negroes, but they did take pride in the day-to-day schooling the whole of white society gave to the blacks. In the mists of the future, Negroes might graduate to full independence, having been lifted out of the dark past by training at the foot of white masters, but it seemed more likely that they were destined to be forever wards. This belief had the inestimable virtue of at the same time flattering whites and permitting them in good conscience to deny Negroes education on an equal footing with themselves.

In stressing the educational value to the Negro of his living among advanced people, white men liked to recall the benefits of slavery. Thus they castigated Frederick Douglass for railing against the race to which he owed all of his culture. They wanted to know who was it that took Africans from their native jungles and in a mere two centuries taught them what they had failed to learn in forty. If the blacks had not been enslaved, they would have been wasted in tribal wars, buried with dead kings, eaten at cannibal feasts, or left without religion and without hope.[1]

Even though Southerners complimented themselves for having brought a measure of civilization to drum-beating savages, they also argued that they must continue indefinitely to elevate this childlike race not yet capable of becoming independent through formal education. In consequence, it was entirely consistent with the Southern mind for Bishop T. U. Dudley of the Kentucky diocese of the Protestant Episcopal Church to issue a call in 1885 to all Southerners to join in uplifting by personal contact their ignorant and untaught neighbors, exhibiting before their wondering eyes in daily life the principles of truth and justice, purity and charity, honesty and courage. The bishop claimed that enactments of Congresses and proclamations of Presidents were powerless to vivify the dead mass, but he expressed great hope in the patient counsel of neighbors. The time had come to reestablish tutelage over Negroes; otherwise they must retrograde to barbarism, and the South might then be forced to wage relentless war against them for self-protection.[2] It was also consistent with the white man's belief in the superiority of his race for him to recommend the imposition of Anglo-Saxon control over backward peoples wherever found—in the South, the West, or in Africa. The New Orleans *Picayune* in 1887 underlined the correctness of the South's program for educating Negroes through contact with the superior white race by urging that Indians, like Negroes, be subjected to strict discipline; attempts at formal education for red or black savages had been a wretched failure.[3] As for the primitives of the African continent, did not the Negro Bishop Turner of Georgia write from Liberia in 1895 advising the enslavement of these people? Then "millions and jillions of Africans, who are now running around in a state of nudity, fighting, necromancing, masquerading and doing everything that God disapproves of, would be working and benefiting the world."[4]

To disarm critics of this long-range educational policy,

[1] Stevenson, *The Southern Side*, 291-92; *Sunny South*, January 12, 1884.
[2] *Century Magazine*, VIII (1885), 275-79. See also Lilly, in Southern Society, *Race Problems of the South*, 119-21; *Christian Advocate* (Nashville), May 5, 1892, December 29, 1894, August 9, 1898.
[3] August 16, 28, 1887.
[4] Cited in Curry, *Difficulties, Complications, and Limitations*, 14.

Southerners were compelled to see themselves as kind guardians
of the subordinate race. As proof of their kindness, propagandists narrated incidents in which whites condescended to
instruct the simple Negroes, such as when Governor Alfred H.
Colquitt appeared at a colored Sunday school to teach be-
nighted freedmen. There was in the South, said the white
Southerner, a humanity that linked the homestead and the
cabin and bridged the present to the past, and to this humanity
the destiny of Negroes should be intrusted. Negroes therefore
ought to rely upon the magnanimity of their white fellow
citizens as a guarantee that they would be treated with the
generosity due to their unfortunate condition. Moreover, personal relations between Negroes and whites were friendlier in
the South than in the North because in the South they were
based on the recognition, by both races, of the superiority of
the white race.[5]

When the temptation to intervene in Southern affairs
appeared to be dangerously stirring in the enemy camp, Southern spokesmen hastened to reaffirm the South's interest in the
elevation of Negroes. A brief against threatened interference
published in 1890 praised Alabamians for providing care, protection, education, and "all sorts of advantages" to Negroes
since Alabama was redeemed in 1874. This was convincing
proof that Negroes prospered most where the power of white
men was greatest; whites were the best friends the Negro had.[6]
Such propaganda had its effect upon the Northerner seeking an
excuse to abandon the reformer's role. Satisfied of the Southerners' good intentions, E. L. Godkin announced his willingness
to give them a free hand in training Negroes, and John R.
Commons, an important liberal economist, accepted the South's
management of the "domesticated" race, although he believed

[5] *Sunny South*, June 8, 1878; Watterson, *North American Review*,
CXXVIII (1879), 47-58; Eustis, *Forum*, VI (1888), 154; Morgan, *ibid.*,
588.
[6] Herbert, ed., *Why the Solid South?* 67.

that the brightest among them should be permitted to vote and to attend a university.[7]

Southerners could not educate Negroes as white men and then deprive them of a large measure of freedom, nor would they frankly admit that Negroes should be educated for subordination no matter what their capabilities. If it could be shown that the black race was actually incapable of profiting by the advanced education upon which Anglo-Saxons thrived, then the limitations which the South placed upon the education of Negroes would appear simply a commonsense recognition of the facts of life. Thus white men, as we have seen, undertook to prove that Negroes were dull. That blacks occupied a low level in the scale of ability, all agreed; divergence of opinion occurred on whether Negro inferiority was irrevocably fixed or could be eliminated by centuries of training under the supervision of advanced whites. Only an occasional independent thinker, such as George W. Cable, could not see the marked incapacity of the Negro, which Southerners in general deemed axiomatic.

Some uncompromising propagandists of Negro inferiority denied that the blacks had any ability whatever to profit from traditional education. A little schooling, they believed, could not elevate a people ordained for manual labor, and must spoil them. Even Booker T. Washington's manual education, only mildly disturbing to most Southerners, was sufficiently intellectual to be regarded by the unbending minority as an experiment in the impossible.[8]

It was difficult to maintain such a view when thousands of Negro children daily proved the presence of scholastic aptitude in the black race. Most Southerners were therefore compelled to admit that the Negro child could learn reading and writing

[7] Godkin, "The Republican Party and the Negro," Forum, VII (1889), 257; Commons, Races and Immigrants in America (New York, 1907), 39-62.

[8] [Puryear], The Public School, 17-18; Norwood, Address on the Negro, 24.

and arithmetic. Some said that Negro and white children learned at an equal pace up to age fourteen, beyond which the Negro mind ceased to advance. Another group rejected this observation on the ground that brightness in the Negro child always revealed the uplifting presence of white blood. Still others, fearing the destruction of the Anglo-Saxon through enfeebling miscegenation, condemned the mulatto to certain failure, holding that only pure blacks possessed the necessary endurance for education.[9]

A more popular belief was that the Negro child might stay abreast of the superior Caucasian in simple learning, where imitative faculties functioned, but that complex material soon revealed the true character of the Negro's primitive mind. In exercises where memory was relied upon, black pupils might seem up to the standard of the whites of equal age and opportunities, but the race had developed no talent for abstract study of any sort. As for adult Negroes, the Southerner was surprised at their capacity for self-sustenance during the cataclysmic changes of the Civil War and Reconstruction, but assigned this triumph not to intelligence but to endurance.[10]

Many white apologists, content with the assertion that the ablest Negro fell below the average white in educational achievement, did not bother to analyze Negro learning power closely. Negroes, it seemed to them, had at first rushed to school to avoid hard labor, but had soon become disenchanted by their inability to reach the level of mediocre whites. Blacks achieved a deceptive success until they reached a low ceiling through which they could not break, a ceiling imposed by mental inferiority and marked instability of character, both inherent.

Most whites found it safest to direct attention from the

9 R. W. Wright, "Richmond since the War," *Scribner's Monthly*, XIV (1877), 312; Perry, *Twelve Years among the Colored People*, 95.

10 [Strother], *Harper's Magazine*, XLIX (1874), 462-64; Bond, *Negro Education in Alabama*, 147; Lilly, in Southern Society, *Race Problems of the South*, 118.

individual to the race. To compare a Negro with a white man, especially if the Negro were a Douglass, a Washington, or a Du Bois, could be embarrassing, but when the white and Negro races were compared historically, the white man's intellect seemed to expand while the Negro's contracted. William H. Ruffner, superintendent of Virginia's public schools, following this popular line of justification, conceded that in the great future the Negro race might possibly, though not probably, attain an equal rank with the foremost race. Accordingly, he supported the education of Negroes, but with little expectation of success in the foreseeable future.[11] J. L. M. Curry, one of the most influential advocates of Negro education, believed that the Negroes' limited capacity justified special and segregated education for them because they could not at once attain what the dominant race had attained after centuries of evolution. Curry thought, however, that they should be judged charitably. Behind the Caucasian lay centuries of uplifting influences. Behind the Negro were centuries of ignorance, superstition, idolatry, and fetishism.[12]

Despite his reputation as a Southern white champion of Negroes, it is clear that Curry's thinking on the Negro question sustained the caste system and that the sort of education he favored for Negroes would only inadvertently advance them toward equality with whites.

The trouble was, education designed for whites spoiled the Negro worker. Immediately after the war a large class of Southern people objected that education of the freedmen would result in increasing the numbers of those who sought to escape labor, and the South would then be saddled with the idle and vicious. "To educate a Negro is to spoil a laborer and train up a candidate for the penitentiary," the Southern mind ran.

[11] *Scribner's Monthly,* VIII (1874), 86-90.
[12] *Difficulties, Complications, and Limitations,* 5-13. See also J. L. M. Curry, *Report of the Chairman of the Educational Committee, Proceedings of the Trustees of the John F. Slater Fund for the Education of Freedmen, 1899* (Baltimore, 1899), 29.

Bootblacks, hoehands, and other manual workers, constituting the very foundations of civilized society, required little or no training. There must be mudsills. The educated Negro, however, felt degraded by his lowly calling. Unhappy, he worked less efficiently than the simple laborer by his side, whose guileless heart was made happy by a word of praise. Furthermore, the Negro laborer would never become excited by impossible ambition unless the spirit of unrest were stirred within him by education for which he was unfitted.[13] Frederick Douglass did his people a great disservice by urging them to shed the abjectness of cart drivers and servants and to compel the world to recognize them as equals.[14]

Since the South had very little appreciation of an educational system which unsettled its laborers, the change in attitude between the end of the war and the end of the century was barely noticeable. In 1893, Charles H. Smith still argued, as the disbanded Confederates had argued, that too much education and too little work was bad for Negroes. As the professions and trades were closed to them, their only recourse was manual labor, and the education they were receiving ruined them for that. Educated Negroes became tramps and vagabonds and supplied the convict camps. "Cinda's bright boy is in the chain-gang for forgery," Smith wrote; "he got a little too much education and it ruined him for honest work." When Negroes advanced to higher mathematics, they became "the dudes and vagabonds of towns, dressing well at somebody else's expense."[15]

Professor Paul B. Barringer, in an address before the Southern Education Association in Richmond, December 29, 1900, re-

[13] Booker T. Washington, "The Awakening of the Negro," *Atlantic Monthly*, LXXVIII (1896), 327-28; Tindall, *South Carolina Negroes*, 215-16; Bond, *Negro Education in Alabama*, 114; Alfred M. Waddell, "The Franchise in the South," in Southern Society, *Race Problems of the South*, 46; [Puryear], *The Public School*, 10.

[14] Charles K. Marshall, *The Exodus: Its Effects upon the People of the South* (Washington, 1880), 7; Jackson, Miss., *Clarion*, October 3, 1883; [Puryear], *The Public School*, 4.

[15] *Forum*, XVI (1893), 179-80. See also *Christian Advocate* (Nashville), December 13, 1890.

viewed the education of the Negro, and judged it a failure. The Negro, he said, had received as a gift from the South residence in a civilized society, the English tongue, the Christian religion, and the domestic arts; from the North he had received freedom, citizenship, and the ballot. In the next generation the race had received as a gift $200 million in education. Notwithstanding this, the black still stood at the door of the South, now as a criminal beggar. "As he has grown in criminality and physical depravity, since receiving what he has of education," Barringer said, "that kind of education is surely a failure." Moreover, the Negro had used his education, given in compassion, as a weapon of political offense against his benefactors. Nor would industrial education train the Negro for efficient labor without inducing him to attack the social order; even this education would be used to promote racial warfare. The need was for a new style of education that would specifically fit the degraded black for his role as an agricultural laborer.[16]

That was the heart of the question. Accepting his role, the Negro would be protected; rejecting it, he would invite attack from the master class. Let him attempt to move out of his natural status and compete with the white man for work above his aptitude, and then he would find every inch of ground fiercely contested.

Education of the Negro in the white man's tradition was indeed revolutionary in its tendency. Some future generation would face the specter of the educated Negro. What, then? "Suppose our educational schemes succeeded," the educator Lawton B. Evans wondered; "suppose we elevate him [the Negro] as a race until he has the instincts and drives of a white man?" What would be the consequence? The Negro, having been taught his social and political rights, would demand their recognition. "Being trained for office he will demand office," Evans foresaw. "Being taught as a Negro child the same things and in the same way as the white child, when he becomes a

[16] Printed in Charleston, S.C., *News and Courier*, December 29, 1900.

Negro man he will want the same things and demand them in the same way as a white man."[17]

A few Southerners were not frightened by the specter of educated Negroes demanding privileges supposedly restricted by right to white men. Among them, Sidney Lanier expected the freedmen to make giant strides from a lowly condition associated not with race but with slavery. Another Southern writer, George Washington Cable, scornfully rejecting his region's defense of its educational policy, wanted to give individual Negroes every opportunity to advance, regardless of the overall quality of the black race. Other sympathetic whites rejected all notions of Negro dullness as fictions based on prejudice. The mind of the black as well as of the white man, they believed, was formed for light.[18]

The danger of political revolution and subsequent social and economic revolution particularly worried Conservatives, North and South, and led some of them to favor education for Negroes as a preventive of chaos. Desiring a conservative South, with a reliable working force, they believed that illiteracy was worse than foreign invasion, that it incited domestic violence and perpetually menaced republican institutions. Education, on the other hand, would keep Negroes from succumbing to the false ideas of agitators. Conservative classes, realizing the danger of Populism and other isms, thus stood for Negro education—but against the Negro vote.[19]

The trustees of the Peabody Fund, impressed with the need of giving safe education to a mass of potentially dangerous

17 "The South and Its Problems," *Educational Review*, VII (1894), 339-40.

18 Lanier, "The New South," *Scribner's Monthly*, XX (1880), 844-45; Southern White Man, "Letter to the Editor," in New Orleans *Bulletin*, September 26, 1874, reprinted in Cable, *The Negro Question: A Selection of Writings on Civil Rights in the South*, ed. by Arlin Turner (New York, 1958), 26-29; Waterbury, *Seven Years among the Freedmen*, 125; Guion Griffis Johnson, "Southern Paternalism toward Negroes after Emancipation," *Journal of Southern History*, XXIII (1957), 488.

19 Merle Curti, *The Social Ideas of American Educators* (New York, 1935), 271, 281-82.

citizens in the poverty-stricken South, went so far as to call for federal aid, provided that it could be administered by the states. They sought support in the writings of Washington and Jefferson, but perhaps their most telling argument was to point to the danger of insurrection. Where large masses of population were ignorant and in need of common necessities, the trustees warned, nothing was easier than for scheming demagogues to influence their minds against their more fortunate countrymen, who by patient industry had been able to surround themselves and their families with comfort and luxury. Noting that four-fifths of all the bonds, and even a larger proportion of stocks, were owned by capitalists of the Northern states, and that the people of the South and West, especially the colored people, owned very few of them, the trustees asked: "What security have the people of the United States that these jarring interests of debtors and creditors, of numbers and property, may not in the future give rise to serious conflicts?" If to the turbulent element of the North were added "seven hundred thousand untutored and non-property-holding colored votes, whose interest is opposed to these kinds of property because of the taxation which they entail upon them, it requires no spirit of prophecy to foresee that the danger will be greatly increased."[20] Education therefore could be a conservative bulwark against the formation of an aggressive and politically organized proletariat. It could also save Negroes from superstition, shiftlessness, vulgarity, and vice.[21]

This was true even after the mass of blacks had been disfranchised. When Negro voters had marched to the polls in a cloud of ignorance, they had been susceptible to manipulation

[20] *Memorial of the Trustees of the Peabody Fund, with the Report of Their Committee on the Subject of the Education of the Colored Population of the Southern States, February 19, 1880* (Cambridge, Mass., 1880), 1-15, 21-22.

[21] A. D. Mayo, *The Opportunity and Obligation of the Educated Class of the Colored Race in the Southern States: An Address at the Agricultural and Mechanical College for Negroes at Normal, Alabama, May 29, 1899,* (Normal, 1899), 7-9.

and, according to the prevailing view, had thrown the South into the hands of demagogues, threatening the existence of the social order. Even if the Negroes were presently barred from the polls, how long could they be excluded? As a result of this fear an occasional Southerner urged the common school to prepare colored people for the right discharge of their duties as citizens. The Reverend Edgar Gardner Murphy, for example, favored Negro education on the ground that an ignorant class "cannot exist in a popular government without finally bringing it to disorder, distress, and ruin." "Each year," he said, "more and more there comes the danger of political disintegration among the whites, and a consequent disposition to call in the Negro vote as umpire. Shall we keep him in the condition which best fits him to follow vile leaders, with low appeals and evil passions, to bad government; or shall we guard against that day by educating him enough to make him amenable to the influence of reason and right?"[22]

But the typical Southerner did not approve training Negroes for politics. He wished their education limited to what might be necessary to encourage good behavior among them. In view of the system of thought which assigned a servant status to the Negroes, the definition of the goals of education was at once prescribed: Negro schools should turn out obedient, orderly workmen well versed in the duties of their station in life. Domestic servants should improve in honesty, 'possum hunting decline, and Negroes become more disposed to look up to whites.[23]

The Negro historian Carter G. Woodson has testified that the "mis-education" Southern whites provided for the Negro was an overwhelming success. It permitted the master class to manipulate the Negro's actions by the control of his thinking. This education stimulated the whites, while it depressed and crushed the Negro, drilling into him the thought of his

[22] The White Man and the Negro, 22-23.
[23] [Strother], Harper's Magazine, XLIX (1874), 462; Page, The Negro, 80.

own inferiority. Woodson denounced this education as the worst sort of lynching. It taught the student that his color was a curse and that struggle to change his condition was hopeless. In geography, Woodson complained, a poet of distinction would be pictured as representing the white race; a bedecked chief, the red; a prince, the yellow; and a savage with a ring in his nose, the black. The content of the curricula encouraged the inference that the Negro belonged where he was found in society. Moreover, Negro children were not permitted to use texts which contained the Declaration of Independence and the Constitution, for the study of these documents might lead them to contend for their rights.[24]

The dilemma involved in educating Negroes and, at the same time, keeping them subservient caused the South to boast of its achievement in providing a colored educational establishment even as it subtly discriminated against that establishment. Discrimination showed itself in the legislation of Southern states as they were redeemed. Tennessee Conservatives in 1870 repealed the public education law, thereby producing discouragement among the blacks and the loss of 104 schools, 326 teachers, and 7,655 pupils—all because of the dominance of a political element hostile to Negroes. In the same year Conservatives in North Carolina began their attack on Negro education; before long the schools were practically closed. Redeemed Alabama inaugurated retrenchment and restored education to local reactionary control. During 1874 and 1875 Arkansas closed its schools. In 1875 the Mississippi legislature, over the desperate opposition of the remaining Negroes among its members, seriously cramped Negro education by drastically cutting school appropriations. In South Carolina most Negro schools closed during the anarchy of the Red Shirts' triumphant campaign of 1876. The redeemed South's explanation for this decline in

[24] *The Mis-education of the Negro*, xiii, 2-3, 17-22, 82-83. Senator James B. Eustis of Louisiana argued that "the Negro at the South having been educated to rest content with his allotted rank, has no aspirations to attain equality with the white race." *Forum*, VI (1888), 149.

education, especially in Negro education, was that irresponsible Radicals had engendered race hatred and had destroyed financial resources.[25]

In Texas the constitution of 1866 had provided for the education of "white scholastics" exclusively.[26] Though this constitution was superseded, concern for the whites to the disadvantage of Negroes continued to be manifested throughout the rest of the century. For a time the Radicals successfully swept aside white privilege. Following redemption, Texans repealed the advanced school law the Radicals had initiated, thus destroying the burgeoning "centralized despotism" of the state over local communities and securing the practical abolition of the public schools, despite pledges to the contrary. Negroes protested, and so did their sometime allies, the Republicans, the Greenbackers, and the Populists. These groups, supported in a general way by the Peabody Fund and a growing public sentiment in favor of free schools, gradually forced the "solid Democracy" to abandon empty promises for concrete action. The result was a movement back toward the "centralized despotism" of the Radicals with the enactment of the school law of 1884. The new superintendent of schools, in his report for 1885-1886, was then able to refer to the Radical program as without fault, except for its financial extravagance and its partisan motivation. The law of 1884, however, was by no means designed to undermine Anglo-Saxon supremacy; the whites retained total control of its administration, including the "separate but equal" provision. Nor was there the same flaming spirit of mission, nor the sense of justice, which had moved the Radicals.

[25] Taylor, *The Negro in Tennessee,* 176; Whitener, "Public Education in North Carolina during Reconstruction, 1865-1876," in Green, ed., *Essays in Southern History,* 67-90; Du Bois, *Black Reconstruction,* 653-59; Bond, *Negro Education in Alabama,* 148-50; Wharton, *The Negro in Mississippi,* 247-48; Jackson, Miss., *Clarion,* August 18, 1875; Tindall, *South Carolina Negroes,* 209; Dabney, *Universal Education in the South,* I, 235.

[26] The following account is adapted from documents in Eby, ed., *Education in Texas,* 449-819.

The South's defense of its educational failings ran about as follows: (1) the white Johnson governments justifiably neglected education out of fear that freedmen would be admitted to the schools; (2) the Carpetbagger educators created a good system of public education in theory, but impoverished the South and incited race war; (3) therefore, Radicals were responsible for the redeemed South's neglect of education, for the white as well as for the Negro child.

White children at first did suffer almost as much as Negro children from near destruction of the school system, brought on partly by poverty, but principally because the new democratic system of education, even for white children, was inconsistent with the old order. Fewer than one-half the enumerated school children attended classes in eight of twelve Southern states in 1879-1880, and illiteracy among the whites increased by 100,000 during the decade 1870 to 1880. In many counties in Texas the value of the jail exceeded that of all school property during the 1887-1888 school year. A Mississippian observed in 1885 that most school buildings in his state would be judged by a Northern farmer as unfit for cattle. In these schools, he said, maps, charts, and globes would "create quite a sensation."[27]

When it eventually proved necessary to do something toward educating the Negro in order to give weight to the Southerner's contention that he would treat the blacks right if left alone, opposition to Negro education was diverted to the question of distribution of school funds among white and colored children. Equal apportionment of school revenue to sustain the "equal but separate" school facilities was objectionable on several grounds. It would in time eliminate the gap between the white and black races. Propertied groups would be forced to contribute a part of their property for the purpose of making Negro laborers less dependent and less exploitable. Black workers might then set up for themselves or go off to the state legislature

[27] Dabney, *Universal Education in the South*, I, 115; Jackson, Miss., *Clarion*, June 10, July 10, 1885; Eby, ed., *Education in Texas*, 832.

to appropriate more of the white man's money for their own benefit.

The editors of the *Southern Review* in 1872 therefore doubted if there were better grounds in taxing the whites to give the Negro child an education than in taxing whites to give the Negro adult a farm.[28] Similarly, an opponent of public education, Bennett Puryear, in 1877 denounced the Virginia school tax because it was enacted by those who had votes but no money. Puryear argued that universal suffrage was, *ipso facto*, a confiscation of property; therefore, the poor man had no right to control that which did not belong to him; in other words, "he has no right to suffrage." Since the poorest of the poor were the Negroes, they above all had the right neither to free education nor to suffrage.[29]

In the Texas constitutional convention of 1866, O. M. Roberts moved to tax one race and not the other, or the two races at different rates, in order to eliminate or minimize white support of Negro schools. Other delegates hoped to raise funds for Negro school children exclusively from taxes paid by "Africans, or persons of African descent." This was done in Kentucky until 1879. The Charlottesville, Virginia, *Chronicle* in 1879 proposed the Kentucky system for Virginia. The Mississippi Convention of 1890 provided for "equal" support of separate schools, although several delegates conducted a spirited fight to deny Negro schools any funds collected from white taxpayers. Their minority report, after noting the large number of children belonging to a race that hardly paid taxes but yearly became alienated from the whites, then warned the people to look with a jealous eye on the distribution of the school fund. In 1901, 1903, and 1905, bills were introduced in the legislature of North Carolina to provide for division of school funds in accordance with tax income from the two races but were defeated out of fear that the courts would

28 "Religion and Civil Government," *Southern Review*, XI (1872), 387.
29 *The Public School*, 19-39.

overthrow the proposed amendment along with Negro disfranchisement if it appeared that the state wished to keep the Negro in ignorance at the same time it disfranchised him for ignorance.[30]

Unable and perhaps unwilling to deprive Negroes of all education, white Southerners parried criticism of their deliberate restriction of Negro education by boasting of their generosity. According to them, colored education was at first reluctantly conceded and grudgingly supported, but finally perfected at heavy cost. A few years after emancipation, Southerners had provided the freedmen with a school system chiefly by the self-imposed taxes of those who, a few years before, claimed their labor as slaves. The scholar W. P. Trent defended the Southern people for unequally distributing school money and commended them for having spent millions for the education of a race that

is hardly capable of appreciating the benefits it receives. They have done this in spite of the fact that no good results of any moment will ever be seen by them or their children. They know the negro well. And they know it is idle to hope that this race can be really elevated for centuries; they know also that with him it is especially true that "a little learning is a dangerous thing"; but they have acted on the principle that they must do for their wards (for the negro is the ward of the South, not the nation) the best that is in their power, as they have built schoolhouses and trained colored teachers, and are willing to raise whatever money may be necessary to render the work more efficient.[31]

If the South deserved praise for its financial sacrifice on

[30] Texas Constitutional Convention (1870), *Journal of the Convention,* 2 vols. (Austin, 1870), I, 209; Dabney, *Universal Education in the South,* I, 278-79; Charlottesville, Va., *Chronicle,* February 14, 1879; Mississippi *Constitutional Convention, Journal,* 132; Louis R. Harlan, *Separate and Unequal: Public School Campaigns and Racism in the Southern Seaboard States, 1901-1915* (Chapel Hill, 1958), 63-65.

[31] *Atlantic Monthly,* LXXIX (1897), 772. See also Charleston, S.C., *News and Courier,* November 4, 1876; J. L. M. Curry, *Education of the Negroes since 1860* (Baltimore, 1894), 7; Eby, *The Development of Education in Texas,* 269-70; Page, *The Negro,* 60-61.

behalf of the Negro, then surely it could not be condemned for providing inferior facilities because any measure of free education for this inferior and alien race was more than just.

For a time the South flirted with the idea that all America should be invited to help support the burden of Negro education. Some whites praised the memorial of the trustees of the Peabody Fund to Congress on the need for federal assistance in the education of the colored people and declared themselves for such assistance, provided no federal control was attached. Others commented somewhat sourly that the reason Northerners were becoming aware of responsibility for the education of Negroes was not benevolence but a growing fear of Negro voters. Still others, agreeing that it was unsafe to leave the Negroes in ignorance and believing that nine out of ten needed the discipline and training of the public schools, advocated the use of funds from the sale of United States public lands for allotment to the states on the basis of the number of illiterates.[32]

The repeated failure of the Blair bill, which would have allocated public land revenues to the states according to need, moved J. L. M. Curry to complain that Congress deliberately refused aid for the removal of illiteracy, leaving the unaided and impoverished South to carry that burden. Curry hoped to disarm Northern critics by citing state legislation forbidding discrimination against Negro children in the allocation of school funds; he expected to allay Southern fears by demanding federal funds with no strings attached. Public schools, he said, were teachers of the duties of citizenship and potent agencies for binding heterogeneous elements into homogeneity. He was, of course, repeating Northern statements about the value of education in Americanizing immigrants, but he did not explain how segregated education in the South could achieve this

[32] Charlottesville, Va., *Chronicle*, March 26, 1880; *Sunny South*, April 2, 1881; Charleston, S.C., *News and Courier*, December 21, 1880, August 3, 1882; Jackson, Miss., *Clarion*, January 2, 1884, January 4, February 23, 1888.

exalted purpose. In truth, it was not his intention that it should, even though he was an influential advocate of public education for Negroes and wished them to have their fair share of public money.[33] A major reason Southerners had such a high regard for Curry and the Peabody Foundation, which imported Northern money, was that they never challenged white supremacy.

The Blair bill, on the other hand, a threat to white supremacy, induced in the South both criticism and applause. The Texas Democratic conventions of 1884 and 1886 opposed it as an unconstitutional and dangerous encroachment upon the rights of the states and another step toward the destruction of the Republic. As might have been expected, the Texas Republican convention of 1886, with colored people in control, took an opposite position, endorsing the education of the masses in general and supporting the Blair bill in particular. Two years earlier both the "straight-out" and regular Republican conventions had denounced the Texas senators for voting against the bill. In other Southern states some white leaders favored the Blair bill, evidently believing that the states could administer federal aid in such a way as to benefit whites at the expense of Negroes. Senator John T. Morgan of Alabama feared, however, that federal aid would seriously disturb labor conditions in his state by lengthening the school term for Negro children, thus drawing them from the cotton fields in which they were most needed.[34]

In the first years of the twentieth century the Southern Education Board, an intersectional partnership of Northern industrialists and Southern progressives who advocated education as the key solution to the race problem, bowed to white supremacists who insisted that education for Negroes should be

[33] *Difficulties, Complications, and Limitations,* 16-18. See also Curti, *The Social Ideas of American Educators,* 279-80.

[34] Eby, ed., *Education in Texas,* 780-813; Allen J. Going, "The South and the Blair Education Bill," *Mississippi Valley Historical Review,* XLIV (1957), 269-90; Bond, *Negro Education in Alabama,* 142.

inferior. Adopting a policy of expediency, Northern philanthropists joined forces with Southern Conservatives who administered school discrimination. Yet Northerners did work timidly
for racial justice in education. The Rockefeller-financed General Education Board in 1915 considered the securing of
increased allotments from public funds for Negro education,
still disproportionately small, one of its major purposes. Other
Northern foundations concerned themselves solely with the
improvement of Negro education in the South.[35]

In 1900 the Southern states spent approximately three times
as much in educating the white child as in educating the Negro
child. During this year in South Carolina expenditure for each
white pupil was $5.75 for every dollar spent in educating the
Negro child; by 1915 the ratio had increased to 12 to 1. In
Alabama, as late as 1914-1915, 80 percent of the Negro children
lived in rural areas, and fewer than half of them attended
school; practically all who did were enrolled in the first five
grades.[36]

Southern whites segregated the children of their black laborers in financially starved schools in order to perpetuate
supposed racial differences that must, in fact, be deliberately
induced. But the white Southerners persuaded themselves, as
well as citizens of the North, that Negroes wished to be left
to themselves in educational affairs.

[35] Louis R. Harlan, "The Southern Education Board and the Race
Issue in Public Education," *Journal of Southern History*, XXIII (1957),
193-96; *The General Education Board: An Account of Its Activities, 1902-
1914* (New York, 1915), 196. The General Education Board, endowed
by John D. Rockefeller, aimed to promote education without distinction
of race, sex, or creed. A number of other philanthropists, such as John F.
Slater, Daniel Hand, Anna T. Jeanes, Caroline Phelps Stokes, and Julius
Rosenwald, created funds specifically for the improvement of Negro education.
[36] Harlan, *Journal of Southern History*, XXIII (1957), 196-202; Harlan,
Separate and Unequal, 8-40; Bond, *Negro Education in Alabama*, 161-63;
Bond, *The Education of the Negro in the American Social Order* (New
York, 1934), 151-67; General Education Board, *Report of the Secretary,
1914-1915* (New York, n.d.), 37.

CHAPTER TEN

The Industrial Education Movement

SOUTHERNERS entertained the belief that higher education was unsuited to Negroes. Any attempt to educate them as white men was an attempt to treat children as adults. Manual education, on the other hand, would, in addition to providing the type of education suited to Negroes' abilities, equip them for greater efficiency in agricultural pursuits and, for a handful of the most gifted, as artisans. Masked by these beliefs was the realization that the college-bred black man not only contradicted the Southern image of the Negro but also dangerously threatened white supremacy. In consequence, around the end of the century, when Negroes born in the redeemed South were old enough for college, industrial education became a great subject for controversy.

The Southerner thought college instruction beneficial only in training prospective immigrants to Africa. Merely to turn out colored men to float about "with Homer in one pocket and a shoe-brush in the other" was to ask for trouble. Higher education simply encouraged the Negro male to avoid hard labor and the female to shun cooking. The numerous little Negro colleges in the South, maintained by well-meaning Northerners, dispensed just such nonsense. Misguided philanthropy opened universities and offered courses in languages, theology, and philosophy to those who might benefit from carpentry. Such miseducation encouraged the foolish inclination of so many to become preachers and teachers.[1]

The Southerner, who retailed the widely held notion that there were too many Negro preachers abroad, failed to see that the abundance of clergymen, if such there was, might well be explained by the fact that Negro intelligence and capacity for leadership were blocked in other directions. The South did have good reason to worry about these clergymen. Negro churches were relatively independent of white control, so that their pastors were in a position to encourage aspirations for liberty. It was a notorious fact that the Negro clergyman could keep his people in a state of agitation over white supremacy.[2]

In developing the argument against book learning for cotton-hands, Southerners looked for evidence that academic instruction violated the black man's nature. They discovered from a searching inquiry of employers that education generally detracted from the Negro's efficiency. This was true, however, only because the wrong kind of education was offered. Founding Negro universities in the South was about as preposterous as founding universities in the heart of Africa to develop the natives there, but industrial training guaranteed colored people work by teaching them how to work intelligently. It was a curse to turn them out of school lacking skill in the labor they were called upon to perform, especially since nature had endowed them with sharp vision so that they might develop skill in dealing with objects but had deprived them of capacity for the abstract studies in which so many were ineffectually engaged. Many whites therefore welcomed the movement for industrial education as the Negro's salvation, some of them, such as G. T. Winston, simply because "the negro is our labor unit . . . and he is less skilled than during slavery."[3]

[1] Marshall, *The Exodus*, 11; Murphy, *The White Man and the Negro*, 23-24; Curry, *Difficulties, Complications, and Limitations*, 19-20.

[2] Woodson, *The Mis-education of the Negro*, 144; Waddell, "The Franchise in the South," in Southern Society, *Race Problems of the South*, 46.

[3] Charleston, S.C., *News and Courier*, December 29, 1900. See also Chattanooga *Tradesman* and New Orleans *Times-Democrat*, cited in

Radicals, Southerners complained, had taught the Negroes to quit the field to seek positions for which they were unsuited, with the result that the new generation had lost the manners, morals, and skills their fathers had learned as slaves. But the great educators of Negroes, notably Armstrong and Washington, wisely had reversed this policy by establishing the type of school which the plantations themselves had been, agricultural and mechanical training schools.[4]

Distinguished Southern educators were often propagandists for industrial education partly because they knew that most positions requiring advanced education were not available to Negroes outside the Negro communities and partly because they were defenders of the caste system. Thus J. L. M. Curry, representative though he was of professional men, editors, politicians, and educators, seldom made a speech or wrote a report without advising industrial education for Negroes. Curry was quick to criticize their private liberal arts colleges, while he gladly reported that in the "special colored schools established or aided by the State, of a higher order than the public schools" (a phrase pregnant in significance), such as those in Georgia, Alabama, Mississippi, and Texas, manual training was required. Disregarding speculative opinions concerning the progress of which the Negro might be ultimately capable, Curry could see no reasonable objection to the fact that in the South the Negro's hope was to be found, not in university instruction or in schools of technology, but in manual training.

"Education of the Colored Race," in *Report of the Secretary of Interior* (Washington, 1897), 2085-87; John Gilmer Speed, "New Light in the Blackbelt," *Century Magazine*, XXVIII (1895), 797-98; Atlanta *Constitution*, October 18, 1892; Jerome Dowd, "Paths of Hope for the Negro: Practical Suggestions of a Southerner," *Century Magazine*, XXXIX (1900-1901), 278-81.

[4] Robert Lowery, "The Negro as a Mechanic," *North American Review*, CLVI (1893), 472-77; Dabney, *Universal Education in the South*, I, 436-37; Hollis Burke Frissell, "Popular Education in the South," in Southern Society, *Race Problems of the South*, 84-89.

Consequently, he lauded Hampton, Spelman, Claflin, Tuskegee, and other schools which emphasized manual arts.[5]

W. P. Trent, like Curry, despised the half-baked instruction offered in small denominational colleges and favored schools of the Booker T. Washington type. This kind of education recommended itself because it would develop the reliable labor force the South needed.[6]

Daniel C. Gilman, president of Johns Hopkins University, also envisioned the Negro's salvation in terms of hard labor. In an address at the opening of the Armstrong-Slater Trade School in November, 1896, Gilman stressed the blessings of labor. "Work, work, work," he said, "has distinguished every progressive and prosperous race," while "sloth, sloth, sloth, has been the characteristic of decadence and imbecility." Gilman expected to win the resigned acquiescence of the Negro race to manual labor by explaining that the distinction between the races was permanent, "that this distinction is natural and cannot be set aside by human action; that the lessons of history make it clear that differences of race are ineffaceable, by legislation or volition." Each race must recognize these differences and develop such qualities as it had.[7]

Walter B. Hill, chancellor of the University of Georgia, also based endorsement of manual education on the ground of Negro inferiority. Hill described three steps in the education of the Negro: "Uncle Tom in his master's cabin," when he received training in the virtues of order, fidelity, temperance, and obedience; "Uncle Tom without a cabin," when he failed to benefit by the academic education for which his superior the Anglo-Saxon had been prepared through centuries of

[5] *Difficulties, Complications, and Limitations*, 9, 19. See also Curti, *The Social Ideas of American Educators*, 278.

[6] "Tendencies of Higher Life in the South," *Atlantic Monthly*, LXXIX (1897), 772-73. See also Evans, *Educational Review*, VII (1894), 333-34.

[7] *A Study in Black and White: An Address at the Opening of the Armstrong-Slater Trade School Building, November 18, 1896* (Baltimore, 1896), 11-14.

growth; and "Uncle Tom in his own cabin," when he received training which supplemented and developed the education begun under slavery, a realistic type of education ushered in by Armstrong and Washington.[8]

So effective was the South's propaganda, and so well adjusted to the prevailing *laissez faire* conception of labor's role in the economy, that Northern industrial magnates gave their support to the movement for manual education. Not until 1926 did the General Education Board begin to promote cultural as well as industrial education of Southern Negroes. The John F. Slater Fund, created in 1882 to uplift the freedmen and their posterity by means of Christian education, concentrated its attention on manual training schools. The Southern Education Board channeled Northern funds into Negro industrial institutes and white colleges.[9] Foreign observers, as well as Northerners, fell easy victims to Southern propaganda to the effect that races followed the same evolutionary process as individuals, only much more slowly, and that Negroes therefore required manual training.[10]

Adherents to the labor education movement were gained among the Negro community itself. Booker T. Washington helped persuade whites at least that a large proportion of the colored men and women in the colleges should take up industrial pursuits. Mere book education, he said, took the young man from the farm and made "him yield to the temptation of trying to earn a living in a city by the use of his wits."[11] No wonder Washington was celebrated by Southerners as the wisest leader of his race. But when the historian John Spencer

[8] Cited in Dabney, *Universal Education in the South*, II, 100-102.

[9] Curti, *The Social Ideas of American Educators*, 305; Elwood P. Cubberly, *Public Education in the United States: A Study and Interpretation of American Educational History* (Boston, 1934), 441-42; Harlan, *Journal of Southern History*, XXIII (1951), 195.

[10] James Bryce, "Thoughts on the Negro Problem," *North American Review*, CLIII (1891), 642-57; Klein, *In the Land of the Strenuous Life*, 301-303.

[11] New Orleans *Times-Democrat*, January 24, 1897, cited in *Report of the Secretary of Interior*, 2090.

Bassett, then a young professor at Trinity College in North Carolina, suggested that Booker T. Washington, next to Lee, was the greatest modern Southerner, he raised a tempest of protest that nearly cost him his job.[12]

Washington's style of education had been brought from Hawaii by General Samuel Armstrong, who, as a Freedmen's Bureau officer, turned from leading Negro troops during the war and protecting them immediately after emancipation, to educating them for the future. The general's father had been one of the missionary founders of manual labor schools in the islands and longtime minister of public instruction there. The Hawaiian experiment in uplifting humble people was reenacted at Hampton Normal and Agricultural Institute, where Washington obtained his training.[13]

Armstrong's Hampton Institute and Washington's Tuskegee envisioned a long-range training program to elevate the Negro by teaching him the dignity of labor and the value of orderly habits. The purpose of teacher training at Hampton was to equip the recipient to be a light of civilization in his community, elevating his race by the power of example. Washington taught his students that labor was a spiritual force which not only increased wage-earning capacity but promoted fidelity, accuracy, honesty, and perseverance. He wished to make his people indispensable to the ruling class at home. If that were done, the Negro could, silently and unnoticed, work out of the trough.[14]

Washington appealed to Northern industrialists for assistance

[12] Edgar W. Knight and Clifton L. Hall, "Educational and Other Rights of Negroes," in Readings in American Educational History (New York, 1951), 682-85. Andrew Carnegie called Washington "a modern Moses and Jesus combined." Cited in Bond, Negro Education in Alabama, 212.

[13] Frissell, in Southern Society, Race Problems of the South, 95-97; Ludlow, Harper's Magazine, XLVIII (1873), 672.

[14] Ludlow, Harper's Magazine, XLVIII (1873), 672-81; Washington, Atlantic Monthly, LXXVIII (1896), 323-26; Curti, The Social Ideas of American Educators, 291-97.

and obtained financial support from the Peabody and Slater funds and from Collis Huntington, Andrew Carnegie, H. H. Rogers of Standard Oil, and others. In return he promised a skilled, docile, and cheap labor supply, and diminishing social friction. Insofar as Washington defended the *status quo*, he was their man, and the industrial barons raised him to great heights.[15]

Washington did not wish to consign his race to perpetual servitude; indeed, his goal was integration, though he could not afford to say so. Aware of the weakness of Northern support and of the Negro's vulnerability to attack by white supremacists within the South, he expected neither the states nor the federal government to promote the interests of his people. Nor could Negroes resort to outright agitation. In place of political means, which had been taken away, Washington offered economic means to achieve integration and advised the Negro to accept a despised status for a time, while seeking to destroy the oppressive system from within, laying the foundation upon which his children and grandchildren could build.[16] The increasing wealth of a self-reliant people would overthrow a structure unassailable by the impatient and aggressive politician. This was the strategy of determined weakness, the method of the conquered who avoids certain defeat in a bold encounter, but who cannot and will not be subdued in patient conflict.

Washington found that he could win friends in Boston to sustain Tuskegee without alienating white supporters at home. He seldom made the mistake of forgetting the watchful South,

[15] Curti, *The Social Ideas of American Educators*, 299. Huntington gave Washington only $2 when first solicited, but eventually donated thousands; among Carnegie's numerous gifts was one of $600,000. Bond, *Negro Education in Alabama*, 212-13. See also Jay Saunders Redding, *The Lonesome Road: The Story of the Negro's Part in America* (New York, 1958), 169.

[16] Spencer, *Booker T. Washington*, 195-202. Horace Mann Bond declared that Washington failed to achieve these goals but that his elevating influence might have been great over the long span. *Negro Education in Alabama*, 217-25.

and when he did so on one occasion in Chicago with President McKinley in the audience, he hastily interpreted his remarks to meet the complaints of the Birmingham *Age-Herald*. On another occasion, fearing that whites might get the impression that Tuskegee was interested in things of the mind, he reprimanded E. Franklin Frazier, later an important sociologist, for walking across campus with an armful of books.[17]

Washington gave a deceptive appearance of freely bowing to Southern demands by repeating much of the white man's propaganda. Reconstruction policy, he said, had been artificial and forced; a Northern element had used the ignorance of the black race to punish the South; politics drew the Negro's attention from self-help; and a Negro who had been a lieutenant governor during Reconstruction was deservedly a bricklayer's helper later on. He agreed that the Negro sought advice from Southern white friends on everything but voting and that suffrage tests were needed. At least half the reliable colored men in any Southern town, he said, were artisans who had learned their trades under slavery; it was sad, on the other hand, to observe a young Negro "with grease on his clothing . . . and weeds in the yard, engaged in studying a French grammar."[18]

In preparing his speech to be delivered at the Atlanta Exposition in 1895, Washington was painfully conscious that "an ill-timed address" would prevent any similar invitation "to a black man for years to come." Uppermost in his mind was a need to "cement the friendship of the races." The address was, therefore, practically a distillation of Southern thought on the Negro question. The wisest of his race understood the folly of agitating for social equality, he said. It was right that the Negro be prepared for the exercise of privileges before he demanded them. The Negro would be patient and sympathetic in "your effort to work out the great and intricate problem

17 Booker T. Washington, *Up from Slavery* (New York, 1900), 137, 200-202, 255-56; Louis Lomax, *Negro Revolt* (New York, 1962), 47-48.
18 *Up from Slavery*, 84-85, 121-22, 236-37.

which God has laid at the doors of the South." Ignorant, the Negro began "at the top instead of at the bottom." The Negro was given a "chance in the commercial world" in the South. "Cast down your bucket among these people who have, without strikes and labor wars, tilled your fields, cleared your forests, builded your railroads and cities." No foreigner can approach our devotion. We will "lay down our lives, if need be, in defense of yours." We accept segregation: "In all things that are purely social we can be as separate as the fingers, yet one as the hand in all things essential to mutual progress."[19]

This speech was a national sensation, probably because it appeared to say that Negroes were satisfied with subordination. America knew that the Negro had reason to be bitter and that Washington might possibly jettison his well-known policy and publicly demand justice. When he did not, nervousness and a sense of guilt were followed by elation. Everyone from President Cleveland down to the lowliest white man could rejoice in Washington's trial and acquittal of the white American. The Negro problem was being solved in a satisfactory manner, and there was no need for a painful attack on caste. Racial and sectional harmony prevailed—so said the outstanding Negro leader.

But in this address Washington objected to injustice, though in a low key in order to avoid exciting hostility among the dominant whites. He looked forward to the time when the South would "administer absolute justice, in a willing obedience . . . to the mandate of the law." Furthermore, he spoke of his people as beginning at the bottom, implying that they would not be satisfied to remain there.[20]

On other occasions, Washington stated that *some* carpet-baggers were honorable and competent; that the Negro would not make the mistakes he had during Reconstruction if again permitted to exercise his political rights; that franchise tests

[19] *Ibid.*, 211-25.
[20] *Ibid.*, 218-24.

should apply with absolute honesty to both races alike, because the present system was unfair to the black man, to the white man, and to the rest of the Union; that segregation on trains should not be permitted; that little, prejudiced men were barred from what was highest and best in the world; that a race willing to die for its country during the Spanish-American War should be given the opportunity to live for its country in peace; that the Louisiana Constitutional Convention ought not to disfranchise the black man.[21]

Though Washington appeared to accept the Southern white as the Negro's master and seemed to encourage Negroes to vote Democratic, he himself voted Republican and against the solid South and used all his influence to maintain the alliance between the Republican party and the Negroes.[22] Moreover, he dined with President Roosevelt and raised a storm in doing so. Washington, in short, condemned the Southern social order and employed the strategy of weakness in patient warfare against the powerful white caste. Thus he adjusted his educational system to restrictive conditions laid down by a hostile South. For having done so, his reputation has declined. Not his picture, but that of the uncompromising Frederick Douglass now hangs in the offices of Negro leaders.[23]

Though many people were persuaded that Negroes should give up their ambition for higher education in favor of the manual arts, various Negroes and Northerners and a few Southerners called attention to the tendency of this policy to bar Negroes from cultural and professional achievement and to prepare them for permanent subjection. These dissenters insisted that traditional university education be made available to the blacks.

Colored leaders in Texas saw the movement toward manual training as an effort to keep their people in a status of peonage. A Committee on Industrial Education at the Colored Teachers'

---

[21] *Ibid.*, 85-87, 100-101, 229, 255, 318.
[22] Spencer, *Booker T. Washington*, 167-68.
[23] Earl Conrad, *Jim Crow America* (New York, 1947), 191.

Association meeting in 1900 denounced the view that practical training was most suitable for the colored man as "unjust, illogical, spurious, and antagonistic to American peace and prosperity, and entirely out of harmony with the soundest philosophy of the age. We disagree with those who hold that conditions force us to take the lower order of occupations exclusively."[24]   In replying to a questionnaire of the New Orleans *Times-Democrat* touching on industrial education, Bishop A. Grant, a Negro, went to the heart of the question: "The Negro should not be educated as a race but as anybody else."[25] The Negro clergyman, Charles T. Walker, in an address before the National Education Association, stated that in addition to skilled craftsmen the Negro race needed the "most highly educated men and women to train and prepare the future leaders of the race."[26]

The Negro scholar, W. E. B. Du Bois, the leading critic of Booker T. Washington's kind of education, resented the emphasis upon industrial training as frustrating the Negro's desires for professional, literary, and artistic distinction, and as tending to keep him on the mudsill of the social order. Unlike Southerners who argued that Tuskegee Institute was adapted to the nature of the Negro, Du Bois maintained that it nurtured him in the psychology of slavery and violated the rights of the "talented tenth." Du Bois believed that the Radical effort to open higher education to Negroes had been the salvation of the South and the Negro. When reaction triumphed, there was a little group of trained colored people which grew by leaps and bounds. Had it not been for the Negro school and college, "the Negro would, to all intents and purposes, have been driven back to slavery."[27]

Some Northern leaders supported the demands of colored

[24] Cited in Eby, *The Development of Education in Texas*, 271.
[25] January 24, 1887, cited in *Report of the Secretary of Interior*, 2091.
[26] "The Educational Needs of the Southern Negro," in *Journal of the Proceedings of the National Education Association*, 1903, 127.
[27] *Black Reconstruction*, 667. See also Curti, *The Social Ideas of American Educators*, 304, 305; Spencer, *Booker T. Washington*, 154-73.

people for traditional college, as well as industrial, education. S. W. Powell, to cite an example, pointed out that Southerners promoted manual training as a means to give the Negro just enough education "to keep him from voting on the side of anarchy and to make him more efficient as a hewer of wood and a drawer of water."[28] He himself favored industrial education mixed with liberal doses of intellectual and moral training as a practical thing. As another example, William T. Harris, the great Northern educator, in an address at Atlanta University in 1895, urged Negro students to strive for excellence even in classical studies. Industrial education was appropriate for some Negroes, he admitted, but "the colored man is not always going to be the person who draws water and cuts wood; he is going to help on with civilization." If this were so, he needed to learn mathematics, science, literature, and language.[29]

Not a few critics penetrated the South's subterfuge in seeming to support Negro education by agitating for manual training. They saw plainly that the prime motive of many of those who most strongly advocated industrial education was the conviction that the Negro was and should be doomed to servitude. As the New York *Independent* declared:

This is a denial of the manhood of the Negro, of his equality in any sense with the white man, and of his right to compete with him in any of the higher walks of life. The Negro is not to hold office; he is not to vote as other men vote, freely, and have his vote fairly counted; he is not to be called upon to contribute anything in the way of brain force to the national life; he is not to aspire to professional attainment; he must lay aside all ambition for literary or artistic recognition, and must be absolutely content with his lot as a servant. If educated at all, he must regard it as great boon to be allowed to read and write and have a little smattering of a knowledge of numbers.[30]

[28] "Industrial Education for the Negro: Is It a Craze?" *Century Magazine*, XVI (1889), 472-73.
[29] *Higher Education for Negroes: An Address Made to the Students of Atlanta University, Atlanta, Ga., October 29, 1895* (Atlanta, 1895).
[30] Quoted in *Liberia*, Bulletin No. 10 (February, 1897), 71-72.

Although Negroes maintained their right to higher education, industrial training prevailed to a large degree in the state schools for Negroes and was included to a lesser degree in the private institutions. Furthermore, except for a few universities of the caliber of Howard, Fisk, and Atlanta, Negro institutions of higher learning, both state and private, were financially impoverished, inadequately staffed, and pitifully small in enrollment. Most of them did not deserve the designation of college. In few of them were more than 10 percent of the students doing college work. In 1914 the total number of competent students was so small that there were Negro colleges with as few as eight or ten students; elementary and secondary education had to be their principal concern. Of eight Negro colleges in Texas in 1914-1915, only three were accredited by the state, and their total enrollment, excluding elementary and high school pupils, was 129.[31]

Tougaloo and Alcorn universities may be taken as examples of higher education for Negroes in Mississippi. From their foundation, white supremacists denounced them, calling Alcorn "a miserable sham—an abortion—a den of iniquity" that "ought to be beaten down and sown with salt." After taking strong doses of vocational education, including blacksmithing, wagon-making, carpentering, and agriculture, the colleges in time won reluctant toleration from local whites. In 1885 Tougaloo had an enrollment of 269 students, most of them in the elementary grades, and graduated that year five prospective teachers from what amounted to a high school normal program. A year earlier Alcorn was able to offer advanced instruction to a mere handful of the student body of 166.[32]

The South's refusal to jettison its intellectual baggage when

[31] *The General Education Board*, 203-206; Charles Forster Smith, "The Negro in Nashville," *Century Magazine*, XX (1891), 154-56; Eby, *The Development of Education in Texas*, 272-78; Wharton, *The Negro in Mississippi*, 251-53.

[32] Jackson, Miss., *Clarion*, April 24, 1873, March 4, 1875, January 12, 1876, June 10, December 31, 1884, January 28, 1885.

its slaves gained freedom conditioned its educational treatment of the freedmen. Developing a social policy which consigned Negroes to a subservient caste, differing little from that worked out in the Old South, Southern leaders repeated and adapted the old phrases, and fought to hold on to the old order. It was impossible to educate freedmen and their descendants in company with whites and on the same principles, and continue at the same time to reserve the master's privileges. The South therefore created a special educational establishment designed to confirm the Negro in his status of subordination. This was done in a context of Negro striving encouraged by more or less feeble support from the federal government and private organizations, and aided by a spirit of humanity in the South.

PART FOUR

Labor

CHAPTER ELEVEN

Coercion of the Black Worker

RIGHT AFTER emancipation, Southerners revealed their intention toward the freedmen. Unable or unwilling to understand that the work of Negroes could be other than a form of slavery, or that it could be accomplished without binding the hireling to the employer, planters inserted in contracts provisions pregnant with meaning: Negroes must be respectful; they must not keep too many dogs; they must not leave the plantation without the landlord's permission. The idea seemed to be that the laborer must be bound body and soul.[1] Partly from habit, partly from calculation, the planter hoped to maintain a control of his labor force almost as rigid as it had even been. As a result, some Negroes could hardly tell the difference between slavery and freedom: "Missus done keep me in slave times totin' milk, an' pickin' cotton, an' now de black 'uns is free, an' gwine to de skule 'cept us 'uns, an' 'pears like we hev to tote all de milk, an' pick de cotton, an' work jes' de same."[2]

In order to avoid any semblance of a free labor market, planters began to hold meetings as early as 1865 to establish a common front. In many counties of Virginia, especially where the Negro element was large and powerful, planters organized to set wages and, in some instances, agreed not to hire all those who applied for work without recommendations. This policy was understood by freedmen and their guardians as an effort to keep Negroes landless and assure whites the benefits of slavery without its inconvenience. A Virginia district commander of the Freedmen's Bureau therefore issued a general order in July, 1865, forbidding citizens to band themselves together for the purpose of agreeing on remuneration for the labor of freedmen. To Virginians the bureau's intervention was the work of "nigger-radicals" and vindictive politicians.[3]

In other states, planters formed associations to keep down the price of labor, agreeing in some instances to offer no more than five dollars a month. Dissatisfied freedmen appealed to bureau officers, who insisted upon a much higher wage, and the cry was then raised that freedmen had been encouraged in idleness.[4] Negro and bureau opposition proved sufficient to defeat the first attempts to fix countywide wages by means of associations. The failure was, however, only in open and formal combination. General agreement on wages and conditions of labor tended to be reached in practice and to become customary.

Agitation for uniform labor policies was kept up until the planters got what they wanted. In 1870 Colonel D. Wyatt Aiken, before the Agricultural Society of Barnwell, South Carolina, warned planters against admitting to agricultural partnership men whose stock in trade was animal strength. "Their presumption assured our submission; our submission is their ruin; their ruin is our failure." Such had been the state of agriculture since the inception of the new order of plantation economy. Aiken proposed the buying and selling of agricultural labor as any other commodity. But the price of this commodity should not be set in a free market; rather, it must be fixed by the planters, who by proper combination could secure them-

[1] De Forest, A Union Officer, 58-60.

[2] Waterbury, Seven Years among the Freedmen, 71.

[3] McConnell, Negroes and Their Treatment in Virginia, 33-44. General O. O. Howard thought of the bureau as the freedmen's shield against "the imposition of employers, the cruelty of enemies, and unfairness of the courts." Freedmen's Bureau, Report of the Commissioner (1866), 2. See also Wharton, The Negro in Mississippi, 94.

[4] Freedmen's Bureau, Report of the Commissioner (1866), 2. See also Saloutos, Farmer Movements in the South, 16.

selves "against the preponderant influence of the inferior race."[5]
On rare occasions Negroes ventured publicly to object to the
policy that Colonel Aiken advocated, as when a colored state
convention in Nashville in 1871 dispatched a memorial to
Congress praying for protection against clubs and associations
formed to control Negro labor.[6]

White leaders proposed and endorsed the resolutions of
citizens' committees which urged planters to dominate their
hands. Local committees requested planters to refuse work to
any Negro who had been fired, who was still in debt to a
former employer, or who had made himself obnoxious to the
community. The united action of employers was, however,
never thorough enough to suit the whites, who often complained that discipline was lax and wages exorbitant.[7]

Legislation was needed to make legal and effective the
coercion deemed necessary to manage the freedmen's labor.
Could not white men use the power of the state against Negroes
as they were accustomed to doing? Soon after Lee's surrender,
Virginia leaders declared that magistrates and municipal officers
should "hold a rod in *terrorem*" over wandering, idle creatures.
Nothing short of the most efficient police system would prevent
the utter destruction of the economy. The penalty for vagrancy
should be virtual servitude: unless goaded, Negroes would not
work.[8] Here is the spirit of the black codes, the later vagrancy
legislation, and the convict lease system.

The black codes were enacted in response to a demand for
extraordinary control over the freedmen. The Louisiana code
abridged the freedom of agricultural labor, limited its mobility,
and authorized the use of force to make Negroes work. Negroes

[5] *A Practical Paper on Plantation Economy* (Columbia, S.C., 1872),
extract in Carrollton *West Alabamian*, January 29, 1873.

[6] Cited in Taylor, *The Negro in Tennessee*, 131.

[7] *Banner of the South and Planters Journal*, September 16, 1871; Carrollton *West Alabamian*, June 12, 1872, December 23, 1874; "Letter to
the Editor," from Madison Station, Mississippi, in Louisville *Home and
Farm*, January 15, 1880.

[8] McConnell, *Negroes and Their Treatment in Virginia*, 45-46.

were enjoined not to form unions nor to strike, while anyone tampering with them was subject to fine and imprisonment. The freedman must contract for a year's labor and include his family in the agreement. If he quit, he forfeited his wages. If he was refractory, fines were exacted from him. Justices of the peace, planters themselves, were charged with the protection of the Negro workers.[9]

The labor legislation of Texas in 1866 permitted the planter to fine his laborers and to deduct the fine from wages. Fines could be imposed for neglect, disobedience, impertinence, malingering, and like offenses. If the Negro refused to work, he could be jailed. When he deserted an employer, no other was allowed to hire him under penalty of heavy fine. Although the Freedmen's Bureau suspended the operation of these laws, and similar ones in other states, its power was not felt in every community. Especially was this true in Texas, where the bureau was unable to reach more than one-third of the state.[10]

The Johnson governments, together with their labor legislation, were shoved aside by the Radicals; yet Southerners continued to demand special legislation to govern the labor of freedmen. The Negro was unproductive, it was widely believed, because he had escaped from authority or had been alienated from the men who knew him well. Planters blamed the army, the Freedmen's Bureau, the Loyal League, and the whole of the national government for turning industrious slaves into idlers. The Freedmen's Bureau, an especial object of complaint, did not merely take the place of the old master in distributing food and clothing; it also subverted his authority by setting up special courts and by regulating conditions of labor and determining wages. It went so far as to provide dissatisfied Negroes with free transportation from a district in South

[9] Roger W. Shugg, *Origin of Class Struggle in Louisiana: A Social History of White Farmers and Laborers during Slavery and After, 1840-1875* (Baton Rouge, 1939), 212-14.

[10] Freedmen's Bureau, *Report of the Commissioner for the Year 1867* (Washington, 1867), 65-66.

Carolina to more promising areas in order to force local planters to raise wages and offer better conditions.[11]

In view of the South's definition of the Negro's role as laborer, any agency which interposed itself between planter and worker was sure to be denounced. According to the plantation interest, the bureau had transferred an army of clergymen from their pulpits in New England to its offices in the South, where the fanatics acted on the assumption that the planter was a monster and the Negro a darling. Teaching the Negro to expect immunity for any act, they undermined Southern agriculture; they encouraged the Negro's inclination to idleness and assisted him to abandon the farm where he was needed and go off to cities where he was unwanted. Nevertheless, planters ought not to lose hope, for the impracticable views of a fanatical pulpit could not long obstruct the prosperity of agriculture.[12]

To Governor Benjamin G. Humphreys of Mississippi, four years of cruel war, marked by vandalism, was scarcely more destructive to the homes of white men and impoverishing and degrading to Negroes than the administration of this black incubus.[13] Less dignified critics lambasted the Freedmen's Bureau as an agency of robbery and tyranny administered by cutthroats who delighted in organizing racial strife. These villains taught Negroes "to be idle; to be thriftless; to hate the whites; to look to the general government as the fountain of every blessing, and the sky from which not only food would drop into their mouths but raiment would descend upon their bodies."[14]

[11] *Ibid.* (1866, 1867, 1868, 1869), *passim;* Freedmen's Bureau, *Circulars, passim.* For a detailed account see Paul S. Pierce, *The Freedmen's Bureau: A Chapter in the History of Reconstruction* (Iowa City, 1904), 129-60.

[12] New Orleans *Crescent,* October 16, 19, 23, 1865, December 11, 1867, February 7, 1868.

[13] Quoted in "Monthly Record of Events," *Harper's Magazine,* XXXII (1866), 261.

[14] Jackson, Miss., *Clarion,* December 25, 1873, January 20, 1879.

The Southern mind entertained few variations on the theme that the bureau ruined the Negro and set him against the white man. A generation after its demise, Hilary A. Herbert censured the bureau in retrospect for having organized chaos by demoralizing labor, when the first lesson for the freedman was that in the sweat of his brow he must earn his bread. H. G. Turner charged the bureau with attracting the Negroes to the towns where it located schools and dispensed mendicancy. Thomas Nelson Page complained that the work of the army and then of the bureau in luring freedmen from field to ration dispensary had initiated the lamentable change in the relations between the planter and his laborers.[15]

The Freedmen's Bureau existed only for a moment, but it was succeeded by militant carpetbagger governments which brought Negroes actively into politics. Southerners vehemently opposed this development both because they believed that uneducated servants had no business in government and because they knew that political power would be used to destroy white supremacy. A principal lesser complaint against the Negro's participation in politics was that it disturbed his labor. Flattered by his importance as a political element, he was no longer content to plow the land or chop the cotton. Lofty duties of citizenship called him from field and barnyard. When he was inspired by the chance for office, perhaps a seat in Congress, and the opportunity to rearrange the social order, was there any reason to wonder, the white employer asked, that the Negro had become involved in party organization, riots, marching, and drum beating to the neglect of his plantation duties?[16]

[15] Herbert, "Reconstruction at Washington," in Herbert, ed., *Why the Solid South?* 18; Turner, *ibid.*, 118-19; Page, *The Negro*, 30-31.
[16] [Puryear], *The Public School*, 20-21; Richard B. Elder, "Country Life in Virginia Now-a-days," *Lippincott's Magazine*, IX (1872), 347-51; De Leon, *Harper's Magazine*, XLVII (1874), 271; King, *Scribner's Monthly*, VIII (1874), 653-54; Carrollton *West Alabamian*, October 30, 1872, September 1, September 29, 1875.

With the shiftless character of the Negro accepted as an axiom, the question arose during Reconstruction, "How can the freedman's labor be managed best?" Whatever system was adopted, be it sharecropping or wages or some variation of these, the Negro, sheltered, clothed, and directed by the planter, tended to revert to a routine like that of slavery, though one less severe in discipline.

In the search for suitable labor policies to replace bondage, whites sometimes debated in confusion and occasionally surrendered to despair. In his gloomier moods, the Southerner felt there was no hope for his region. A Texas planter, unable to deal with Negroes under changed circumstances, turned his plantation over to a son who managed the freedmen by means his father could not adjust to. A Louisianian, weary of the whole subject of black versus white, expected fresh humiliations in a thousand changes and would have been glad to see the last Negro vanish from the soil. An old South Carolinian resolved to raise a little corn and a few hogs, but never again to plant cotton, because "the niggers won't work and all the spirit was out of him anyway."[17]

Yet the South's purpose to hold its black labor force in subjection was generally firm despite moments of indecision. The first impulse was to refuse work to freedmen in order to force them to acknowledge dependence. This strategy would not be adopted, however, for the war-crippled planter, though loath to admit it, was as dependent upon the Negro as the Negro was upon him. Failing to compel the freedman to come begging, he decided to employ the old discipline in combination with low wages or to turn to sharecropping. Either system was compatible with a status verging on slavery. On some plantations there might be a dozen squads, each working on a different plan, the planter hoping to find out which system would be

[17] King, *Scribner's Monthly*, VIII (1874), 134-35; Hancock, *The South after Gettysburg*, 198.

most advantageous to him and most binding upon the freed-men.[18]

The lease system was quickly rejected. Aside from the fact that a freedman owning nothing but his labor could hardly get sufficient capital to rent and work land, leasing did not commend itself to the whites who were reluctant to abandon authority over the freedman's activities. Indeed, a good deal of hysterical opposition was raised at the thought that Negroes might become renters. To lease land, according to some, was to set up a pesthouse. Others objected to the lease system because freedmen, like children, required direction; else their ineradicable carelessness led to general neglect. Planters who rented land to Negroes were sometimes denounced as undermining the labor system by setting up lazy and impecunious renters who consumed improvements while raising nothing more than grass. But under proper restraints, 500 fieldhands could produce 1,500 bales of cotton.[19]

Sharecropping was another possibility. Some liked this arrangement because it bound the Negro to the land for at least a season. Though whites as well as blacks became sharecroppers, Negroes were the more vulnerable to exploitation. Despite the opportunities for advancement that steady workers might seem to enjoy in good times, in practice the sharecropper did not get ahead. The system made impossible demands on a people trained in slavery, and merchants and plantation storekeepers, with their markups, high interest rates, and opportuni-

[18] N. E. Cobleigh, "Southern Reconstruction," *Methodist Quarterly Review*, XLII (1870), 389; Caroline E. MacGill, "Immigration into the Southern States," in Julian A. C. Chandler and others, *The South in the Building of the Nation*, 13 vols. (Richmond, 1909), VI, 592; George K. Holmes, "The Peons of the South," *Annals of the American Academy of Political and Social Science*, IV (1893), 265-74; Freedmen's Bureau, *Report of the Commissioner* (1866, 1867), *passim*; King, *Scribner's Monthly*, VIII (1874), 663.

[19] Carrollton *West Alabamian*, February 16, 1870; De Leon, *Harper's Magazine*, XLVII (1874), 276; E. Merton Coulter, *The South during Reconstruction, 1865-1877* (Baton Rouge, 1947), 79; Wharton, *The Negro in Mississippi*, 64.

ties for deceit and fraud, often relieved the sharecropper of the potential savings needed to climb the agricultural ladder. Rarely did a freedman find that his season's toil had done anything more than square accounts. But to the planter, sharecropping had the advantage of making the laborer more reliable: "the pleasant uncertainty of the result and the stimulant to personal exertion which this plan holds forth—will usually keep the laborers quiet and contented to the close of the year."[20] But there were serious weaknesses in the system. The black cropper wanted a part in planning, the employer complained, he was inclined to neglect the crop, and more often than not he was dissatisfied with his portion of the profits.[21]

The wagehand's time belonged entirely to the planter. There was, however, the danger that wage payments could lead to weekly declarations of independence. To prevent this, it was suggested that the laborer be hired for a year and that he receive only one-half his wages each month until the year's end. And the planter should furnish rations. Wages, some openly asserted, should be low enough to bring in hunger, even more effective than the lash used to be, as an ally. Necessity had become the true "higher law" for the freedman. Here and there a few whites, incensed at the Negro's power to bargain, urged planters to reduce wages because labor ought not dictate to capital; then they might come up to the standard which prevailed in Georgia, where determined planters had brought their laborers under splendid control. Although many planters were scrupulous to avoid abuses in the payment of wages, low though they may have been, it is not surprising that some of them were charged with retardation of wages during the existence of the Freedmen's Bureau or were later inclined to hand out

[20] Jackson, Miss., *Clarion*, March 18, 1869.
[21] Freedmen's Bureau, *Report of the Commissioner* (1867), 52; King, *Scribner's Monthly*, VII (1873), 133; Matthew Brown Hammond, "Agricultural Credit and Crop Mortgages," in Chandler and others, *The South in the Building of the Nation*, VI, 422-24; De Leon, *Harper's Magazine*, XLVII (1874), 272.

tickets redeemable in staples at the end of the month. In any case, white Southerners persuaded themselves and all who would listen that Negroes willingly accepted low wages and remained content with the humblest living conditions.[22]

Sometimes whites were rudely shocked, as they were on the eve of the Radical collapse in South Carolina, when workers along the Combahee River struck the rice plantations in protest against a wage cut.[23] Planters of the region, acting as a body, had reduced the daily wage from fifty to forty cents. Lower income, together with the grievance of some workers against being paid in checks good only at the plantation store, led the Negroes to join together in "insurrection." The strikers went from plantation to plantation calling on all hands to quit work and carrying away by force those who refused. Committees approached planters with an offer to return to work if the wage cut was rescinded, but the planters, sticking together, refused. Whites from outside the district sent in volunteers, Negro leaders were arrested, planters relented, and the strike ended in June.

How could the strike be explained? The Negroes surely were not responsible, for they lacked the intelligence, the capacity for organization, and the desire for improvement implied by the extent and nature of the strike. Radicals, low whites, and rebellious mulattoes must have worked up the insurrection as a political device to marshal the slavish blacks for the fall elections and to win support from Yankee meddlers. Although

[22] *Southern Farm and Home,* reprinted in Carrollton *West Alabamian,* June 1, 1870; Carrollton *West Alabamian,* December 25, 1872, February 23, 1873; De Leon, *Harper's Magazine,* XLVII (1874), 271-73; King, *Scribner's Monthly,* VIII (1874), 649; De Forest, *A Union Officer,* 29-30; Freedmen's Bureau, *Report of the Commissioner* (1867), *passim*; Bruce, *The Rise of the New South,* 5.

[23] The account which follows is based on the editorials and news stories of the Charleston *Journal of Commerce* and the Charleston *News and Courier.* See *Journal of Commerce,* May 22, 23, 24, 26, 27, 29, August 14, 17, 23, 25, September 12, 18, 21, 22, 28, October 11, 27, 28, November 2, 4, 8, 1876. See *News and Courier,* May 23, 27, 29, 30, 31, June 1, August 25, September 5, 9, 15, 16, October 27, 28, 30, November 9, 1876.

Radicals were not in evidence and Negro leaders marched the mobs through the plantation country, investigation would undoubtedly show that Radicals harangued the Negroes at midnight, in cabin and grove, because the strike manifested a "well defined policy of communistic demagoguery." When the Negroes rose again at harvesttime in August, local white people advocated force to compel a return to duty. Extralegal volunteers were again called upon to apply the required force. Whites from neighboring regions exercised a restraining but temporary influence. Wade Hampton then marched through the state with a large semimilitary entourage seeking to sweep out of office the Radical government which permitted such things as the Combahee strike. Hampton made a tactical error. When he came into the Combahee region with only 600-800 cavalry, he encountered heckling, but when his "Red Shirt" escort was reinforced to approximately 1,200 mounted men and 2,000 foot soldiers, he was not again interrupted. Although Hampton lost at some of the polls in the region, he won the state. Thereafter, with the machinery of government in the hands of whites, the Negro worker was helpless indeed.

Southerners had defended the black codes as being impolitic but not unjust. When whites regained control of Southern governments, the objects of the black codes were achieved both through the unequal application of the laws and through measures aimed particularly at the Negro laborer. Examples are to be found in legislation against enticing Negroes from the landlord, providing for imprisonment or fine of laborers who received an advance but refused to do the work agreed in contract, and legalizing verbal contracts—all of which enabled the planter to keep his Negroes in a state of virtual peonage.

Negroes of Tennessee in convention at Nashville in May, 1875, complained of a vagrancy act by which unemployed members of their race were put in the county workhouse and of a labor law which compelled them to remain with their employers. Noting that the legislation nominally did not dis-

criminate between races, the convention stated that it knew of
not one instance when it had been applied to whites, nor did
anyone expect this to be done. The Nashville convention also
focused attention on the uses of convict labor. Penal labor,
employed on farms and railroads and in the mines, it pointed
out, drove the Negro's wages below the subsistence level.
Moreover, Negroes themselves were compelled to do the work of
driving down wages, many of them having been sentenced
under the vagrancy law.[24] In fact, nine-tenths of the convict
laborers were Negroes. Most white convicts were kept within
the prison.[25]

Whites corroborated the Negro's accusations. They warned
colored men who loafed in the shade or congregated about the
railroad station that the authorities were liable to view them
as tramps and set them to work with dispatch. Recognizing the
coercive effect of the convict-lease system on the Negro community, white leaders demanded that idle and vicious Negroes
in town and city be driven to the fields or sentenced to the
chain gang, both to make them useful and to warn others that
they must labor or endure a like fate.[26]

Southerners generally reasoned that slavery had had a deter-
rent effect upon the criminal instinct of Negroes and that
when the instinct broke through anyway, the master had seen
to the punishment. Freeing the slaves had resulted in an ever-
increasing number of criminals. Liberty meant license, and the
jails overflowed. The convict-lease system followed, went the
explanation, because there were too many criminals for the

[24] Taylor, The Negro in Tennessee, 115-16. See also Tindall, South
Carolina Negroes, 112-13; Wharton, The Negro in Mississippi, 87-93.

[25] William O. Scroggs, "Convict and Apprenticed Labor in the South,"
in Chandler and others, The South in the Building of the Nation, VI, 49.
See also Fletcher M. Green, "Some Aspects of the Convict Lease System
in the Southern States," in Green, ed., Essays in Southern History, 122;
Clarence A. Bacote, "Negro Proscription, Protests, and Proposed Solutions
in Georgia, 1880-1908" Journal of Southern History, XXV (1959), 486-87.

[26] Jackson, Miss., Clarion, June 9, 1880; Charleston, S.C., News and
Courier, September 10, 1898.

few jails to handle, and the states were too poor to build new ones. Besides, leasing proved profitable to the states and to the lessee. By 1877 every one of the former Confederate states leased its convicts, mostly Negroes.[27]

Under the system, convicts worked in gangs, usually controlled entirely by the lessees, who employed them on canals and railroads, on farms, and in mines. Much of the tunneling of the Blue Ridge Mountains for the old Western Carolina Railway was done by convicts. In 1878 Georgia's convicts were scattered about the state in fourteen camps. In 1882 Alabama convicts were in the hands of numerous lessees. In 1880 Mississippi turned over practically all of its convicts to the highest bidder. In this state and in Louisiana and Arkansas, subleasing was practiced. In Florida most of the prisoners were leased to turpentine farms. The convict was regarded by the state and the lessee as a source of revenue, a slave under a new dispensation. Few entertained any idea of rehabilitation. Discipline in the camps was severe, and the death rate was appalling.[28]

Charges by Northern radicals that the penal system discriminated against Negroes and reestablished a form of slavery were, according to the white Southerner, mere maudlin sentiment; a convict system that did not involve the severest form

[27] Philip A. Bruce, "A Tobacco Plantation," *Lippincott's Magazine,* XXXVI (1885), 533-36; Robert L. Dabney, "What the Negro Did for the Old South," *Southern States Farm Magazine,* V (1898), 477-82; W. A. Guerry, "The Negro in Relation to Religion," Southern Society, *Race Problems of the South,* 124-34; *Sunny South,* August 31, 1901; Scroggs, in Chandler and others, *The South in the Building of the Nation,* VI, 48-50.

[28] For a devastating indictment of the lease system on these grounds see George W. Cable, "The Convict Lease System in the Southern States," Century Magazine, V (1884), 582-99. In 1879 Governor O. M. Roberts of Texas stated: "To put a man or boy, who is not used to work, in a wood-chopping camp and require him to do a good day's work in the heat of summer and in the cold of winter, is simply to kill him." *Governors' Messages: Coke to Ross,* 332. A reform movement made some headway in the nineteenth century. See Jane Zimmerman, "The Penal Reform Movement in the South during the Progressive Era, 1890-1917," *Journal of Southern History,* XVII (1951), 462-92.

of slavery failed to punish crime. It was true that there were more convict Negroes than whites, but the law was applied with equal justice to both races, and the differential existed because of the instinctive inaptitude of Negroes in distinguishing between what was theirs and what they wanted to be theirs. If there were instances of extreme cruelty, the same was true under any other system.[29]

South Carolinians, as other Southerners, liked to make a substantial profit from their black convicts. The old penal methods, before 1898, had brought in profits to the state of only $1,600 because of administrative costs, but new arrangements whereby 1,800 convicts were hired out for $185,000 a year promised to return a profit of $100,000. Louisianians also expected to make money from their convict-lease system. Private citizens, they said, worked prisoners more efficiently than the state did, and this was the best way to lift the burden of maintaining convicts from the treasury. The crazy sentimentality which attacked the system as an outrage on humanity failed to take into account the fact that the essence of punishment was the infliction of suffering.[30]

If the infliction of suffering was the aim, the Mississippi penal system was efficient. In 1887 the grand jury of Hinds County found in the prison hospital

twenty-six inmates, all of whom have been lately brought there off the farms and railroads, many of them with consumption and other incurable diseases, and all bearing on their persons marks of the most inhuman and brutal treatment. Most of them have their backs cut in great wales, scars and blisters, some with the skin peeling off in pieces as the result of severe beatings. . . . We do inveigh against the principle and system of this great State taking a poor creature's liberty and turning him over to one whose interest is to coin his blood into money.

As a fair sample of this system, on January 6, 1887, 204 convicts

29 Atlanta *Constitution*, October 3, 1879.
30 Charleston, S.C., *News and Courier*, April 11, 1898; Baton Rouge *Capitolian-Advocate*, August 1, December 29, 1882.

were leased to McDonald up to June 6, 1887, and during this six months 20 died, and 19 were discharged and escaped and 23 were returned to the walls disabled and sick, many of whom have since died. God will never smile upon a State that treats its convicts as Mississippi does.[31]

The white community's willingness to coerce Negro laborers, convict or free, was on occasion dramatically illustrated. For example, whites near Morehouse, Louisiana, in 1890 complained that Negroes under contract to them had escaped across the border into Arkansas. The people of northern Louisiana had called meeting after meeting to which they had invited their Arkansas neighbors to cooperate in regulating labor. Despite this, Arkansans encouraged Negro desertion by their mad course in harboring labor fugitives and were "in truth, arming them with Winchester rifles, in order that they may resist any attempt on the part of the people of North Louisiana to recover . . . their deserting labor that is seeking refuge in their midst." Let the Negro become dissatisfied, then off he fled to the "pest hole" of Chicot County, land of the black man, "the worst negro-ridden county in the South." Arkansas whites might allow Negroes to carry things with a high hand in Chicot County, but they should understand that if they disturbed labor belonging to Louisianians, they must take the consequences, that is, a military invasion to return the fugitives.[32]

There were Southerners who endorsed paternalistic means as more effective than naked coercion in controlling Negro labor. They thought that the well-being of the South rested upon the contentment of its Negroes. Induce the laborer to settle down and become docile by furnishing him a comfortable house and a garden spot, they advised. Teach him how to use machinery

[31] Jackson, Miss., *Clarion*, July 13, 1887. For other attacks on and defense of convict leasing in Mississippi see the *Clarion*, March 5, 1884, March 17, 1886, September 4, 11, 1890.

[32] Morehouse *Clarion*, reprinted in New Orleans *Picayune*, August 26, 1890.

and make him more efficient and trustworthy. Build a school-house on the farm to bring contentment to the parent and to educate his children in more intelligent labor. Permit him to sing, be loud, enjoy his recreation. Pay him good wages with incentive increases according to merit. Be kind and just. Make only reasonable rules but enforce them rigidly. "Thus let the negro become identified with and attached to the soil upon which he lives," J. B. Killebrew counseled, "and he himself, the land-owner and the country will be advanced by his labor."[33]

To their credit, many Southerners protected exposed Negroes from the ruthless power generated by the white community and concerned themselves with the welfare of their laborers. This type of Southerner was represented by a Mississippi widow who had been so kind to her slaves that not one would leave her after the war. Her wish was their law. They deferred to her as to a mother.[34]

More often than not, paternalistic Southerners were sincere when they declared that they were friends of the Negro in his place and spoke and wrote about the white man's duty to the black. Such leaders of opinion as J. L. M. Curry, Hilary Herbert, Thomas Nelson Page, along with many others, repeatedly admonished fellow Southerners to deal justly with the lowly Negro.[35] These proponents of kindness usually entertained no thoughts of radical change. They rated blacks as farm laborers to be humored, not worked too hard, given nominal benefits, but restrained from emulating the whites. But even they endorsed coercion; they defended the caste system, which was, ultimately, based on force.

[33] *Southern States Farm Magazine,* V (1898), 490-91. See also Stone, *North American Review,* CLVIII (1894), 506.

[34] Waterbury, *Seven Years among the Freedmen,* 39.

[35] On this point see Johnson, *Journal of Southern History,* XXIII (1957), 483-503. See also *Sunny South,* June 19, 1886, April 20, 1889, April 26, 1890.

CHAPTER TWELVE

Migration of Labor

INTIMATELY associated with the labor question was the South's agitation over the immigration of whites and the emigration of Negroes. From the end of the Civil War on through the nineteenth century, Southerners conducted a campaign, varying in intensity though weakening as the century wore on, to attract white immigrants. As voters they would guarantee that "Negro rule" would become an impossibility; as laborers they would force Negroes to work humbly at their appointed task, if they wished to work at all.

Newspapers early began agitating for immigration, pointing out in 1865 the political and practical advantages that immigrant labor could bring to the South, and gave their support to the immigration movements then being initiated in South Carolina, Georgia, Virginia, and other Southern states. In October of that year the Charleston *Courier* declared that since emancipation had spoiled the slaves, South Carolina would be ruined if it continued to depend upon the unreliable and unstable freedmen. During the spring and summer of 1869 Father Abram Ryan's *Banner of the South* trumpeted for thrifty white immigrants both to provide labor and to help restore white supremacy by their votes. Louisianians found immigration to be necessary; the only question was how to procure it. During the summer of that year North Carolinians favored every effort to secure immigration of white laborers despite the opposition of Radicals and Negroes. Early in 1870 the arrival in Mississippi of Danes, Swedes, Norwegians, Swiss, and Irish, "brawny looking fellows, giving every indication of usage to labor and the will to work," was hailed "as the dawn of a new era in Southern labor." Mississippians hoped that an active campaign for immigrants would save the state from the doom of Africanization like that which befell Santo Domingo.[1]

A clergyman in Tennessee responded to the immigration fervor by ironically observing that the proud Southerner proposed to lay aside to some extent his prejudices and invite the immigrant to come and bring his skilled labor—and money —with him.[2] Despite the scoffing of occasional dissenters, immigrant associations sprang up in the states; even localities, among them sparsely populated Sebastian County, Arkansas, and little Holly Springs, Mississippi, formed their own societies.[3]

Farmers' associations joined in the clamor. The Alabama State Planters' Society, in February, 1871, bewailed the sloth, waste, and dishonesty resulting from the disruption of the labor system caused by emancipation of slaves and their participation in politics, and noted that labor was scarce, dear, and unsatisfactory. Pointing out that Western states were attracting foreigners, the society requested Alabama to create a bureau of immigration to get its share of good white workers.[4]

Yet the South could be expected to abandon its plan to replace the Negro with the foreigner if the Negro would only put himself in right relation with the white employers: "If he thus meets their wants, and supplies, reliably, a labor so neces-

[1] Charleston, S.C., *Courier*, August 19, October 3, 1865; *Banner of the South*, May 1, June 19, June 26, July 3, 1869; New Orleans *Picayune*, June 9, 1869; Wilmington, N.C., *Journal*, August 24, 1869; Carrollton *West Alabamian*, February 2, 1870; Jackson, Miss., *Clarion*, May 1, 1873.

[2] Cobleigh, *Methodist Quarterly Review*, XLII (1870), 393.

[3] Jackson, Miss., *Clarion*, September 5, 1872; Fort Smith, Ark., *Herald*, June 26, 1875; Charles H. Wesley, *Negro Labor in the United States, 1850-1925* (New York, 1927), 195. County immigration societies in Mississippi accomplished little or nothing. Wharton, *The Negro in Mississippi*, 102. See also Rowland T. Berthoff, "Southern Attitudes toward Immigration, 1865-1914," *Journal of Southern History*, XVII (1951), 328-30, 336-38.

[4] Carrollton *West Alabamian*, April 19, 1871.

sary, he insures not only that they will not seek other labor, but . . . having a useful place for his race, they will not invite any other to come; and by this accord he is guarded against a competition which otherwise they would be compelled, in self preservation to invite, nay, to strive for by every appliance they can invent, and which would destroy him."[5]

Slavery having been abolished, Southerners imagined that immigrants would find the South attractive. They would flow South because free labor, hitherto unable to compete with slave labor, would no longer be turned away by such a barrier.[6] It was at last discovered, however, that free Negroes who were practically slaves presented a stumbling block to immigration; yet efforts to bring in whites went on.

In January, 1870, planters in Alabama imported a force of laborers sufficient to pick their cotton and grind their cane "independent of the unreliable negroes." Here was an experiment with migratory labor, such as the West later used in harvesting wheat and the South in chopping and picking cotton, foreshadowing a major trend of the future. Ten years later, Louisiana sugar planters contracted for 700 Portuguese to replace refractory Negroes—and treated them like Negroes. In the winter of 1881 and for the three following winters, Italian laborers who worked in summer on road construction were employed by operators of South Carolina phosphate mines to show Negro workers that the miners were not dependent upon them. But by 1890 the less manageable Italians had been succeeded by Negroes.[7]

The most striking illustration of the South's desire to force Negroes to work, or to get rid of them, was the movement to

[5] "The African in the United States," *Southern Review*, XIV (1874), 152. See also Charleston, S.C., *Journal of Commerce*, October 3, 1876.

[6] F. Schaler, "Immigration of Capital and of Population to the South," *Southern Magazine*, X (1872), 545; T. M. Logan, "The Southern Industrial Prospect," *Harper's Magazine*, LII (1876), 592-93.

[7] Carrollton *West Alabamian*, January 26, 1870; Shrugg, *Origin of Class Struggle in Louisiana*, 265-66; Berthoff, *Journal of Southern History*, XVII (1951), 331; Tindall, *South Carolina Negroes*, 126.

import cheap Oriental labor. Western railroad builders worked gangs of coolies; why could not the South? In the fall of 1865 a few Southerners responded to the emancipation of their slaves by suggesting that coolie labor, in addition to being more slavelike and cheaper than the newly freed Negro labor, was acceptable to the North. But as an early end to difficulties in the way of "applying negro labor to the fields" could be anticipated, there was no reason to add to the superfluous colored and mongrel races in the South.[8]

Radical Reconstruction replaced military government, and the difficulties in the way of "applying negro labor to the fields" increased. A commercial convention in Memphis then gave renewed impetus to the Chinese immigration project. The Southerner now began to discover that although European immigrants performed twice as much work as Negroes, Chinese were best for plantation agriculture because of their remarkable powers of endurance and adaptability to malaria. Another great advantage of "John Chinaman" appeared to be that he would work steadily and faithfully for wages that would starve a white man, or even a Negro. Unlike the white immigrant from the North or from Europe, he would not seek to become an independent farmer. If he did, the South could expect support from the other sections, particularly the West, in thwarting this ambition.[9]

The experience of the last few years, a Georgian noted in 1869, proved the futility of attempting to replace Negroes with European peasants, who, at the close of the first year, set out on their own; thus the planter lost his outlay and became merely a successful immigrant agent. But the Negro was lazy, was being slain by whisky and disease, or went off to town. The solution to this problem was to import indentured Asiatics. The "descendants of Shem" were vastly superior to the

[8] New Orleans *Crescent*, October 27, 1865.
[9] Wilmington, N.C., *Journal*, November 26, 1868; New Orleans *Picayune*, July 30, 1869; Wesley, *Negro Labor in the United States*, 196-97.

descendants of Ham and could be trained up as Negroes had been. Furthermore, Chinese, like Negroes, were "decreed to be hewers of wood and drawers of water." There was, however, some danger that the meddling spirit of New England might inaugurate a fresh agitation and bestow on the Chinese all the privileges of citizenship.[10]

A Louisiana editor supposed that the Negro could leave the Chinese far behind in cottonpicking, as he had been trained from childhood in that art; nevertheless, even though Negro labor was better, it was diminishing, and Chinese coolies would make excellent replacements. Debating with the editor, a reader argued that Chinese were better workers than Negroes and were adapted to the cultivation of cotton, corn, and sugar, while their women made excellent domestics. The editor conceded that the Negroes' plan to bring about the equality of races through subdivision of land might be defeated by the importation of gangs of coolies.[11]

Others thought that the rapid completion of the Central Pacific demonstrated the energy of the Chinese and the availability of their work for a merely nominal sum. The 10,000 Orientals thrown out of work by the completion of this railroad might be induced to move South as the vanguard of an inexhaustible supply from overpopulated China. Since the cost of Chinese labor was no more than a third the cost of Negro labor, the full demands of the South could be satisfied at rates which would make it the cheapest and best labor in the world. In addition, it was hopefully observed, the Chinese neither fraternized with Americans nor wished to intermarry with them. In view of all these advantages, some complained, there was a lack of public spirit in the failure to import large numbers of Chinese when all knew that many planters would next year adopt any shift to entice their neighbors' hands from them in a general

[10] Cuthbert, Ga., *Appeal*, clipped in Fort Smith, Ark., *Herald*, August 14, 1869.
[11] Shreveport *South-Western*, June 19, August 8, 10, 27, 1869.

scramble for freedmen at ruinous prices. This was just the sort of thing that, if Negroes were to be kept under control, had to be avoided. A convention of Negroes in New Orleans in October, 1869, taking threats to replace them with Chinese seriously, objected, as white unions did, to the proposed introduction of Chinese coolies into Louisiana as a means of driving down their wages and depriving them of economic liberty.[12]

Planters could not compete with western railroads for Chinese labor. And Chinese had no history of servitude in the South to render them as amenable as freedmen. In abandoning their propaganda for coolie labor, Southerners began to insult the Chinese as unfit to live in their region. Before the winds of propaganda had excited great expectations of Oriental bondage replacing vanished Negro slavery, an opponent of Chinese immigration had warned that if John Chinaman was a source of profit, he was also a serious danger: "Every one knows that he is shockingly degraded in morals, that he is dishonest, corrupt, thievish, cowardly, a natural born serf, and a ready assassin on the most trifling inducement."[13] Planters dampened enthusiasm by reporting that they had found Chinese more refractory than Negroes. From Terrebonne Parish, Louisiana, came the report that a gang of twenty-five Chinese became so dangerous that their employer had to shoot and kill one, wound another, and run the rest off the plantation.[14]

In California, it was found, Chinese filled the asylums and hospitals at the expense of white taxpayers, and their homes were dens of iniquity. Because it was impossible for the two races to coalesce, Californians had rightly determined that "the Chinese pest must be utterly stamped out."[15] Former advocates

[12] New Orleans *Picayune*, August 6, 1869; Jackson, Miss., *Clarion*, May 20, 1869; Wilmington *Journal*, September 7, October 5, 1869; Shreveport *South-Western*, September 17, 1869; Wesley, *Negro Labor in the United States*, 197.
[13] *Banner of the South*, July 31, 1869.
[14] Jackson, Miss., *Clarion*, November 20, 1872.
[15] Charleston, S.C., *News and Courier*, May 30, 1876.

of coolie labor turned to denouncing industrialists for sacrificing their country's welfare for cheap labor. They wanted Chinese barred from the country.[16]

With victory over Negro workers assured after the fall of Radical Reconstruction, the Chinese lost their appeal. Fear of adding a "yellow peril" to the South's "black peril" doubtless had some effect. The Chinese experiment, though it collapsed speedily, revealed that Southerners were unwilling to accept their former slaves as really free and that racist allies waited to be cultivated all over the nation, particularly in California and in other Western states.[17]

Southerners had never really wanted Chinese, but they did fondly hope to obtain appreciable numbers of white immigrants to offset Radical-taught freedmen. Perceptive observers noticed, however, that the South could never secure white immigration, so much desired, until it raised the status of the laboring man. White laborers, offered strong inducements to come, found conditions so bad that they soon gave up. Fifty-four Germans, for example, "mutinied" against a Texas landlord and scattered like leaves. A perspicacious Mississippian explained such incidents: "If Southern people expect white immigrants to come here and live, and cultivate their lands as mere hirelings, they had as well abandon the delusion."[18] Judge Albion W. Tourgee, once a carpetbagger in North Carolina, observed that immigrants shunned the South because "The negro will work more hours for less money, wait longer for his pay, live in cheaper houses, endure more hardships, claim fewer privileges, and increase more rapidly than the northern or foreign white laborer."[19]

[16] Fort Smith, Ark., *Herald*, March 8, 1879; Jackson, Miss., *Clarion*, April 12, 19, 1882.

[17] Berthoff, *Journal of Southern History*, XVII (1951), 359.

[18] "J. J. W." in Jackson, Miss., *Clarion*, November 3, 1881. See also King, *Scribner's Monthly*, VIII (1874), 649. Italians found that many native whites regarded them as another inferior people to be disciplined. Berthoff, *Journal of Southern History*, XVII (1951), 344.

[19] *Forum*, VII (1889), 146.

Most Southern whites were inclined to offer, innocent of his irony, Tourgee's explanation. They said that no day laborer could compete with the Negro because his wants were few and his endurance great. Admittedly he was ungrateful, idle, and worthless generally, but hirelings of the white race were no less objectionable. The better class of immigrants went West to take up land, while the others, a scurvy lot, made more unreliable laborers in the North than Negroes did in the South. Incessant immigration to the South would be ruinous, anyway, for the region was not a manufacturing or food producing area but a cotton country, and experience had taught that the successful cultivation of this crop was a science known only to Southern planters and their Negroes.[20]

Although some Southerners realized that the South was obliged to give up its schemes of immigration because of the unwillingness of foreigners to work alongside Negroes, many believed that white immigrants did not compete with Negroes because they were physically incapable of doing so: they were not so made by nature. To them the idea that white laborers avoided the social degradation of working alongside Negroes was nothing but a myth. The simple fact was that Negroes were perfect laborers. In the Old South it had invariably been true that contractors with hired slaves completed their projects more rapidly, more peaceably, and with better profits than Northerners who brought down white labor for the same purpose. The difference was in the inherent quality of the labor.[21]

The failures born of numerous attempts to obtain cheap immigrant labor to carry on large enterprises led to equally unsuccessful efforts to secure immigration of farmers rather than laborers. The Louisiana Emigration and Homestead Company, directed by General P. G. T. Beauregard and other prominent citizens, organized a great campaign in 1873 to

---

[20] Carrollton *West Alabamian*, March 19, 1873.
[21] Dabney, *Southern States Farm Magazine*, V (1898), 478-79.

regenerate the state's economic and political life by offering small homesteads as an inducement to prospective farmers from the North.[22] In this way Louisiana whites hoped to gain numbers to overcome the Negro majority. Pleas for white homesteaders came also from individuals and communities throughout the South. The Louisville *Home and Farm* provided a clearinghouse of information, printing letters showing the advantages of every Southern locality.[23] A Louisianian thought that freedmen might be drawn to the sugar region as day laborers, inducing immigration of small farmers to supply their places in the cotton region. Similarly, a Mississippian expected white homesteaders to occupy hill country as the Negroes moved into the big planters' bottom lands. As a result, political and economic dominance over Negroes could be assured.[24]

New Englanders certainly were not wanted as homesteaders. Though intelligent, energetic, and persevering, their intelligence was "not of that comprehensive character which respects the views of others; their energy is directed chiefly to the attainment of purely selfish ends; and their perseverance is as often marked by an obstinate persistence in wrong as in the pursuit of a rightful end." Their "earnestness degenerates into a spirit of propagandism," which leads them to legislate away the rights of an entire people, while declaring and believing "that they are displaying the utmost magnanimity." Such dangerous characters "would not be a desirable acquisition."[25] Before the war these undesirables sought "intercourse with the servile population in preference to people of their own color." After the war they hurried South as greedy carpetbaggers, swindlers, and revolutionaries. The South needed immigrants with pride in

[22] King, *Scribner's Monthly*, VII (1873), 150; see also Edward King, "The Great South: In the Cotton States: II," *Scribner's Monthly*, VIII (1874), 519-22; Carrollton *West Alabamian*, March 12, 1873.

[23] Louisville *Home and Farm*, June 15, July 1, 15, August 15, September 1, 1879, April 15, November 1, 1880.

[24] New Orleans *Picayune*, May 7, 1869; Jackson, Miss., *Clarion*, January 15, 1874, February 22, 1881.

[25] New Orleans *Crescent*, June 25, 1866.

their race, not those who would form "social equality societies with the native freedmen."[26]

Some advocates of the immigration of homesteaders were unaffected by antagonism toward Negroes or New Englanders. The poet Sidney Lanier, who hoped that the common interests of farmers of both races would eliminate the color line in politics, believed that the South would benefit from the rise of the small farm to a position of dominance over the plantation. In the Ocmulgee River region of Georgia, Lanier wrote, "the whole prospect seems distinctly to yearn for men. Everywhere the huge and gentle slopes kneel and pray for vineyards, for corn fields, for cottages, for spires to rise up from beyond the oak groves." Lanier hoped for communities, ornamented by schools, drama societies, and village orchestras, to blossom in the South. The small farming to be found in their environs

means . . . meat and bread for which there are no notes in bank; pigs fed with home-made corn . . . ; yarn spun, stockings knit, butter made and sold (instead of bought); eggs, chickens, peaches, water-melons, the four extra sheep and a little wool; two calves and a beef—all to sell every year, besides a colt who is now suddenly become, all of himself, a good, serviceable horse; the four oxen, who are as good as gifts made by the grass; and a hundred other items, all representing income from a hundred sources to a small farmer, which equally represents outgo to the large farmer.[27]

If the presence of Negroes constituted a stumbling block to white immigration, perhaps they should be sent to the North or Latin America or Africa to make way for white people. Negro emigration coupled with white immigration would guarantee white supremacy against the possibility of future revolution, preventing amalgamation absolutely by rendering it physically impossible. Thus was population migration, with the good coming into the South and the bad leaving, offered as a way to make the South a democracy of Caucasians, who alone were capable of self-government. Emigration schemes, no

26 New Orleans *Picayune*, September 18, 1868, June 13, 1869.
27 *Scribner's Monthly*, XX (1880), 843-51.

matter what the avowed motive, were based in reality on the intention of the whites to control Negroes. If they would not work for white men, they should be driven from the country. Even agitation of the question served to show the alien race that it would be tolerated only if subservient.

Would white farmers come South if Negroes were expelled? General Robert E. Lee, testifying before the Committee of Fifteen on Reconstruction against the proposed amendment enfranchising freedmen, said in May, 1866: "I think Virginia is peculiarly adapted to that kind of labor that would flow into the State, if it were made more attractive by the absence of the colored race."[28] Most African colonizers were more direct than Lee. In laying down the hoe and taking up the "howlings of political hustings and caucuses," one wrote, the colored population made it clear that the sooner they departed, the better for the South. "We can see no good end to be subserved by keeping these people among us to foster our enemies and to corrupt our people." Negro farming, or farming with free Negro labor, had proven to be a disastrous experiment. "Sunbeams from cucumbers are as easy of extraction as thrifty cultivation from the emancipated slave . . . we say again go, GO, GO!"[29] The Reverend Charles K. Marshall of Vicksburg, Mississippi, also believed that colored labor was far from being indispensable. As slaves, he claimed, the blacks had been more comfortably fed, clothed, and lodged, and happier than any other peasantry; since emancipation, they had become less comfortable, less moral, and less happy. They had learned the multiplication table and forgotten their prayers. All told, they were no longer useful to the South.[30]

Some Southerners wondered if the Negro should be exiled from the white South as an alternative to bitter racial wars.

[28] Cited in "Monthly Record of Events," *Harper's Magazine,* XXXII (1866), 807.

[29] Mobile *Register,* clipped in Carrollton *West Alabamian,* January 14, 1874.

[30] *The Exodus, passim.*

They saw the Negroes being continually driven back to the labor line. Every higher step of their progress, every deepening of their aspiration, would carry with it increased humiliation. Because white repugnance to amalgamation rested upon a scientific basis, the black race could never be obliterated by absorption, and struggles of growing intensity promising malignant evils could be avoided only by colonization. Reminding Northerners of their alarm over the yellow patch on the Pacific coast, these Southerners advocated forcible expulsion of the inferior races from the nation.[31]

The race problem could never be settled as long as Negroes constituted a large element in the South, the emigrationist asserted. They could not be indefinitely denied the privileges of citizenship against the will of a section which was victorious in war on their account and which persisted in regarding them as good enough citizens for the South. If the "Force Bill" to make the federal government the guarantor of Negro suffrage passed, efforts to secure the emigration of Negroes must be redoubled. The choice lay between securing their departure or keeping them in the South and trying to make of them white people. "Which of the two lies further out of the bounds of sanity is the real question at issue, and on this point we have not a moment's doubt."[32] Amid debate over the best way to assure white supremacy in Mississippi by constitutional amendment, a proposal was made to solve the problem once for all by dispatching the Negroes to the Congo.[33]

John Temple Graves, perhaps the most eloquent and active champion of Negro deportation, stated at the Montgomery Conference on Race Relations in 1900 that absolute physical separation of the Anglo-Saxon and Negro races was imperative, for the presence of Negroes among whites corrupted politics,

[31] E. W. Gilliam, "The African Problem," *North American Review*, CXXXIX (1884), 425-29.
[32] Charleston, S.C., *News and Courier*, October 13, 1892; see also issues of October 9, 1890, January 21, 1891. See *Sunny South*, September 16, 1893.
[33] Jackson, Miss., *Clarion*, October 2, 1890.

throttled independence of thought, and debased labor. There could be "no peace, no purity, no tranquil development, no durable agricultural prosperity . . . no moral growth for the white race outside of separation." While it was an indestructible fact that the white man would never accept the Negro as an equal, the Negro was consumed with an unalterable desire to be equal to the white man above him. Unless the radical surgery of deportation were performed, America would witness the violent destruction of the ambitious but weak race.[34]

Some observers discerned among ex-slaves a universal unrest which portended general migration. The premature and relatively insignificant movement to Kansas by Southern Negroes around 1879 had been only a symptom of a coming general exodus to Africa. One prediction was that by January 1, 1920, the "colored population in the South will scarcely be counted. Perished, migrated, vanished."[35] Noting that enough ships to take the blacks to Africa could not be found, the Negro Richard L. Greener remarked: "Even if Henry Clay's wished-for bridge of boats could span the Atlantic, and the blacks could be induced to cross in a continuous throng, the daily birth rate would more than balance the daily list of emigrants." Greener did think that the exodus might be accomplished in the distant future.[36]

If Africa was too far away, why not turn to the West Indies? The United States might buy land in the Caribbean, or in Mexico, or in Central America. These areas would prove far more attractive than primitive Africa, and an enormous ship-building program would not be required to transfer all the blacks to these nearby lands.[37]

Because deporting millions of Negroes would be a difficult

[34] "Address," in Southern Society, *Race Problems of the South*, 54-56.

[35] Marshall, *The Exodus*, 3-7; see also O. F. Cook, "The Negro and African Colonization," *Forum*, XXVII (1899), 114-19.

[36] Gardiner and others, *North American Review*, CXXXIX (1884), 89-90.

[37] Henry A. Scomp, "Can the Race Problem Be Solved?" *Forum*, VIII (1889), 372-75.

undertaking, Senator J. T. Morgan of Alabama, like John Temple Graves, endeavored to make the project a national objective; and Senator Matthew C. Butler of South Carolina introduced a bill to secure federal appropriations to help finance black emigration to Africa.[38]

Little interest in emigration was found among Negroes until Conservative victories announced the advent of official white supremacy. Then, as a consequence, great numbers thought of moving to freer atmosphere, and some did join the "Exodus" to Kansas in the late 1870's. By 1891 a quarter of a million Negroes had gone North and West. Extreme poverty doubtless restrained many from leaving. Others must have listened to Frederick Douglass, who urged them not to abandon their struggle for dignity by leaving the South to men who sought, by elevating the states above the authority of the federal government in matters concerning human rights, to reverse the outcome of the Civil War. Douglass warned the white Southerner: "Drive out the negro and you drive out Christ, the Bible, and American liberty with him."[39]

The Southerner answered that a door was opened by providence to the Africans who had absorbed Christian civilization while in bondage and were now prepared to enter upon their inheritance. The scholar Basil Gildersleeve cited a "body of eminent men" to support his claim that "the manifest destiny of slavery in America was the regeneration of Africa."[40] The Reverend Charles K. Marshall worked up a less respectable theory that black men, cramped by a race of giants in America, would have room for growth in backward Africa. The Negro's great hopes upon emancipation had been blasted by unequal competition:

[38] Carter G. Woodson, *A Century of Negro Migration* (Washington, 1918), 148; Tindall, *South Carolina Negroes*, 162.

[39] Gardiner and others, *North American Review*, CXXXIX (1884), 85. See also Henry King, "A Year of the Exodus in Kansas," *Scribner's Monthly*, XX (1880), 213; Woodson, *A Century of Negro Migration*, 126, 138-39.

[40] *Atlantic Monthly*, LXIX (1892), 86.

Yesterday at the handles of a plow; to-day at the helm of State. Yesterday an honored barber; to-day the governor of a common-wealth. Yesterday a faithful coachman; to-day a legislator. Yester-day a humble, plain, respectful field-hand; to-day a member of Congress. Poor yesterday and a thrall as well; to-day he is courted, caressed, and taken into the confidence, the counsels, and the patronage of the learned, the powerful and great. Yesterday he drove a cart; to-day he is a justice of the peace;—not for his learning in legal lore, but for his African descent. Penniless to-day he is told, and believes it, that to-morrow he "will receive from the general government forty acres and a mule." Alas! to him it is all dead leaves and chaff. His elevation was transitory. His hopes were not realized. His pretended friends pledged, warned, and promised—only to drop him on the cold rocks. The South fol-lowing the example of the North, has gradually reduced the negro to a plane as unimportant and as destitute of distinction as that of the negro of Massachusetts, Pennsylvania, and New York. A thousand things combine to fill him with feelings of discontent.[41]

A small group of Negroes could be found to support Mar-shall's colonization schemes. W. H. Council spoke for emigra-tion to Africa, though "50,000 professors and preachers" of his race hurled "anathemas of excommunication" at him. Bishop Henry McNeal Turner of the African Methodist Episcopal Church urged Negroes to abandon all hope in America and look to Africa. Bishop Lucius H. Halsey of the Colored Methodist Episcopal Church, agreeing that the South would never accept Negroes other than as a submerged people, re-quested Congress to set aside territory in the West for the blacks.[42]

While some of its thinkers advocated emigration, the South worried about the effect upon its labor system. The very next cotton crop might be endangered. Even the movement of Negroes to the cotton lands of the Southwest was alarming to the planters left behind. Though Negroes were said to be lacking in industry, it was recognized that they performed a

[41] *The Exodus*, 2-3.
[42] Gardiner and others, *North American Review*, CXXXIX (1884), 575-76; Bacote, *Journal of Southern History*, XXV (1957), 489-94.

vast amount of work. Besides, as Dr. E. E. Hoss of the *Christian Advocate* noted, it would take generations to replace the vanished black labor force, and "we should think it a poor exchange to swap off a million . . . negroes for an equal number of Italian Dagoes or Hungarian miners."[43]

Methodist Bishop Charles B. Galloway worried about Negroes taking leave of the South in consequence of a widespread restlessness induced by lynching, the widening gulf of separation, and threatened curtailment of Negro education. They were quietly leaving, and if they continued to do so, the South faced industrial disaster.[44] According to Robert Dabney, the South was on the threshold of a brilliant future if only the Negroes remained to practice their vocation as the world's finest laborers.[45] The South without the Negro, remarked a Mississippian, "would be a wilderness and a waste; and with the exodus of the negro, would begin the exodus of the white man."[46]

Reaction to the migration of Negroes to Kansas and other Northern and Western states during 1879 and thereabouts revealed the Southerner's intention to keep his laborers home despite what he might say to the contrary.[47] A convention of white and black leaders at Vicksburg, May 6-7, 1879, controlled by whites, charged that insidious reports had stimulated the Negroes to emigrate to Kansas. White leaders of the convention sought to halt the exodus by promising to use their influence to protect the Negro's rights. The Negro leader John R. Lynch had told his fellow Mississippians that unless their rights were protected, his people would have no choice but to leave the region to those who claim that "they own all the land,

[43] *Christian Advocate* (Nashville), April 4, 1891.

[44] *The South and the Negro*, 5-7.

[45] *Southern States Farm Magazine*, V (1898), 478-79.

[46] Jackson, Miss., *Clarion*, April 28, 1886.

[47] Saloutos, *Farmer Movements in the South*, 57; L. A. Dutto, "The Negroes in Mississippi," *Catholic World*, XLVI (1888), 578. Small white farmers and tenants were for the exodus. Wharton, *The Negro in Mississippi*, 114-15.

pay all the taxes, and are the possessors of all the education to be found in the South, and are therefore alone entitled to govern."[48]

Negroes were urged to be wary of rascally agents who cared no more for them than for cattle and of politicians who wished to use them to win control of doubtful states; they should stay in the South among their white friends and "pick cotton at good wages." Letters by Negroes against the exodus and news items about the disillusioned returning home were featured. Planters tried to bribe Negro leaders to speak against emigration, laborers were paid in drafts good only at local stores, and officials preferred false charges against departing Negroes. Crowds of emigrants waiting for transportation were broken up and exodus leaders beaten and kidnapped and, perhaps most effective of all, Southern governments restricted the liberty of emigration agents.[49]

Before the fever could be cured, Benjamin Singleton, "the Moses of the colored exodus," had led eighty thousand of his people from the "land of night" toward the light of freedom. The Great Migration, just beginning in the nineteenth century but amounting to an enormous volume in the twentieth, was, according to Earl Conrad, an extension of the escape of slaves: in both the object was to escape from a tyranny-ridden part of the nation to a less oppressive region.[50]

A few whites believed that the South would be a happier country without Negroes, but most of them merely engaged in idle talk until the hint of an exodus revealed to them how much they depended upon black workers. Similarly, many

[48] Jackson, Miss., *Clarion*, February 26, 1879. For the convention see the *Clarion*, May 14, 1879; Woodson, *A Century of Negro Migration*, 135-37; Wharton, *The Negro in Mississippi*, 115.

[49] Atlanta *Constitution*, September 28, 1879; *Sunny South*, May 10, 30, December 27, 1879; Jackson, Miss., *Clarion*, April 23, 30, May 21, July 2, 1879; Tindall, *South Carolina Negroes*, 156, 179-80; Woodson, *A Century of Negro Migration*, 137-38; Wharton, *The Negro in Mississippi*, 115, 195.

[50] *Jim Crow America*, 40-43. See also Redding, *The Lonesome Road*, 182.

whites appeared to be greatly interested in attracting immigrants to their region. But the truth of the matter was, Southerners had little use for immigrants unless they would "work like niggers" and support the white man's party; and few immigrants were willing to come, and fewer still to remain, on these terms.

CHAPTER THIRTEEN

Negro-White Competition

IN THE OLD SOUTH all white men had enjoyed the status conferred by color. Following emancipation, leveling forces were set to work which threatened to obliterate distinction between the poorer whites and the blacks. If this happened, white supremacy could not be maintained. To avoid a union of poorer whites and blacks, Southern leaders had to find the means to preserve the racial loyalty of the most depressed of the whites.

During Radical rule, whites of the Southeast, in order to avoid the possibility of falling to the Negro's level, were tempted to desert the land of their fathers for Texas, or so it seemed: "To come in competition with the negro race as a laborer; to have to work side by side with them in every position where muscle is power, and to see his children growing up side by side with their children as equals and companions, and without the power to prevent it by his honest efforts, are well calculated to make the poor white man gather together his household goods and look for a State where, at least, in a large portion of it, he is free from equality as a laborer."[1] There was in fact a tidal wave of white emigration from the black states to Texas. At the end of the nineteenth century some leaders thought that the only sure way to protect whites from Negro competition was to deport the Negroes. In the meantime, racial antagonism between ordinary whites and Negroes, it appeared, was bound to cause trouble.[2]

The upper class Southerner often said that racial antagonism stemmed from economic competition between whites and blacks and supposed that only small farmers and poorer whites hated Negroes; those who wished Negroes to be like slaves were those who never owned a slave. Believing that these whites needed aid, Edgar Gardner Murphy, like many other Southern gentlemen, warned that it was at the peril "of the South, and of the country, that we forget the poor white boy of the Southern fields!"[3] This persistent concern encouraged Southern leaders to find a way to protect whites from Negro competition and to give them preference in employment, but at the same time to exploit the poor of their own race nearly as much as they exploited Negroes.

To maintain white supremacy the South launched a crusade to establish the factory. On the farm, Negroes set the pace for the agricultural labor market to which whites in the same field were forced to conform, but the factory offered employment to the whites, divided the poor into white and black, and gave the privileged whites reason to believe in the supremacy of their race.[4]

In Louisiana, as in other states, the industrial movement excited much enthusiasm. "It is the duty of State governments and of wealthy men of the South to provide employment for our poor white people," a New Orleans journal declared. "A cotton mill is much better than a poor-house."[5] In this state, however, a mill established in Claiborne Parish failed and actually became a poorhouse. General Nathan B. Forrest, after the war a railroad builder and promoter, said: "We have widows

---

. [1] Carrollton *West Alabamian*, January 15, 1873.

[2] Charleston, S.C., *News and Courier*, December 29, 1900.

[3] *The White Man and the Negro*, 24-26.

[4] Carrollton *West Alabamian*, June 18, 25, July 23, 1873; Broadus Mitchell, *The Rise of the Cotton Mills in the South* (Baltimore, 1921), 77-231; Cash, *The Mind of the South*, 180-85; Shrugg, *Origin of Class Struggle in Louisiana*, 299; Bruce, *The Rise of the New South*, 27-28.

[5] *Commercial Bulletin*, December 25, 1866, cited in Shrugg, *Origin of Class Struggle in Louisiana*, 299-300.

and orphans to provide for—let us open mines, construct railways, that poor orphan boys can be employed; and build factories that our widows and the little orphan girls can also find comfort, and make a subsistence by laboring in them."[6] At the Mississippi Mills, Wesson, Mississippi, in 1876 most of the five hundred employees were white boys and girls.[7]

After a hard struggle, the textile industry was successfully established in the South, and whites were employed in increasing numbers. The extraordinary enthusiasm over the growing industry in South Carolina, Georgia, and Alabama was in large part a consequence of the demand for labor for the surplus white population. The erection of factories was "an act of positive charity to a large class of indigent whites."[8] The two thousand cotton mill workers in and around Petersburg, Virginia, were white, King reported in 1874. He did not foresee that partly because of the threat of cheap Negro labor, the "cotton-mill trash," "lint heads," "cotton tails," and "factory rats," though occupying a niche above Negroes, might find themselves on plantations in a city, housed in company tenements and subjected to unwonted control.[9]

The potential competition in the mills between white and black labor bore severely upon white women and children. As the work of white women was obtained at a low rate of wages, P. A. Bruce observed, there was little or no inducement to the millowners to employ Negroes to take their places, even should the white male operatives offer no opposition.[10] Bruce assumed that if the Negroes came in, all the white women would have to leave, and this was certainly the Southern belief. An Alabama journal, in supporting a strike of white

[6] *Banner of the South*, October 16, 1869.

[7] Jackson, Miss., *Clarion*, April 19, 1876.

[8] *Banner of the South*, January 25, 1871.

[9] *Scribner's Monthly*, VII (1874), 665; Cash, *The Mind of the South*, 207-208.

[10] *The Rise of the New South*, 184. See also Charleston, S.C., *News and Courier*, February 16, 1891; De Leon, *Southern Magazine*, XIV (1874), 570-71.

operatives at the People's Cotton Factory, Montgomery, against
the employment of a Negro, declared: "This attempt to practice
a mingling of the races in a Southern cotton mill is equivalent
to mixing them in schools, and can do nothing but bring
disaster and ruin to any mill that attempts it."[11]

Integrated factories would indeed be as unsettling as mixed
schools. Reasons were found, however, for supposing Negroes
unfit to work alongside white machine operatives. The manager of a cotton mill in Columbus, Georgia, explained that
Negroes were not employed in his mill because the whirl of
spindles put them to sleep. Those who stayed awake were
hypnotized by the humming machinery. The manager of the
Eagle and Phenix mill in Georgia employed only ten Negro
yardworkers among 800 textile workers, because, he said, their
lack of quickness and sensitiveness of touch and their general
sleepiness disqualified them for work which required the
characteristics they lacked. Better equipped for outdoor work,
they would always be so employed. To justify their exclusion
from the mills, in one town Negroes were said to lack dexterity;
in the next town, where they rolled tobacco, they were said to
have great dexterity. In either case their skill or lack of it was
deemed to be evidence of inferiority. Although most cotton
mill owners and managers glibly ruled out skilled factory labor
for Negroes, one manager thought that exceptional Negro
youths might have the capacity to learn textile work; but such
a training program would require much time and, besides, it
was not needed, for there were more than enough whites to
supply the mills.[12]

In 1898 there were five hundred cotton mills in the South,
only three of them employing Negroes. Even in 1957, among

---

[11] Cited in Charleston, S.C., *News and Courier*, September 11, 1898.
[12] De Leon, *Harper's Magazine*, XLVII (1874), 411; Edward King,
"The Great South: The Cotton States: I," *Scribner's Monthly*, VIII
(1874), 406-13; Bryce, *The American Commonwealth*, II, 514; Wesley,
Negro Labor in the United States, 238-39; Edwin R. Embree, *Brown
America* (New York, 1933), 151.

400,000 textile workers in Virginia, North Carolina, and South Carolina, not one Negro was weaver, spinner, or loom fixer.[13] A few experiments with Negro labor in cotton mills were tried and failed. The Elmwood Manufacturing Company, Columbus, Georgia, proposed to employ Negroes, but the white people would not buy the company's securities, and it went out of business before making any goods. An effort to substitute Negro workers for whites in a textile factory in Charleston in 1890 resulted in a victory for the whites. Nine years later, Atlanta textile workers won a strike precipitated by the hiring of Negroes. In 1900 a Charleston cotton mill which employed blacks went bankrupt, an event that Charlestonians took as conclusive proof of the correctness of their preconceptions. Another experiment with Negro labor was made at the Coleman cotton mill at Concord, North Carolina, which was Negro owned and operated, only the manager, a Northerner, being white. The mill opened in 1901 and failed the next year. The Afro-American Cotton Mill Company of Anniston, Alabama, met the same fate.[14]

Negro factories might succeed, at least for a time, so it was thought, if their dull, sluggish, and incompetent workers were thrashed like oarsmen in a galley. The Ashby and Bailey Company, Northern-owned, employed three hundred Negroes, mostly minors, in a textile mill at Fayetteville, North Carolina. The colored superintendent, T. W. Thurston, maintained a harsh discipline in the plant. Because, as he said, kindness would be construed as weakness, he used the lash on children and adults of both sexes; anything less was a waste of time. All under twenty-one years of age came to the plant with certificates from parents permitting corporal punishment. The factory, Thurston said, would fail if operated like white ones,

[13] Charleston, S.C., *News and Courier*, September 11, 1898; William Peters, *The Southern Temper* (New York, 1959), 226.

[14] Charleston, S.C., *News and Courier*, August 11, 1898; Tindall, *South Carolina Negroes*; Bruce, *The Rise of the New South*, 134, 184; Wesley, *Negro Labor in the United States*, 240-41.

for despotism was necessary where Negroes were concerned.[15]

Unlike textile work, certain jobs in phosphate mines, the lumbering industry, railroad construction, and ironworks were thought to be tailored to the black man's nature. He was also expected to do well at tasks in steel plants which required strong muscles, resistance to furnace heat, and qualities of the observer rather than of the thinker. Accordingly, colored laborers were welcomed in Southern ironworks except in positions where judgment was required. And in lumbering their adaptation to rough work kept them "freely and profitably employed" in felling and hewing of trees and in other outdoor work.[16] Although Negroes might handle very well simple jobs in the industrial order, said a spokesman of the planters, "it is obvious . . . negro labor is the ancient and legitimate labor of the planter." This gentleman therefore urged the South to guarantee railroad construction jobs to white immigrants in order to force the Negroes back to the fields.[17]

The reaction to a strike at an iron foundry in Richmond in 1891 illustrated both the determination of whites to control desirable jobs and the continued sway of proslavery thought. On this occasion the apologist of white supremacy noted that although the places at the machines were filled by volunteers, and although there were many nonstriking Negroes in the works, it never occurred to anyone that Negroes might work at the machines, and not one person ever suggested it.[18]

Since Negroes were unorganized, thoroughly controlled, desperately poor, and accustomed to being despised, their condition invited employers to send agents among them to recruit "scabs." Negro scabs were brought into Northern steel plants chiefly to break strikes. They were used in many smaller labor disputes about 1890 and in large numbers in the great Home-

[15] Charleston, S.C., *News and Courier*, November 4, 1900.
[16] *Christian Advocate* (Nashville), February 16, April 13, 1893; De Leon, *Harper's Magazine*, XLVII (1874), 418; Tindall, *South Carolina Negroes*, 126-29; Wharton, *The Negro in Mississippi*, 125-27.
[17] *Banner of the South and Planter's Journal*, March 11, 1871.
[18] Page, *The Negro*, 410.

stead strike of that year. By 1900 the Negro population of Allegheny County, Pennsylvania, had reached 27,753. In 1898, Negro workers from Alabama used in Illinois to break the power of white miners were attacked by mobs. The Republican governor urged on the mobs without, Southerners observed, bringing down upon himself the denunciations of those Northern journals that had censured similar resistance to Negro domination in North Carolina.[19]

In the South, judicious hints by factory managers were sufficient to warn white workers of limits beyond which they would not go in order to maintain white supremacy. Commonly such hints took the form of assurances that Negroes would not be employed unless white labor costs rose too high. Thus did the threat of Negro strikebreakers reduce the incidence of labor disputes. Occasionally, however, they were called in to make good this threat. An ironmaster of Chattanooga acknowledged that whenever he faced a strike, he replaced whites with Negroes.[20] On the Houston and Texas Railroad in 1890, striking switchmen were replaced by Negroes. Other white workers then struck, offering this explanation: "Observation, deep and honest conviction, have taught us that we degenerate in the eyes of all when we acknowledge them [Negroes] our equals, as we are compelled to do, as the position they occupy is on a par, and must necessarily be recognized as equal to ours; and compels us to directly associate with them to an unbearable extent."[21] Accused of undermining white

---

[19] Horace R. Cayton and George S. Mitchell, *Black Workers and the New Unions* (Chapel Hill, 1939), 5-7; Wesley, *Negro Labor in the United States*, 243-45, 261, 279-80; *Christian Advocate* (Nashville), December 1, 1898.

[20] N. P. T. Finch of Birmingham, Alabama, quoted in Charleston, S.C., *News and Courier*, September 11, 1898; Taylor, *The Negro in Tennessee*, 142-43. In 1883 Negroes broke a strike at ironworks in Chattanooga and Nashville and were put to work at every type of job in the industry. Wesley, *Negro Labor in the United States*, 243.

[21] Charleston, S.C., *News and Courier*, October 27, 1890. Between 1882 and 1900, strikes in the United States against the employment of Negroes numbered fifty. Wesley, *Negro Labor in the United States*, 237-38.

supremacy, the company replied that it worked the Negroes under the direction of white men and that it did not employ them by choice but only because the white switchmen refused to work.[22] Many Southern agrarians would have nothing to do with proposals of Midwestern Populists for government ownership of railroads; they feared that with federal ownership, whites, especially the young ladies, would be compelled to associate with Negro conductors, flagmen, and brakemen, and with Negro agents at depots all along the lines.[23] In Louisiana in 1873, white longshoremen had trouble with "low, ignorant negroes, who slept under tarpaulins and in barrel houses, and who . . . could afford to work at lower than regular rates." They managed to have many of the Negroes jailed as rioters.[24]

Partly because of the effective use of the Negro as a preventer and breaker of strikes, the white supremacy publicist could boast that the South knew little of the fierce hostility that divided labor and capital in the North. The Negro could be thankful that his "respect for authority and inaptitude for organization" saved him from the demoralizing labor troubles which prevailed in areas outside the South. Lest Negroes be tempted, Southern leaders felt obliged to warn labor agitators, such as W. H. Bailey of the Knights of Labor, to get out of the country and leave their workers in peace.[25]

Unions might declare that they welcomed laborers without regard to creed, color, or sex; in practice they excluded blacks. Even so, Negroes sometimes managed, particularly in towns, to form their own unions, such as longshoremen's, carpenters', and mechanics' associations; and the Knights of Labor endeavored to organize both town and country Negroes. Whites were able, however, either to destroy Negro organizations or to render them ineffective. When a Negro union supposed itself

[22] Charleston, S.C., *News and Courier*, October 27, 1890.
[23] Saloutos, *Farmer Movements in the South*, 104.
[24] New Orleans *Picayune*, August 24, 1874.
[25] Grady, *Century Magazine*, VII (1885), 916; Eustis, *Forum*, VI (1888), 154; editorial, *Southern Bivouac*, IX (1887), 712.

strong enough to demand higher wages, the usual outcome was announcement within a few days that the conspiracy had failed and the deluded blacks were quietly at work.[26]

The presence of two sets of workers, one enjoying slight privileges over the other, and the occasional overt use of the disadvantaged workers to threaten the privileged workers indicate the heavy burden that whites themselves carried in subordinating Negroes.

This effect of competition, actual or potential, between white and Negro is exhibited in the discussion of the labor problem in P. A. Bruce's *The Rise of the New South*. As long as white operatives could be obtained at low wages, Bruce noted, there was little probability that blacks would be employed in cotton mills. A vast body of poor whites who lived in the hills and mountains without comfort but who possessed a hardy spirit and physical vigor found mill wages very attractive. These most contented factory workers in the nation, said Bruce, unlike the disreputable immigrants of the North, were good Anglo-Saxons; their names on the payrolls of the principal Southern mills were identical with the names on the regimental rosters of the Revolutionary, Mexican, and Civil wars. The great reserve of poorer whites, and the numbers of women and children employed in the mills, tended to prevent the formation of labor unions in the South. If the whites became refractory, the mill-owners would supplant them with Negroes. Strikes which did occur were "likely to be only brief in duration, chiefly as the result of the Southern employer's ability to hold the great mass of negro mechanics *in terrorem* over the heads of the whites."

[26] Wesley, *Negro Labor in the United States*, 259. In 1900 Samuel Gompers advised Negroes to establish separate organizations. See also John R. Commons and Associates, *History of Labor in the United States*, 4 vols. (2d ed., New York, 1946), II, 114, 116, 118, 135; Charlottesville, Va., *Weekly Chronicle*, June 20, 1879; S. M. Matison, "The Labor Movement and the Negro during Reconstruction," *Journal of Negro History*, XXXIII (1948), 426-69; Sidney F. Kessler, "The Organization of Negroes in the Knights of Labor," *Journal of Negro History*, XXXVII (1952), 248-76.

There was and would be peaceful relations between employer and employee.[27]

Southerners proved adept in adjusting the idea of white supremacy to *laissez faire* economic doctrine, to the great disadvantage of many whites as well as of the Negroes. It seemed to them logical to assert that Negroes would accept the lowest of low wages, when they really meant that Negroes would be forced to accept whatever was offered. Negroes were not permitted to bargain; as a consequence, neither were the lowly whites. Despite hardship borne by these whites in competition with Negroes, even they derived benefits from membership in a privileged race. And so they, too, championed the ideology of white supremacy to keep the Negro in his place.

[27] Pages 165, 185-86.

CHAPTER FOURTEEN

Persistence and Change

FROM EARLY IN THE seventeenth century until the Civil War, white Southerners defended slavery by a system of thought which, in its simplest terms, portrayed the Negro race as inherently subject to the white race. When ruled by their superiors, Negroes made excellent contributions to the welfare of society; when free, they became a drag on the community and posed a danger to good order. Emancipation, defeated Confederates believed, could not change the character of Negroes or the natural relation between the races. And so they derived an ideology of white supremacy from proslavery thought and on its basis created a social order in which they were able to dominate semifree Negroes.

To prevent amalgamation of the races, to make possible thoroughgoing discrimination, and to keep individuals of the dominant and subordinate groups from forming ties of friendship, Southern whites kept strict watch over racial contacts and regulated them with elaborate ritual. Although the Creator, they argued, had implanted in each race an instinct of aversion toward other races, fallen men often refused to heed the promptings of this instinct. It was necessary, they claimed, to segregate the races, for if mongrelization of the South did not result in the extinction of the population, it would bring cultural disaster. To strengthen revulsion against racial fusion, white Southerners described their race as beautiful and the black race as ugly.

With the abolition of slavery went the abolition of the slave law, but to subordinate free Negroes, the South required distinct legal systems for the two races. So the dominant class enacted black codes, which, when nullified by Congress, they reestablished in practice by discriminatory administration of the law. Ultimately this discrimination was achieved and maintained by violence. To justify the violence of lynch mobs, terroristic organizations, the white man's party, and the white man's government, whites said that when two races occupied the same territory, a struggle ensued until the weaker race submitted.

During the early campaigns of the so-called race warfare for dominance precipitated by emancipation, Negroes helped elect Radical state governments and were on the way to overcoming the vestiges of slavery. But whites counterattacked, regained monopoly of governmental power, and disfranchised Negroes. To keep Negroes out of politics, whites developed a one-party system; second or third parties might call out the Negro vote, held out of political battle by administrative devices and threats.

Freedmen, hungering for the pleasures and profits of education, flocked to schools opened by missionary teachers and, later, by Radical governments. But the educated Negro did not conform to the white man's notion of the Negro, and besides, he had ambition for place and prestige. Upon regaining political control of the states, whites, asserting that blacks could not profit from an education designed for the superior race, provided inferior education in segregated schools for Negroes. They did not discriminate against Negro school children to the same degree that they discriminated against Negro adults in the political and economic spheres. In this way they left room for the slow elevation of Negroes.

Whether slave or free, said the white Southerner, Negroes were born to labor for their betters. For a season the Freedmen's Bureau and the Radical governments interposed their authority between master and servant and offered the servant opportunity to escape from bondage, but with the restoration of white rule the opportunity was all but lost. Whites claimed that to prevent Negroes from ruining themselves and the planters too, it was necessary to impose upon them many of the controls from which they had been freed by fanatics and knaves. By means of the sharecrop system, segregation in the labor force, and political coercion, whites reduced hopeful black workers to a condition of virtual peonage. In the midst of their struggle to reconquer the freedmen, whites threatened to replace Negroes with less difficult workers. Negroes, for their part, hoping to escape from the tightening system of caste, began to migrate from the South. During the last quarter of the nineteenth century they departed in the thousands; during the next six decades the exodus turned into one of the most significant population movements in American history.

The ideology of white supremacy and the social order of which it was both a cause and reflection were fully developed around 1900. The idea that white men, being superior, ought to rule black men made possible the creation of the caste system as a successor to slavery. In the workings of this system there was a circularity: command over resources led to command over persons; command over persons led to command over resources. With political power came control over social and economic policy. Controlling social and economic policy, whites were able to get and keep a monopoly of political power. In the same fashion the doctrines of the ideological system strengthened one another. What is important is that the ideology of white supremacy and the actual practical supremacy of whites are creations of men and are sustained by men.

That whites did not see fit to be as harsh as they might have been can be explained by their general adherence to Christian and democratic principles and by their long association with Negroes. They were able to transcend the barriers of the caste structure and to see through the fog of ideology just enough to penetrate behind the masks of race to the human

qualities of Negroes. By private acts of charity, many avowed
white supremacists sapped and mined the foundations of
racism.

Even though Christianity slowly worked against the social
order, for a good part of the period since 1900 clergymen did
their part to justify the "Southern way of life." As a group they
ameliorated the system when and where they could by criti-
cizing cases of individual cruelty and by urging their flocks to
deal fairly with colored people. Whites must give opportunities
to Negroes, they said, but providence required segregation in
church and school and society and political supremacy for
whites. Their program for the improvement of Negroes did
not include a particle of social equality. They did find support
for a gentle sort of white supremacy in St. Paul's injunction to
the servant to be obedient to his master. They took the
absence from the New Testament of specific denunciation of
caste as showing the conformity of this institution with Christianity, and Christ never, they pointed out, cried out against
slavery, which was practiced in the Roman Empire of His time.
The sense of brotherly love did not mean equality for all men.
Further, there was the long tradition of comfortable dualism
between divine and secular law which made caste systems
acceptable on this earth as part of the natural order of fallen
human nature. Moreover, it was pointed out that the idea of
equality emerged among materialists and atheists of the En-
lightenment. So, while clergymen condemned unkindness and
lack of charity on the part of any person to any other person,
black or white, this did not mean that they condemned the
social order. On such a basis many Christian Southerners felt
justified in maintaining a belief either in slavery or in post-Civil
War caste society.

From 1900 until after World War II Negroes received little
encouragement from the churches in the South. Now these
churches have repudiated white supremacy, and by so doing
have made a decision of the utmost importance in Southern

history. Before the recent shift most Southern clergymen and their flocks would have given endorsement, with few qualifications, to Thomas Pearce Bailey's statement in 1914 of the racial doctrines of the Southern people, which, Bailey pointed out, were a part of the religious culture. These doctrines were:

1. "Blood will tell."
2. The white race must dominate.
3. The Teutonic peoples stand for race purity.
4. The negro is inferior and will remain so.
5. "This is a white man's country."
6. No social equality.
7. No political equality.
8. In matters of civil rights and legal adjustments give the white man, as opposed to the colored man, the benefit of the doubt; and under no circumstances interfere with the prestige of the white race.
9. In educational policy let the negro have the crumbs that fall from the white man's table.
10. Let there be such industrial education of the negro as will best fit him to serve the white man.
11. Only Southerners understand the negro question.
12. Let the South settle the negro question.
13. The status of peasantry is all the negro may hope for, if the races are to live together in peace.
14. Let the lowest white man count for more than the highest negro.
15. The above statements indicate the leadings of Providence.[1]

Other Southern leaders also defended things as they were. Educators might advocate improved education for Negroes; very few opposed segregation or some measure of discrimination in education. Similarly, business and labor leaders as well as planters supported economic discrimination against Negroes. In many books Southern historians gave approval to the triumph of white supremacy. They depicted freedmen as ignorant creatures manipulated by conscienceless or foolish carpet-

[1] Thomas Pearce Bailey, *Race Orthodoxy in the South and Other Aspects of the Negro Question* (New York, 1914), 93.

baggers and scalawags. Whites, on the other hand, after a bitter struggle in which they unfortunately had to use illegal means, broke the unnatural alliance between Negroes and the white opportunists and reestablished home rule. Most readers of these histories concluded that only the South could or should handle the Negro problem and that no attempt at reconstructing the South ought ever again be tried.

During the first half of the twentieth century when the question of disfranchisement came up, politicians said that Negroes did not vote because they were not interested or because they could not qualify under the impartially administered suffrage regulations. Most of them, unless challenged, acted as if the political situation was permanently prescribed; others, such as Tom Heflin of Alabama and Theodore Bilbo of Mississippi, vociferously championed white man's government. Before the New Deal, and to some extent before the beginning of the great assault on white supremacy around 1945, Southern politicians did not have much explaining to do. The national parties and the various branches of the federal government were not concerned about the condition of Negroes. From time to time Congress threatened to enact antilynching legislation, but Southern congressmen and their Northern allies were able to prevent that. No strong movement existed to force the South to enroll black voters. In the executive branch of government the Presidents from McKinley to Hoover tried to extend their support among Southern whites while almost completely disregarding the Negroes.

While the ideology of white supremacy persisted in the South, changes in the Negro community and in its geographical distribution combined with other forces to make possible the explosive confrontation of the civil rights movement and white supremacy in the 1960's. The improvement of the mass of Negroes through education (as inadequate as much of it was) and through relatively greater participation in the economy, and the achievements of the elite of the race in literature, in the arts, especially in music, and in sports, gradually raised the status of the black race in the eyes of white Southerners. Of great importance was the migration of Negroes from the cotton, tobacco, and cane fields to urban areas.

Depression, war, technological developments in agriculture, and the hope of gaining freedom and prosperity set the rural Negro population on the move. As the races drifted apart in the urban environment, a strong sense of solidarity among Negroes emerged. Advances in education put them into possession of the techniques of communication and organization and contributed to their consolidation within the white world. With increasing solidarity went increasing sensitivity to prejudice and strengthened will and capacity to resist discrimination. In Northern cities they regained the political influence lost in the South.

Other important factors affecting race relations included the effects of the national communication media, the gradual change in the climate of opinion brought about by twentieth-century researches in the social sciences, the growing integration of the South in an urbanized and industrialized America, and the domestic repercussions of the nation's role as defender of freedom in the world community.

As a consequence of these changes a considerable number of whites began to see the race question in a different context. This group conceded that Negroes might not, after all, be inherently inferior. Although the mass of Negroes, they believed, continued to be disorderly, shiftless, given to stealing, and sexually promiscuous, perhaps this was so because of their cultural, rather than their biological heritage. With further advancement in education and a strengthened resolve on the part of Negroes to improve themselves, within a generation or so whites might be able to admit them to a larger measure of racial equality.

For the present, Negroes should, however, be satisfied with recent gains. If they pushed for full-scale integration in the schools, on the job, and in the neighborhood before they had lifted themselves to the white man's standard, they could only injure what cause they had. Southerners taking this position exhibited a great deal of arrogance, but they had, ideologically if not in practice, advanced somewhat beyond the notion that white supremacy had been ordained by God and nature.

A distinct minority of whites, more significant than at any time in the past, advocated, with little or no qualification, straight-out racial equality. This group was helped by the fact that the South's intellectual leaders had practically ceased to write articles and books, and to deliver lectures, on the natural inferiority of Negroes. Adamant defenders of white supremacy had, therefore, no fresh and clever defense against attacks on racism.

Negroes have opposed white supremacy for as long as they have been subjected to it, and a small but persistent group of whites, by appealing to religious and democratic principles, have always urged their fellow citizens to take up the banner of human rights. In 1910, the year the program to disfranchise Southern Negroes by constitutional amendment was completed, educated Negroes and idealistic whites formed the National Association for the Advancement of Colored People. Although the NAACP was more militant and national in scope than Booker T. Washington's Negro improvement group, its first successes consisted in the dissemination of propaganda and the chipping away in the courts of the legal paraphernalia of white supremacy. In the 1920's Marcus Garvey's Universal Negro Improvement Association, with its black nationalism, rejection of the white world, and back-to-Africa schemes, stirred the Negro masses and dismayed and frightened the whites. During the New Deal era and World War II Negroes gained further opportunities in the industrial and military establishments and enhanced their political strength in national affairs. These evolutionary changes prepared the way for the powerful assaults on white supremacy of post-World War II America.[2]

After the war, pressure against white supremacy began to gather such force that it became obvious that a Second Reconstruction, as C. Vann Woodward has called it, had gotten underway. Southern Negroes cast off the habits of Sambo and, with magnificent courage, formed great processions on streets and highways in protest against white supremacy. In their support, federal courts handed down decision after decision, Congress passed civil rights bills, and Presidents sent armed forces into the South.

White supremacists met the onslaught with cleverness and fury. In Congress they blocked and delayed and weakened civil rights legislation. In the states they secured the adoption of a complex variety of school laws under the cover of which they hoped to preserve segregation. And they attempted to clog the courts with prolonged litigation. Where necessary, they inaugurated token integration. As in the past, they used the weapons of economic coercion and intimidation. When eviction, the denial of credit and supplies, loss of job, and threats failed to work, the violent were stirred to battle. Snipers felled and mobs flogged and lynched the enemy. In some places municipal police, sheriff's forces, and state troopers assaulted civil rights demonstrators with whips, clubs, and tear gas, and jailed thousands.

Whipping up resistance to the Second Reconstruction were the folk propagandists. They released a flood of speeches, pamphlets, and letters in which they discussed God's intent concerning white supremacy, depicted Ham as the ancestor of the servant race, and denounced integration as the aim of

[2] For an outstanding analysis of changes in the Negro community, see Robert Ezra Park, *Race and Culture*, ed. by Everett Cherrington Hughes (New York, 1964); for changes in the South, both black and white, consult Thomas D. Clark, *The Emerging South* (New York, 1961); and for a detailed account of the Second Reconstruction, refer to Woodward, *The Strange Career of Jim Crow*, 119-91.

outside agitators, Communists, and traitors to the white race. These energetic defenders of the old order proposed various schemes to bring the federal government in line with the unwritten constitution of white man's government.

In respect to the past there were a surprising number of whites who spoke out against the extremists. Some were forced back into the ranks of the Silent South; others left the region; still others held their ground with courage. It must be said, however, that the old unity of the South on the Negro question had been broken and that outside the areas of hard-core resistance, a white dissenter was altogether less likely than formerly to be ostracized, beaten, or have his house dynamited.

By the mid sixties Southern Negroes had regained the franchise, breached the white man's school, obtained equal right to the use of public facilities, and secured a measure of economic betterment. Most of these gains, however, were forced on the South by the various branches of the federal government over the stiff opposition of the region's politicians. And as the Negro vote within the states increased, political opposition of the white supremacists hardened. During the summer and early fall of 1966, for example, segregationist candidates won the Democratic gubernatorial primaries in Alabama, Arkansas, and Georgia principally because they convinced enough voters that they were more determined and able than their opponents to halt the advance of Negroes and to check the federal government's efforts to enforce civil rights legislation. Nevertheless, even though a majority of Southerners tenaciously clung to the remnants of white supremacy, by 1966 there had occurred a substantial change for the better in the attitude of whites toward Negroes, a change engendered in part by the Negroes' rising level of educational, economic, and professional achievement. There had occurred also a profound change in the willingness and ability of Negroes to press hard for continued improvement in race relations. Little doubt exists that these changes are more enduring and pregnant with significance than short-range political trends: witness the Arkansas gubernatorial election in November, 1966, in the outcome of which white supremacy apparently was not the ultimate factor. Thus the outlook for Negroes to achieve unfettered citizenship in the South is bright.

Bibliographical Essay

THE SOURCES discussed in this note constitute a sample of the enormous body of literature touching on white supremacy in the South. Other materials not here discussed are cited in the footnotes.

Most of the leaders who developed the white supremacy of the New South were brought up in the slave South. For the climate of opinion then current refer to: Albert T. Bledsoe, *An Essay on Liberty and Slavery* (Philadelphia, 1856); John C. Calhoun, *A Disquisition on Government and Selections from the Discourse* (edited by C. Gordon Post, New York, 1953); Langdon Cheves, *Speech of the Honorable Langdon Cheves, delivered before the Delegates of the Nashville Convention, on Friday, November 13, 1850* (Columbia, S.C., 1850); Howell Cobb, A *Scriptural Examination of the Institution of Slavery in the United States with Its Objects and Purposes* (Georgia, 1856); E. N. Elliot, ed., *Cotton Is King and Pro-slavery Arguments* (Augusta, Ga., 1860); George Fitzhugh, *Cannibals All! or, Slaves without Masters* (Richmond, Va., 1857) and *Sociology for the South, or the Failure of Free Society* (Richmond, Va., 1854); and James H. Hammond, *Selections from the Letters and Speeches of James H. Hammond* (New York, 1866).

Newspapers give expression to the public mind on every aspect of race relations and are wonderful sources of fact and opinion. Since white supremacy could not be sustained in a local community alone, even small-town editors kept alert to regional developments and tied their ideas to the network of Southern thought. Thus local journals such as the vigorous Carrollton *West Alabamian* are rewarding sources. The *Banner of the South* and the *Sunny South,* both Georgia newspapers, were regional in orientation, literary in pretension, and conservative of "Southern civilization" in intent. The Charleston (S.C.) *Courier* (later *News and Courier*), the Jackson (Miss.) *Clarion,* and the New Orleans *Picayune* are important. Because of its religious connection the Nashville *Christian Advocate* (Methodist) has special interest. The Atlanta *Constitution,* Austin *Democratic-Statesman,* Baton Rouge *Capitolian-Advo-*

cate, Charleston (S.C.) *Journal of Commerce*, Charlottesville (Va.) *Chronicle*, Fort Smith (Ark.) *Herald*, Houston *Chronicle*, Houston *Post*, Louisville *Farm and Home*, New Orleans *Crescent*, New Orleans *Republican*, Shreveport *South-Western*, and Wilmington (N.C.) *Journal* are filled with material on the white man and the Negro.

Numerous books and pamphlets deal with white supremacy in one form or another. Bennett Puryear's *The Public School in its Relation to the Negro* (Richmond, Va., 1877) is an exceptionally interesting and able brief work on all aspects of the "Negro question" by an ardent white supremacist. Thomas M. Norwood's *Address on the Negro* (Savannah, Ga., 1908) is also a representative statement of Southerners who entertained no doubts whatever about white men's right to rule Negroes. Southern Society for the Promotion of the Study of Race Conditions and Problems in the South, *Race Problems of the South: Proceedings of the First Annual Conference* (Richmond, Va., 1900) is a comprehensive discussion by politicians, propagandists, and clergymen. See also: *America's Race Problems: Addresses at the Annual Meeting of the American Academy of Political and Social Science, Philadelphia, April Twelfth and Thirteenth, MCMI* (Philadelphia, 1901). Other general defenses of the South's racial policy are: Thomas Pearce Bailey, *Race Orthodoxy in the South and Other Aspects of the Negro Question* (New York, 1914); Robert F. Campbell, *Some Aspects of the Race Problem in the South* (2nd ed., Ashville, N.C., 1899); Charles B. Galloway, *The South and the Negro* (New York, 1904); Joseph Le Conte, *The Race Problem in the South* (New York, 1892); and Edgar Gardner Murphy, *The White Man and the Negro at the South* (Philadelphia, 1900). Thomas Dixon's novel *The Leopard's Spots: A Romance of the White Man's Burden, 1865-1900* (New York, 1902) has all the segregationist's arguments. Albion Tourgee's *A Fool's Errand* (edited by John Hope Franklin, Cambridge, Mass., 1961) is an entertaining novel by a Carpetbagger of his failure to reconstruct North Carolina. Philip A. Bruce's history of *The Rise of the New South* (Philadelphia, 1905) and Thomas Nelson Page's *The Negro: The Southerner's Problem* (New York, 1904) are authoritative expositions of Southern attitudes at a time when the finishing touches were being put on the structure of white supremacy. A sharp criticism of this structure may be found in Wilbur J. Cash's provocative *The Mind of the South* (New York, 1941).

For examples of the crazy literature which portrayed Negroes as almost human or nonhuman see: Robert Buchanan, *Calaban: A Sequel to Ariel* (New York, 1868); Buckner H. Payne, *Ariel's Reply to the Rev. John A. Seiss, D.D., of Philadelphia: Also, His Reply to the Scientific Geologist and Other Learned Men in their Attacks on the Credibility of the Mosaic Account of the Creation and of the Flood* (Nashville, 1876); Charles Carroll, *The Negro a Beast or in the Image of God?* (St. Louis, 1900); and Albert Stowe Lee-Craft, *The Devil's Inkwell: A Story of Humanity, Embracing Biblical Evidence Establishing Irrefutable and Utter Supremacy of the White Man on the Earth since the Beginning of Historical Time* (Houston, 1923).

There are a number of histories of Negroes and of Negro-white relations in the states. Some of the good ones are: John Preston McConnell, *Negroes and Their Treatment in Virginia from 1865-1867* (Pulaski, Va., 1910); Roger W. Shugg, *Origin of Class Struggle in Louisiana: A Social History of White Farmers and Laborers during Slavery and After, 1840-1875* (Baton Rouge, 1939); A. A. Taylor, *The Negro in Tennessee, 1865-1880* (Washington, 1941); George B. Tindall, *South Carolina Negroes, 1877-1900* (Columbia, S.C., 1952); Vernon Lane Wharton, *The Negro in Mississippi, 1865-1890* (Chapel Hill, 1947); and Charles E. Wynes, *Race Relations in Virginia, 1870-1902* (Charlottesville, Va., 1961). Francis Butler Simkins' *Pitchfork Ben Tillman: South Carolinian* (Baton Rouge, 1944) has chapters on the frenzied anti-Negro thought of one of the South's most violent and dynamic politicians. John William De Forest's *A Union Officer in the Reconstruction* (edited by James H. Croushore and David Morris Potter, New Haven, 1948) is the highly interesting story of a Freedmen's Bureau officer's dealings with South Carolina Negroes and "Southrons" of every class.

Two distinguished Southern historians, Thomas D. Clark and C. Vann Woodward, have excellent books dealing with the South and the Negro. See, for example, relevant chapters in Clark's *The Emerging South* (New York, 1961); and Woodward's *The Burden of Southern History* (Baton Rouge, 1960) and *The Strange Career of Jim Crow* (New York, 1966). Robert Ezra Park's *Race and Culture* (edited by Everett Cherrington Hughes, New York, 1964), a fine work on the general subject of race relations, devotes considerable attention to the South.

Lewis Hanke, *Aristotle and the American Indians: A Study in Race Prejudice in the Modern World* (Chicago, 1959); Donald

Pierson, *Negroes in Brazil: A Study of Race Contact at Bahia* (Chicago, 1942); Stanley J. Stein, *Vasouras: A Brazilian Coffee County, 1850-1900* (Cambridge, Mass., 1957); and Frank Tannenbaum, *Slave and Citizen: The Negro in the Americas* (New York, 1947) offer descriptions of race relations in Latin America with which to contrast race relations in the South.

There is a wealth of useful periodical literature. George W. Cable's "The Freedmen's Case in Equity," *Century Magazine*, VII (1885), 409-18, is a criticism of white supremacy by a Confederate veteran and writer of distinction. The best known journalist of the New South, Henry W. Grady, "In Plain Black and White: A Reply to Mr. Cable," *Century Magazine*, VII (1885), 909-17, defends the South's treatment of Negroes. Two articles by William P. Trent are exceptional: "Dominant Forces in Southern Life," *Atlantic Monthly*, LXXIX (1897), 42-53, and "Tendencies of Higher Life in the South," *Atlantic Monthly*, LXXIX (1897), 766-78. Guion Griffis Johnson, "Southern Paternalism toward Negroes after Emancipation," *Journal of Southern History*, XXIII (1957), 483-509, is excellent. See T. U. Dudley, "How Shall We Help the Negro?" *Century Magazine*, VIII (1885), 273-80, for a paternalist's argument. In a series of articles on "The Great South" in *Scribner's Monthly*, VII-IX (1874), Edward King superbly reports on every facet of the "Negro problem."

Violence against Negroes is treated in Frederick Douglass, "Lynch Law in the South," *North American Review*, CLV (1892), 17-25; Atticus G. Haygood, "The Black Shadow in the South," *Forum*, XVI (1893), 167-75; Walter Hines Page, "The Last Hold of the Southern Bully," *Forum*, XVI (1893), 303-14; George Braden, "Ku Klux Klan, an Apology," *Southern Bivouac*, IV (1885), 103-109; Stuart Omer Landry, *The Battle of Liberty Place: The Overthrow of Carpet-bag Rule in New Orleans, September 14, 1874* (New Orleans, 1955); and National Association for the Advancement of Colored People, *Thirty Years of Lynching in the United States, 1889-1918* (New York, 1919).

Paul Lewinson offers a general study of Negroes in Southern politics in *Race, Class, and Party: A History of Negro Suffrage and White Politics in the South* (New York, 1932), and Republican policy is analyzed in Vincent P. De Santis, *Republicans Face the Southern Question: The New Departure Years, 1877-1897* (Baltimore, 1959). Traditional indictments of Reconstruction and defenses of white man's government are: Hilary Herbert, ed., *Why the Solid South? or, Reconstruction and Its Results* (Baltimore, 1890); W. J. Northen, *The Negro at the South: An Address before the Congregational Club, Boston, Massachusetts, May 22, 1899* (Atlanta, 1899); and Charles W. Dabney, *The Meaning of the Solid South: An Address at the Commencement of the University of Alabama, May 26, 1909* (n.p., 1909). Moorfield Storey, *Negro Suffrage Is Not a Failure: An Address before the New England Suffrage Conference, March 30, 1903* (Boston, 1903) defends Negro suffrage but reluctantly accepts practical disfranchisement. Arkansas Constitutional Convention (1868), *Proceedings* (Little Rock, 1868) describes the making of a Negro-white government, and Mississippi Constitutional Convention (1890), *Journal of the Convention* (Jackson, 1890) records the legitimation of a white man's government that had existed since 1875.

Views on Negroes, in and out of politics, of the important politicians James G. Blaine, L. Q. C. Lamar, Wade Hampton, James A. Garfield, Alexander H. Stephens, Wendell Phillips, Montgomery Blair, and Thomas A. Hendricks are presented in the symposium "Ought the Negro to Be Disfranchised? Ought He to Have Been Franchised?" *North American Review*, CXXVII (1879), 225-83. Another informative symposium is that of Charles A. Gardiner, John T. Morgan, Frederick Douglass, Z. B. Vance, Joel Chandler Harris, Richard L. Greener, Alvin Johnson, C. S. Armstrong, J. H. Walworth, and J. A. Emerson, "The Future of the Negro," *North American Review*, CXXXIX (1884), 78-99. See also the statement of the Alabama Senator John T. Morgan, "Shall Negro Majorities Rule?" *Forum*, VI (1888), 586-99, and the reply of the former Carpetbagger Albion Tourgee, "Shall White Minorities Rule?" *Forum*, VII (1889), 143-55. Other revealing articles on the attitudes of white people toward Negroes in politics are: H. H. Chalmers, "The Effects of Negro Suffrage," *North American Review*, CXXXII (1881), 239-48; Alfred H. Colquitt, "Is the Negro Vote Suppressed?" *Forum*, IV (1887), 267-78; Charles Gayarré, "The Southern Question," *North American Review*, CXXV (1877), 472-90; Andrew C. McLaughlin, "Mississippi and the Negro Question," *Atlantic Monthly*, LXX (1892), 828-37; J. M. Stone, "The Suppression of Lawlessness in the South," *North American Review*, CLVIII (1894), 500-506; Henry Watterson, "The Solid South," *North American Review*, CXXVIII (1879), 47-58; and Alexander Winchell, "The Experiment of Negro Suffrage," *North American Review*, CXXXVI (1883), 119-34. The historical journals contain informative articles, for example, Elsie M. Lewis, "The Political Mind of the Negro, 1865-1900," *Journal of Southern History*, XXI (1955), 189-202, and T. Harry Williams, "The Louisiana Unification Movement of 1873," *Journal of Southern History*, XI (1945), 349-69.

Charles W. Dabney's *Universal Education in the South*, 2 vols. (Chapel Hill, 1936) is a survey with a strong Southern bias by a distinguished educator. General Education Board, *The General Education Board: An Account of the Activities, 1902-1914* (New York, 1915) describes a Northern fund's educational efforts among black and white Southerners. Louis R. Harlan's *Separate and Unequal: Public School Campaigns and Racism in the Southern Seaboard States 1901-1915* (Chapel Hill, 1958), and "The Southern Education Board and the Race Issue in Public Education," *Journal of Southern History*, XXIII (1957), 189-202, are good histories of policies and practices of racial discrimination in education. So is Horace Mann Bond's *The Education of the Negro in the American Social Order* (New York, 1934). Carter C. Woodson's *The Miseducation of the Negro* (Washington, 1933) is an indictment by an important Negro historian of white-controlled Negro education.

Horace Mann Bond, *Negro Education in Alabama: A Study in Cotton and Steel* (Washington, D.C., 1939); Frederick Eby, ed., *Education in Texas: Source Materials* (Austin, 1918) and *The Development of Education in Texas* (New York, 1925); and Dorothy Orr, *A History of Education in Georgia* (Chapel Hill, 1950) are enlightening state histories of the education of whites and blacks.

A Brief Sketch of George Peabody and a History of the Peabody Education Fund through Thirty Years (Cambridge, Mass., 1898); *Difficulties, Complications, and Limitations Connected with the Education of the Negro* (Baltimore, 1895); and *Education of the Negroes since 1860* (Baltimore, 1894) are by one of the South's great educators, J. L. M. Curry, who supported practical education for Negroes within the limitations imposed by segregation. Merle Curti's outstanding *The Social Ideas of American Educators* (New York, 1935) has an appraisal of Curry's career, and of Booker T. Washington's, too.

The story of the "Yankee teachers" is told in: Henry Lee Swint, *The Northern Teacher in the South* (Nashville, 1941), which is useful despite its Southern bias against "outside agitators"; *Fifth Annual Report of the General Assembly's Committee on Freedmen*

*of the Presbyterian Church in the United States of America, May,
1870* (Pittsburgh, 1870); New England Educational Commission for
Freedmen, *First Annual Report of the Educational Commission for
Freedmen with Extracts of Letters of Teachers and Superintendents*
(Boston, 1863); Edward L. Pierce, *The Freedmen of Port Royal,
South Carolina: Official Reports of Edward L. Pierce* (New York,
1863); Cornelia Hancock, *The South after Gettysburg: Letters of
Cornelia Hancock, 1863-1868* (edited by Henrietta Stratton Jaqu-
ette, New York, 1956); Maria Waterbury, *Seven Years among the
Freedmen* (Chicago, 1890), an especially good book; and *The
Freedmen's Record*, I-IV (1865-1871). For the educational efforts
of the Freedmen's Bureau consult United States Bureau of Refugees, Freedmen, and Abandoned Lands, *Circulars*, 1-30 (Washington, D.C., 1865-1867), *Report of the Commissioner of the
Bureau of Refugees, Freedmen and Abandoned Lands for the Year
1866* (Washington, D.C., 1866), and *Report of the Commissioner
of the Bureau of Refugees, Freedmen and Abandoned Lands for the
Year 1867* (Washington, D.C., 1867).

Louis R. Harlan, "Desegregation in New Orleans Public Schools
during Reconstruction," *American Historical Review*, LXVII (1962),
663-75; Alfred H. Kelly, "The Congressional Controversy over
School Segregation, 1867-1875," *American Historical Review*,
LXIV (1959), 537-63; T. M. Logan, "The Opposition in the South
to the Free School System," *Journal of Social Sciences*, IX (1878),
92-100; and William H. Ruffner, "Co-education of the White and
Colored Races," *Scribner's Monthly*, VIII (1874), 86-90, discuss
the school integration issue.

The controversy over industrial education is found in: Booker T.
Washington, *Up from Slavery* (New York, 1900) and "The
Awakening of the Negro," *Atlantic Monthly*, LXXVIII (1896),
322-28; Samuel R. Spencer, Jr., *Booker T. Washington and the
Negro's Place in American Life* (Boston, 1955); Daniel C. Gilman,
*A Study in Black and White: An Address at the Opening of the
Armstrong-Slater Trade School Building, November 18, 1896*
(Baltimore, 1896); Walter B. Hill, "Uncle Tom without a Cabin,"
Century Magazine, V (1883-1884), 859-64; Helen W. Ludlow,
"Hampton Normal and Agricultural Institute," *Harper's Magazine*,
XLVIII (1873), 672-85; S. W. Powell, "Industrial Education for
the Negro: Is It a Craze?" *Century Magazine*, XVI (1889), 472-73;
William T. Harris, *Higher Education for Negroes: An Address
Made to the Students of Atlanta University, Atlanta, Ga., October*

29, 1895 (n.p., n.d.); and W. E. B. Du Bois, *Black Reconstruction: An Essay toward a History of the Part which Black Folk Played in the Attempt to Reconstruct Democracy in America, 1860-1880* (New York, 1935).

Negroes as farm laborers are discussed in Philip A. Bruce, "A Tobacco Plantation," *Lippincott's Magazine*, XXXVI (1885), 533-42; Robert L. Dabney, "What the Negro Did for the Old South," *Southern States Farm Magazine*, V (1898), 477-82; Edwin De Leon, "The New South," *Harper's Magazine*, XLVII (1874), 270-80, 406-22, and "Ruin and Reconstruction of the Southern States: A Record of Two Tours in 1868 and 1873," *Southern Magazine*, XIV (1874), 17-41; George K. Holmes, "The Peons of the South," *Annals of the American Academy of Political and Social Science*, IV (1893), 265-74; J. B. Killebrew, "How to Deal with the Negro," *Southern States Farm Magazine*, V (1898), 482-92; and Edward King, "The Great South," *Scribner's Monthly*, VII-IX (1874).

Migration of Negro workers is the topic of Charles K. Marshall, *The Exodus: Its Effect upon the People of the South* (Washington, D.C., 1880); Henry King, "A Year of the Exodus in Kansas," *Scribner's Monthly*, XX (1880), 211-18; and Carter C. Woodson, *A Century of Negro Migration* (Washington, D.C., 1918).

George W. Cable devastatingly attacks convict labor in "The Convict Lease System in the Southern States," *Century Magazine*, V (1884), 582-99. Refer also to William O. Scroggs, "Convict and Apprenticed Labor in the South," in Julian A. Chandler and others, *The South in the Building of the Nation*, 12 vols. (Richmond, Va., 1909), VI, 48-53; and Jane Zimmerman, "The Penal Reform Movement in the South during the Progressive Era, 1890-1917," *Journal of Southern History*, XVII (1951), 462-92.

Negroes as craftsmen and industrial workers, as strikebreakers and union members, are studied in the thorough work of John R. Commons and associates, *History of Labor in the United States*, 4 vols. (New York, 1946); Horace R. Cayton and George S. Mitchell, *Black Workers and the New Unions* (Chapel Hill, 1939); Robert Lowery, "The Negro as a Mechanic," *North American Review*, CLVI (1893), 472-77; Charles H. Wesley, *Negro Labor in the United States, 1850-1925* (New York, 1927); Sidney F. Kessler, "The Organization of Negroes in the Knights of Labor," *Journal of Negro History*, XXXVII (1952), 248-76; and S. M. Matison, "The Labor Movement and the Negro during Reconstruction," *Journal of Negro History*, XXXIII (1948), 426-69.

"No doubt," Claude H. Nolen writes, "my residential experience is quite provincially Southern." Except for a few years in the army during World War II, the author of this book has lived in the South—in Tennessee, in Arkansas, in Louisiana, in Texas, and, for three years, in the border city of St. Louis. A native of Memphis, he graduated at Memphis State University. Mr. Nolen also holds the M.A. degree from Louisiana State University and the Ph.D. degree from the University of Texas. Presently he is professor of history at St. Edward's University, Austin, Texas.

slavery — thiefery

when Negro killed white he was always convicted